The
UNITED STATES
OF **SOCCER**

The
UNITED STATES
OF SOCCER

MLS AND THE RISE OF
AMERICAN SOCCER FANDOM

Phil West

The Overlook Press
New York, NY

This edition first published in hardcover in the United States in 2016
The Overlook Press, Peter Mayer Publishers, Inc.

NEW YORK
141 Wooster Street
New York, NY 10012
www.overlookpress.com
For bulk and special sales, please contact sales@overlookny.com,
or write us at the above address.

Cataloging-in-Publication Data is available from the Library of Congress

Book design and typeformatting by Bernard Schleifer
Manufactured in the United States of America
FIRST EDITION
ISBN 978-1-4683-1241-6
2 4 6 8 10 9 7 5 3 1

*To everyone working to grow soccer
in the United States and Canada*

CONTENTS

ACKNOWLEDGMENTS

THOUGH I'M INCREDIBLY PROUD OF THIS BOOK, IT STARTED LIFE AS A COM-pletely different book. In the summer of 2014, I set out to chronicle how American soccer fans experienced the World Cup, by driving to a different American city every day to experience the World Cup with American fans, no matter how long the distance between cities. (I would log 11,000 miles in a Honda Eclipse that performed valiantly throughout the journey, which would then succumb to a rainstorm-induced flood in my driveway a week after I returned home, bringing me safely from a friend's birthday party before capitulating to the deluge. Such is life.) That trip was funded in large part through an Indiegogo and a Kickstarter campaign, and I'm thankful for everyone who contributed, allowing me to traverse the nation and embark on a life-changing journey. The names of the contributors are proudly displayed at philwest.us/supporters, if you're curious to know more about the village it took to create that book. My dad and stepmother, Larry and Lisa West, deserve a special thanks for their generosity and support.

Also greatly deserving of thanks at the book's inception: Lauren Abramo of Dystel & Goderich Literary Management, who saw enough in my initial vision to shop my idea for a book, and then to bring the mission of telling MLS's story to me, via Peter Mayer and the entire Overlook crew.

I'm appreciative of all those who spoke to me in order to make the book possible, as well as the publicists and gatekeepers behind the scenes who helped connect me to them. Three in particular stand out: Rick Lawes, whose insight and encyclopedic knowledge of MLS history was essential at the project's outset; Dan Wiersema, a friend here in Austin whose important work with American Outlaws galvanized my fandom and fed my curiosity about supporters' culture; and Becky Chabot, a soccer advocate with a penchant for getting things right, who graciously stepped in to read the manuscript at a crucial juncture. (I'd also like to thank Paul DeBruler for reading early versions of the book's first chapters between visits to Providence Park.)

I am especially appreciative of two of the most important people in my life, my sons, Noah and Lucas. Apologies that Thanksgiving 2015 was "the day that Dad emerged from his writing hovel to periodically baste a turkey," and that the rest of the weekend was more of that minus the basting. You've shown that you understand my love of soccer and that it's not going anywhere. Thanks for all you've given me throughout our journey together in life, particularly this part of it.

To my wife Katie: Thank you for your boundless support, your love, your willingness to provide balance and guidance and wisdom, as well as playful snark when it's called for. I knew, when we awoke far too early the day after our wedding, to successfully make the opening of the North London Derby viewing party at Finn McCool's, that I'd chosen wisely in choosing you.

I have one especially important thank you to offer, for an opportunity that came about as I was moving into the editing phase of the book. My interest in MLS led to my writing for MLSSoccer.com, and I'm grateful for the opportunity that the website's given me to document the league I've fallen in love with. In particular, I'd like to thank Arielle Castillo, Andrew Wiebe, and Simon Borg for their guidance and insight. I've been thrilled to draw on the knowledge I've gained from writing this book and feel lucky to be adding to it all the time.

Of course, this book or this league wouldn't exist without the fans who have made this iteration of an American soccer league work. If you're holding this book, you've likely either attended an MLS match or you're pondering attending your first. You, therefore, deserve a thank you for the role you've played—or are about to play—in making this story possible.

PREFACE

MAJOR LEAGUE SOCCER'S HEADQUARTERS ARE HOUSED ON TWO FLOORS of a Midtown Manhattan office building, three blocks north of the Empire State Building. Exit the elevator to the office's reception area and you'll see white-on-white signage with a gleaming silver MLS Cup (officially, the Philip F. Anschutz Trophy) in a clear glass case. The halls are white, but augmented with affirming bursts of solid color—from the current generation of MLS uniforms, logo-embossed shovels from multiple stadium groundbreakings, and photos capturing twenty years of history. It's a league aiming for the enduring inevitability of its more established siblings, such as the National Football League counting its Super Bowls in increasingly unwieldy Roman numerals or the National Basketball Association's logo featuring the silhouette of a player who was a star a half century ago. MLS headquarters is just blocks from the headquarters of the other four major American sports leagues, but there's an approachability and even an accessibility to the league that places it in a whole different neighborhood from its sterner older brothers.

The league commissioner is unfailingly affable in his public appearances, going on halftime shows for the major marquee events in his sport—All-Star Games, finals, and conference championships—to answer questions with candor, even with gratitude to be having the conversation about soccer.

The deputy commissioner—the league's first employee and someone who has been with it since before it was even a league, orchestrating the careful choreography of cities, investors, and TV partners to get MLS off the ground—keeps articles about how the league wouldn't make it (which his wife had framed for him) in his study. Among his fondest memories of the league's early ascendancy: going into a bar called Froggy's in Playa del Ray, California, and asking them to find the satellite signal for a market-specific broadcast of an MLS match.

When the league launched in 1996, Americans were most likely to associate soccer with "soccer mom," a demographic crucial to that year's presidential election. They didn't necessarily hear soccer and recall the World Cup that had blown through the nation just two years prior, in which American players wore a star-spangled monstrosity which has since lovingly, nostalgically, become known as the Denim Kit.

There were fans of soccer, but there was almost a secret-society quality to them. They'd watch a PBS weekly show called *Soccer Made in Germany* with highlights from Bundesliga games and Union of European Football Associations (UEFA) competitions. They'd congregate at English- and Irish-themed pubs to watch top-flight English teams. They'd go to newsstands and bookstores to purchase publications on "football" (for that's how most of the countries, then as now, refer to soccer) that had wended their way across the Atlantic. Before the league launched in 1996, professional soccer was hard to find: there wasn't an Internet to speak of, though it would soon come, albeit in the Pleistocene form of listservs and crudely designed websites and message boards.

Twenty years after the league's inception, of course, that's all changed. For instance, I can watch my beloved Arsenal (I've never been to London, but I love them all the same) on TV and via highlight videos; I can read and talk about them online; I can write about them for a fan-run website where Arsenal fans communicate; and, thanks to the team's first American trip in twenty-five years, in 2014 I was able to be in the same stadium with some of them.

But it's not the same as being in a stadium on a regular basis and having an ongoing relationship with a team. And if you choose the level of dedication that is part and parcel of being a supporters' group member, you have a relationship not only with a team but also with people who feel as irrationally passionate about that team as you do. You might invest time, money, and energy into proclaiming your love for your team in the enemy's stadium. You might paint a giant sheet over the course of several days, to unfurl it for only a mere thirty seconds before the start of a match, knowing that it will in all likelihood be captured by TV cameras—because, after all, that giant sheet is helping to set a fan-generated narrative for the match. You might scream yourself hoarse during ninety minutes of action. And at the end of the match, the players you've been screaming for, about, and very occasionally *at* will come over and clap for you, acknowledge you as the fans who are unabashed about your dedication.

If this sounds like the kind of experience you wish existed in American sports, then you should keep reading, because it exists in MLS.

This is a book about MLS and its first twenty years—but not everything about it. Creating a full history of MLS, even at this stage in its young life, would be staggeringly large and even encyclopedic in its scope. My intent in the following pages is to give you a sense of the arc of the league's competitive, year-to-year action. MLS has a "competitive balance" (the term the commissioner prefers to "parity") that has allowed thirteen teams in the league's first twenty years to play in MLS Cup finals, which is impressive considering that the league hovered between ten and twelve teams until 2007. And to understand the league, it's important to know at the very least who's worn its crown at any given time.

But the league's importance transcends scores, individual feats of brilliance, and even victors. Soccer in the United States is—as hokey as it might sound to the uninitiated, or even the initiated—a *movement*. Though soccer is a sport, and though it's a decidedly American inclination to win at every sport, the movement attached to American soccer is more about learning, about belonging, about syncing our steps with others' around the world. In the international game, the Americans are not favorites, our victories are continental rather than global, and our discernibly American guile and gumption makes us likable underdogs rather than a respected-yet-feared superpower. To draw from the movie *The Karate Kid*, we're more Daniel LaRusso than Cobra Kai, and given how we've fared in the last few World Cups, we're really more Daniel LaRusso before he learned how to crane kick.

MLS doesn't have the longest traditions, the best players in the world, or the most money. But it's a lot further along than it was in 1996, and there's a strong sense among many that as it grows and develops it will get to a place among the world's elite leagues, even if it continues to be slightly out of step with the rest of the world—operating without a promotion and relegation system, and on a different calendar, blithely continuing its regular season through the summer months when the rest of the world is quadrennially, exclusively fixed on the World Cup.

MLS also has a supporters' culture that deserves to be known in greater depth by greater numbers, and that was an impetus for this book from the outset. On its surface, a supporters' group is merely a self-declared group of dedicated fans who like to be loud and boisterous while wearing the colors of a hometown team. But it's clearly more than that. A supporters' group is a self-selecting community that is sometimes coarse in its language and brash in its countenance, yet ultimately an ambassador for soccer—loving the sport with an unparalleled dedication and trying to inspire that in others through example.

Supporters' groups, when they're their best selves, foster camaraderie and enable a sense of humor that is vital to following a soccer team. Even in high-scoring games, goals are events, and most fans' reactions to the majority of game action are exasperated responses to a series of moments of almost. Soccer's a sport that demands community, and supporters' groups are the most dramatic expression of that.

And yet, in 2016, community can be found digitally and instantaneously. With a Twitter account and a hashtag, you can participate in an ongoing game discussion that is constantly moving and continually providing opportunities for commentary. Soccer is best enjoyed when it can be talked about, exulted about, or laughed about. Soccer has humor, personality, anecdotes worth sharing with others, and narrative.

This book has history, to be sure, but it also has stories and voices that go beyond who scored when and which team won. The interview transcriptions that became part of this book—the voices of people who have helped shaped the game, the famous and the not so famous—were periodically punctuated by my own laughter.

The writing of this book has been a personal journey in which I set out to learn more about the sport I love in the country I love. And it all starts on a particularly important July 4.

(No, not *that* one.)

The
UNITED STATES
OF **SOCCER**

Chapter 1

THE PROMISE

In which FIFA makes the United States pledge to
create a league that everyone hopes will be more
successful than the NASL was.

IT'S PERHAPS FITTING THAT THE LATEST ATTEMPT TO CREATE A FIRST-DIVISION
American professional soccer league—the one that's stuck, the one
that's just reached a significant twenty-year milestone, and the one that
is definitively and happily alive—began on July 4. Specifically, it was July
4, 1988, when the powers that be at the Fédération Internationale de
Football (FIFA) awarded the United States the 1994 World Cup. Despite
a member of the Brazilian contingent telling the media, "Taking the
World Cup to the United States is like taking the World Series to Brazil,"
another Brazilian representative noted that if the World Cup came to the
States, "There is a great potential for economic power, and a lot of people
can make a lot of money if the games take off," and that's ultimately
what helped the United States win out over Brazil and Morocco in the
final vote.[1]

It was a bold decision for FIFA to make, in response to what arguably
was an even bolder request from the Americans in the first place. While
the United States undoubtedly had the stadiums and the infrastructure
to host a World Cup, there were certainly questions and doubts that a
nation besotted with baseball and football would turn out for soccer. For
Americans in the late 1980s, soccer was the metric system of sports:
workable for the rest of the world, perhaps, but too unfamiliar to be
officially adopted or embraced by the American masses.

There was one key stipulation in FIFA's decision to grant the United States the World Cup that made it all the more daunting: FIFA wanted the Americans to create a top-tier professional soccer league, preferably before the World Cup commenced. And this was a problem, because just thirty-nine months prior to FIFA's announcement, the prior American top-flight organization, the North American Soccer League (NASL), suspended the 1985 season when only two of the nine teams who played in 1984—the Minnesota Strikers and Toronto Blizzard—expressed interest in resuming play.[2] Despite a promise from the league that there would merely be a year's hiatus and it would return with its eighteenth season in 1986, it did not. The league ultimately best known for its flagship team—the star-studded New York Cosmos of the mid-to-late 1970s, featuring Franz Beckenbauer, Giorgio Chinaglia, and Pelé—ended, to borrow from T. S. Eliot, not with a bang but a whimper. (The actual Cosmos franchise, lasting through the NASL's doomed final season, actually called it quits midway through participation in the 1984–85 season of the Major Indoor Soccer League, which is a whimper even Eliot couldn't have imagined.)

The 1994 World Cup announcement spurred then United States Soccer Federation (USSF) head Werner Fricker to promise a national soccer league—the vision, as the *New York Times* reported, was for "one that will encompass in some way teams from existing semiprofessional indoor and outdoor leagues."[3] But it was two years later, when a Los Angeles–based lawyer named Alan Rothenberg replaced Fricker as the head of the USSF, that the origin story of Major League Soccer began in earnest.

Rothenberg's involvement in soccer began with serving as general counsel to the Los Angeles Wolves (of the United Soccer Association and the NASL's first season) in the late 1960s, and ownership of the NASL's Los Angeles Aztecs in the late 1970s.[4] In his assessment, the USSF he inherited "basically had no money, and was still being run as a grassroots organization, with a lot of good people, but without the professional or business background" needed to make a World Cup happen in four years' time.

"One of the first things I did was to go back to FIFA and indicate to them that their expectation that there would be a pro league created before the World Cup was not going to work," Rothenberg explains.

Laughing, he adds, "There was not yet enough enthusiasm or interest that would cause people to invest millions of dollars to create a league. I thought we should do that afterward, in the hope that we would build up an interest, and that would be the catalyst for the launch of a new professional league. They didn't have much of a choice, but they did agree to that."

Rothenberg notes that as early as 1991 he and his organizing team, at a retreat to carve out a mission statement, "had the audacity to say we were going to put on the best World Cup in history." But Rothenberg wanted more; he told the group he wanted to "leave a legacy for the sport of soccer" that went beyond just hosting the World Cup. He notes, "We didn't want to be the circus, where everyone had a good time and when the elephants leave, the only thing to do is to clean up what they left behind."

For Rothenberg this meant creating pre–World Cup buzz through a series of exhibition matches featuring the U.S. Men's National Team (USMNT), and making sure that cities hosting the events had their own legacy plans in place—perhaps involving franchises for the yet-to-be-planned league. One of the showcase events, the 1993 U.S. Cup, featured the American team hosting Brazil, England, and Germany in a tournament that brought the three world powerhouses (and the Americans) to four stadiums that would serve as World Cup venues—Chicago's Soldier Field, Washington, DC's RFK Stadium, the Boston-adjacent Foxboro Stadium and, for indoor stadium fans, Greater Detroit's Silverdome—along with New Haven's Yale Bowl, which was in contention as a World Cup host site prior to the late-1992 announcements.[5]

"That was a spectacularly successful tournament, and it also got people excited about the sport," Rothenberg says. "It was the precursor to the Confederations Cup, because after that, FIFA said, 'That's a great idea, the year before, we'll have a major cup [in the World Cup host nation], and it'll get the teams acclimated and it'll obviously be a test run for the organizers.'" FIFA's website does point to the Saudi Arabia–hosted International Champions Cup in 1992 and 1995 as the first editions of the actual Confederations Cup, but there's something to Rothenberg's claim about his group inspiring the test-driving of the host nation's stadiums the year before the World Cup—Korea and Japan's cohosting of the 2001 Confederations Cup, prior to their hosting of the 2002 World Cup, started the trend that has now become part of the FIFA World Cup blueprint.[6]

It also helped that the United States fared well—including a 2–0 upset of England (invoking the famous 1–0 World Cup victory in 1950 that invariably comes up whenever the United States faces its former colonial masters in international soccer) and a valiant 4–3 loss, in a comeback that just fell short, to eventual tournament winners Germany (led by Jürgen Klinsmann's four goals in three games).

Despite the good feelings, debatable Confederations Cup inspiration, and clear progress toward delivering FIFA a worthy World Cup, FIFA officials expressed concerns to Rothenberg that the professional league still didn't seem to be happening. "When I took the USSF position, I didn't expect to be the one organizing a league," Rothenberg explains. "I assumed that if we built sufficient excitement and interest, that some sports entrepreneurs would step up and say, hey, the time's right to start a league. Nobody had, and FIFA started breathing down our neck, saying you had this promise. So that's when I brought a team together. That's when I recruited Mark Abbott from my law firm to help out with the writing of the plan."

Abbott did a lot more than that. He became MLS's first employee even before it was officially MLS, rounding up the support that would manifest into sponsors as well as *investor-operators*, the term created for the people who would be running individual or multiple teams within what came to be known as the single-entity system. Abbott grew up with the NASL—at one point in his childhood, he was a ball boy with his hometown Minnesota Kicks—and in his assessment of what it would take for a new league to succeed, he turned to the NASL for lessons in what not to do, for, as he puts it, "We knew one of the first questions we were going to be asked is, 'Hasn't this been tried before? What's different now?'"

What they didn't want was a league in which there were too few haves and too many have-nots. Abbott notes, "The modern business of professional sports is one where team owners are competitors on the field and business partners off the field. And if you take a look at the NASL, you have moments of great success in certain markets, but they're not all operating on the same business plan at that time. The Cosmos in 1975 and '76 and '77 are not even playing the same game, not the game on the field, but the business game, as the San Antonio Thunder or whatever other team." Referencing his beloved NASL team, he adds,

> The Kicks had basically gotten into a million-dollar-a-year business, whereas the Cosmos were in a ten-million-dollar-a-year business, and there was such financial inequity, and such a weak set of common business principles, that ultimately when the weak teams failed, the strong teams had nobody left to play, so the league collapsed.
>
> We needed to have successful teams, but we needed to have a strong league, because even strong teams need to be part of a common enterprise. And that was the idea. The simple idea is that we were business partners, while competitors on the field, and that as a business partnership, we had the active business environment that you see at any given time.
>
> We did not think there was a market for people who wanted to own teams or fans who wanted to follow teams that had absolutely no chance of being successful. That didn't mean there weren't going to be teams that wouldn't be more successful than others. But we did not believe that an old NASL-style league, with one or two dominant teams, would allow us to grow.

Regarding getting interested parties on board, Abbott explains how "you had to get different people attached to it, and when people saw enough of a critical mass" only then would serious investors pledge their support.

"We had some early wins," he says of the nascent league's efforts to garner support. "ESPN and ABC had been involved with the World Cup, and even before the World Cup came had expressed interest in getting involved with the league. A number of potential sponsors who were involved in the World Cup or around it said, 'Hey, when you launch a league, we're interested in that.'"

The new league was also seeking a level of commitment that would extend beyond the inaugural season. "We were gutsy, I guess," says Rothenberg. "There were probably a lot of sponsors that would have given us a one-year deal, to see if this works and if so, we'll commit to something longer. But our experience was that if a sponsor only commits to a short time, they don't spend a lot of money or time giving you the promotion you want. Whereas if they've made a longer commitment, they'll actually get behind and make promotions. So we refused to do short-term deals—we refused to do a deal of less than three years. But that's a bigger sell, so it's more time-consuming."

Of course, the league also had to be sanctioned by the USSF; clearly, the Rothenberg-Abbott plan had the inside track with its Major Professional Soccer League, but there were other suitors who went before the USSF in early December 1993 in Chicago—most notably the American Professional Soccer League, which had been in operation since 1990 (and would ultimately be granted Division II status by the USSF), and League One America, proposed by Chicago marketing executive Jim Paglia, with rules that were decidedly divergent from conventional soccer. (As Beau Dure wrote in his book *Long-Range Goals* covering the early history of MLS, Paglia proposed "dividing the field into zones marked with chevrons and limiting players to specific zones for an entire period."[7])

The USSF awarded Division I status to the Rothenberg-Abbott plan just in time for a five-day soccer convention in Las Vegas involving FIFA and USSF officials; as *Los Angeles Times* reporter Julie Cart cynically assessed, "Soccer's international brain trust has come here, ensconced itself in sumptuous hotels and commenced doing what it does so well—hold meetings."[8] The week culminated with the 1994 World Cup draw on December 19 (involving singer James Brown, President Bill Clinton, actor Robin Williams, and other assorted American luminaries), but also included Rothenberg's December 17 announcement of a twelve-team, single-entity professional league that would operate under the name Major League Soccer.[9]

The coupling of the official MLS announcement with the World Cup draw made sense strategically: what better time, with the eyes of literally hundreds of millions of soccer fans on Las Vegas, to announce the beginning of a new, ambitious American league? And yet, Abbott notes that potential investors and sponsors were "holding off on committing until they saw how the World Cup went, because even in the spring of 1994, there was a lot of skepticism about it. There were polls coming out saying people weren't caring about it, all sorts of things."

The exhibition games leading up to the 1994 World Cup were as much about test-driving potential cities willing to host franchises as they were about enticing potential investors and fans. The games also helped raise the profile of national team players, which Rothenberg noted were being called into meetings with potential investors and sponsors to help the organizers seal deals. Rothenberg describes another early ally during this period, Lamar Hunt, as "really wonderful in joining us and talking to some potential investors."

Kevin Payne, who was then overseeing the U.S. Soccer Partners group responsible for putting on USMNT exhibition games between 1990 and 1994, notes that the games, billed as the "World Series of Soccer," were averaging close to 30,000 fans a game in the year leading up to the World Cup, which led him to consider assembling an ownership group for a team. He met with Rothenberg and Abbott in March 1994 to express his interest in assembling such a group, shortly after Hunt had given indications that he'd go in for at least one team. After the World Cup, when Payne learned that Stuart Subotnick and John Kluge from New York–based Metromedia were looking to create a New York team, he looked to Washington, DC, which had drawn particularly well for the exhibition games it hosted, as a potential site for the team. "We were pretty convinced that, presented properly, the sport would succeed," he says. "We really liked the DC market. At the time, of all the various stadiums that were available, RFK was actually a pretty good soccer venue . . . and we knew the Redskins were going to be moving out in '97. So [a DC MLS team] would have relative control of the stadium."

Payne worked for a British company, API, which "believed in the sport in the U.S." and was committed to being part of the ownership group. It took him about a year to put the original ownership group together, which hinged on the involvement of George Soros and the managers who worked at his Quantum Group of Funds. As Payne recalls,

"They had an internal private equity deal. Basically, anything that his managers wanted to invest in, George would match their investment. So they would have done 100 percent of the team, but our company was going to put in 20 percent, and I already had some other investors lined up, so the Soros group ended up putting in about 55 percent."

But MLS was already establishing expectations before deals were finalized. Two days prior to the start of the World Cup, MLS announced that seven initial markets would receive a franchise, including Boston, Los Angeles, New York *and* northern New Jersey, San Jose, Washington, DC, and—in a seemingly puzzling choice to casual observers—Columbus, Ohio.[10] (Columbus, by gathering nearly 11,500 deposits for season tickets, showed a level of fan support that allowed it to vault more traditional core cities for American sports leagues, and Rothenberg was quoted in the *Columbus Dispatch* on the franchise announcement saying that "'everything' was favorable about the bid from Columbus."[11])

At the time, the official party line was that MLS would still be a twelve-team league, starting in the spring of 1995. According to a *Seattle Times* article analyzing the announcement—at a time when Seattle still considered itself to be a contender for one of the inaugural franchises—the league was already concerned with which venues would be sufficiently "soccer-ready," as well as how the projected audience for soccer, in the range of 15,000 to 20,000 people, would exist inside stadiums geared toward baseball and football crowds three to four times that size:

Reflecting the scarcity of soccer-ready venues, the list of 22 bidding cities shows that most of them plan to use stadiums where college or NFL teams are primary tenants.

MLS officials prefer that teams play in 20,000- to 30,000-seat stadiums with grass fields, but few of the proposed interim facilities meet that criteria.

Of the 22 bidding cities, 10 want to drape off sections of large stadiums used by pro football teams to make the stadiums seem smaller.

Stadiums on college campuses accompany at least seven of the bids, including Phoenix (Sun Devil Stadium) and Columbus, Ohio (Ohio Stadium).

Of the cities proposing to use interim facilities, only two cities, New York and Columbus, have firm plans to build permanent stadiums specifically for soccer.[12]

As it so happened, the size and scale of American football stadiums worked to make the 1994 World Cup the best-attended edition of the tournament in history—a record that has still not been broken. FIFA's official website lists 1994's average attendance at 68,991 per match, with the most recent World Cup, Brazil in 2014, coming in a distant second at 53,592 per match (despite the best efforts of the nearly 80,000-person capacity Maracanã Stadium to skew that).[13]

The Rose Bowl, then hosting nearly 92,000 for soccer, was home to several group stage matches as well as the final; a number of other large stadiums primarily used for NFL football were utilized for the tournament, including Chicago's Soldier Field, New Jersey's Giants Stadium, Washington, DC's RFK Stadium and, perhaps inadvisably, Pontiac, Michigan's Silverdome, which was made acceptable to FIFA and the soccer world by overlaying its artificial turf surface, for the duration of the tournament, with grass grown in large trays. In an *SB Nation* article on the 1994 World Cup, American midfielder Thomas Dooley, recalling the USA–Switzerland match that opened the squad's group stage campaign, called the Silverdome "the worst place I have ever played,"[14] in large part because grass doesn't grow well at all in a domed stadium.

In a 2014 retrospective for the *Los Angeles Times*, Kevin Baxter chronicled how some of the most recognized names on the USMNT were personally inspired by the 1994 World Cup: then six-year-old Michael Bradley watched Norwegian and Italian players train in their New Jersey camps; eleven-year-old Chris Wondolowski watched Brazil train at Santa Clara, California's Buck Shaw Stadium; seven-year-old Graham Zusi ran around the Soldier Field grounds with an inflatable soccer ball as Diana Ross sang as part of the tournament's opening ceremony, and five-year-old Omar Gonzalez, a participant in the pregame festivities at the Cotton Bowl, determined then and there that he would one day play for the national team. Baxter's summation is succinct yet superlative: "Twenty years later it remains the most transformative event in U.S. soccer history, one that rescued the national federation from bankruptcy, gave birth to a top-tier professional league and proved to doubting sponsors and a skeptical public that the sport could make it here."[15]

As Alexi Lalas—the 1994 World Cup hero whose roles in the league have included player, general manager for three teams under the Anschutz Entertainment Group banner, and commentator for ESPN and now Fox Sports—recalls,

> It was a wonderful introduction . . . for people who hadn't in person seen what it could be.
>
> Two weeks before the World Cup, I got on a plane, in a middle seat on coach, as was the norm back then. I sat down next to an older lady, and we struck up a conversation, and she asked, "What do you do?" And I said, "I play soccer." And she said, "Oh, that's nice, but what's your job?" And I said, "I play soccer." And she goes, "But what do you do for money?" And two weeks later, I was playing in front of a billion people.
>
> That summer, the culture changed in relation to soccer. The soccer people came aboveground . . . because it was their thing that was finally here. And the nonsoccer people, some of it was patriotic because it was our country and we love an event, and to be able to chant "USA!" and wear the colors, that's something Americans love to do, and that was evident all summer.

The success of the World Cup—fueled in part by the patriotism Lalas described—allowed MLS to more effectively put its plans in motion. Abbott notes that once all the interested but concerned parties saw how well the World Cup had gone, "We had a series of meetings with potential investors that got really serious in terms about how this could really work, in the late summer and fall of '94. Then we started the process of really almost doing an RFP [request for proposal] with cities who had an interest. We really started to put together all the pieces we would need."

And yet the organizers sprung a surprise on those eager for the league to start up: they announced it wouldn't debut in 1995, as expected, but in 1996. "With the prior unsuccessful league, we couldn't make a mistake coming out of the starting blocks," Rothenberg explains. "If we tripped and fell, nobody would pick us up. It was better to do it right than on a particular time schedule. At the end of the day, we felt we need really substantial finances. While we had a core number of investors, we felt that we were on the margin, and taking that extra year enabled us to add a couple of investors to give us that much more financial comfort."

There was an additional reason to delay the launch. As Rothenberg points out, "Frankly, we wanted to dampen enthusiasm. It sounds crazy, but you'd just come off of this summer in '94—the most exciting soccer, full stadiums—and we knew, starting a new league, that it wouldn't look like that. If we started a new league and there were suddenly only 15,000 to 20,000 people in the stands, we knew that was a great number to hit, but the media and the public would say, 'Oh my God. This thing is a failure.' So, it was to calm everyone down between the euphoria and the launch of the league."

As Payne recalls, "The early conversations were mostly about what levels of support did we need to actually launch the league. We spent a lot of time talking about some really basic structural elements of the league, talking about how the single entity would work. And there was also quite a bit of discussion about who else could be recruited to the league."

There was also discussion about the buy-in required to be an investor-operator; Payne recalls they settled on $5 million per team. There was also an additional call option for $3 million, committing the owners to make that payment if the league needed additional funding in the beginning. The league would eventually attract Phil Anschutz—who would later prove integral to the league's survival—as the investor-operator for the team slated to go to Denver. When the league was stuck on just eight investor-operators, at what Payne characterized as a critical meeting for the nascent league's future, Subotnick pledged an additional $5 million option for a second team in New York, and Anschutz also pledged $5 million for a second team (though he wasn't even present at the meeting) to get the league to its $50 million goal. And yet, MLS would start its inaugural season with two teams—Dallas and Tampa—operated by the league.

Though cities and investors were key, the league also needed players, and felt it was important to draw from the cast who had starred in the World Cup. "There was a lot of interest in terms of U.S. national team players and international players—some of the greats came, like [Carlos] Valderrama and [Jorge] Campos," Abbott says. "There was a focused effort on that. And there were some early successes—Tab Ramos in early '95, he was the first commit. And then [John] Harkes, and [Alexi] Lalas, the names that people had learned coming out of the World Cup, and it felt very important for us to have that."

Ramos was recruited by MLS Deputy Commissioner Sunil Gulati to become MLS's first player; as he recalls, "I was in the middle of a contract with Real Betis in Spain. I was having some difficulties there after my injury in World Cup '94. I had an opportunity to come to Tigres in Mexico. Sunil came in and said, 'How about if we buy you and loan you out to Mexico, and then you sign with us?' And I said, 'But there's no league.' And he said, 'We think if you sign with the league, it'll encourage other Americans to sign.'"

So Ramos signed before any teams were announced, but at least knew there would be a team in New York/New Jersey and one in Washington, DC. As a condition of signing first, he was able to choose where he'd be slotted. In large part because his parents and other family members were in Jersey, he chose to play for what would become the MetroStars.

Once he signed, other American players recruited by MLS contacted him to ask about his commitment, and once Valderrama and Campos came on board, Ramos felt a little bit better about his decision.

MLS held its inaugural draft on February 6–7, 1996, to allow teams to claim players. Notable names included Brian McBride, who went to the Columbus Crew with the first overall pick, and a trio of players who would, upon concluding their playing careers, distinguish themselves as MLS head coaches: Peter Vermes, a third-rounder for the MetroStars who would be at his most impactful in Kansas City; Jason Kreis, a fifth-rounder for the Dallas Burn who would net his first of four double-digit goal seasons his first year; and Frank Yallop, who would round out an England-centric playing career with the Tampa Bay Mutiny.[16]

But the league's initial marquee players were slotted into teams in preparation for the MLS Unveiled launch on October 17, 1995. Ramos was the first MetroStar, Harkes was the first member of D.C. United, Lalas was the first member of the New England Revolution, and flam-

boyantly attired Mexican goalkeeper Campos was the first member of
the Los Angeles Galaxy.

MLS Unveiled was held at New York City's Palladium nightclub and
geared to generate excitement around the league and finally give fans an
idea of what they'd specifically be rooting for—which Nike's creative
team, in particular, had a not-so-subtle hand in.

Rothenberg notes that Nike wanted to be MLS's exclusive uniform
sponsor during its negotiations with the league—certainly appreciated,
as Rothenberg recalls, but not necessarily desired:

> We loved the fact that Nike wanted in like that, but we felt not
> to have the others—Adidas, Reebok at the time, Puma, Mitre—
> that it would be a mistake. We cut them back to half the teams.
> We went out and got a different ball sponsor, other teams had
> Adidas, we included all of them. We even had a referee's uniform
> sponsor, which was kind of unheard of. But the idea was to have
> anyone of any consequence in that industry to be involved with
> us. It's pretty gutsy to tell Nike, "Thanks, but you can only have
> half."

In the end, Nike did indeed end up with the rights to half the teams'
jerseys, creating the identity and multicolored looks for the Dallas
Burn, Los Angeles Galaxy, New York/New Jersey MetroStars, San Jose
Clash, and Tampa Bay Mutiny. *Los Angeles Times* coverage of the event
dutifully reported that the Galaxy's home colors were "black, chili
red, Kenyan gold and juniper," while the Clash would be playing in
"celery green, forest green, red, light teal and black," with a scorpion
for a mascot.[17]

Adidas took a relatively more sober approach with D.C. United and
Columbus Crew's jerseys, but then unleashed its palette for the Kansas
City Wiz's six-color achievement. Reebok made the New England Revolution's red, white, and blue jerseys as crazy as a tricolor jersey could
be, and Puma created a billowy forest-green-and-white look for the Colorado Rapids. The ten team uniforms, taken together, showed a definite
departure from the more traditional American sports leagues, with design elements that borrowed more from skater culture than traditional

soccer culture, and color schemes that helped fix the uniforms firmly in the mid-1990s.

While Abbott stops short of the notion that Nike had free rein over the branding process for its teams, noting that investor-operators (or the league, for teams without investor-operators) had to sign off on team names and other branding elements, he adds, "Nike played a significant role in terms of some of the thinking of team names and branding at that point."

Randy Bernstein, MLS's chief marketing officer from 1995 to 1999, remembers the process being a collaborative one in which Nike worked closely with the league in creating brands, tailoring names and colors to the specific markets where the teams would play, and choosing what he judiciously describes as "what colors were interesting to people during that time."

"We were operating on a shoestring budget compared to what the league has now," Bernstein comments. "When we had the opportunity to use the expertise of global powerhouses like Nike, Adidas, and Reebok, we were so thrilled to be able to have them as resources. At the time, we could have never afforded to hire those people independently."

As the *San Jose Mercury-News* noted in its article on the Clash's branding, there was at least public agreement between ownership and Nike's marketers as to the identity: "Nike spokeswoman Judy Campbell noted that Clash constitutes an image and attitude, the scorpion illustrates 'an attacker that is quick and mean,' and the logos and colors 'reflect the diverse ethnic make-up and heritage of the Bay Area.'" The article also noted that owner Peter Bridgewater "added that the scorpion represents the attacking style of soccer he expects the Clash to play. 'I want us winning 4–3, not 1–0.'"[18]

"It was fun," Abbott now says of MLS Unveiled. "It was a real milestone for us in terms of another step in showing we were on a path to launching a league. We were trying to demonstrate progress toward the ultimate goal of launching a league, and MLS Unveiled was one of the steps toward that."

Yet some were baffled and even perturbed by the branding decisions. Payne, in particular, observed that the uniform designs, at best, were taking their lead from the anime-inspired uniforms of the just-launched J-League in Japan.

"That worked very well in Japan," Payne comments. "That was very culturally relevant there. It wasn't here. And the suppliers thought the reason this is going to succeed is because it'll be looked at as sort of a disruptive sport. The kids like it because their parents don't know anything about it. It's generational, and it's going to have the same kind of look and feel as skateboarding or surf culture. Which just couldn't have been more off-base. You look at those original uniforms and logos and team names, and you compare them with D.C. United and you know, really, everybody else got it completely wrong. It set the league back years."

D.C. United fans witnessing the unveiling seemed to express relief that its team had the most normal of the ten uniform styles. As Paul Sotoudeh, a longtime member of the Screaming Eagles supporters' group observes, "Harkes is standing there in the D.C. United jersey and with everyone else—it looks like you took peyote! All these colors all around you!"

Ramos was a bit wary; looking back today, he notes, "Compared to the rest of the world, they seemed a little bit flashy. They seemed almost too American."

Lalas is more forgiving of the looks that MLS Unveiled brought to the league—perhaps because in the mid-1990s he was an embodiment of not just soccer fashion but the decade itself:

> It was still very much an underground, niche type of sport in the U.S. I think that a lot of that is in the way we went about positioning it, the aesthetic of it—and on the field, it was wild as well. But I think it was needed, and even necessary, as painful as it might have been. We needed to go through that to get to where we are now, twenty years out. I think it's revisionist to a certain extent to say you're against it from the start. A lot of it looks dated only because it happened in the '90s and it's relative to the '90s.

Some were upset with MLS Unveiled for other reasons—namely, that not every team was granted players by the league. Columnist Ann Killion, writing in the *Mercury-News*, groused:

Fifteen months after its momentum peaked, Major League Soccer was launched Tuesday.

Smoke, disco lights and adorable children were brought in to announce that San Jose is the proud home of an exciting, hard-nosed, competitive . . . logo.

That was the gist of a 75-minute, over-choreographed media event for the newest addition to the San Jose sports scene. The local site was connected to New York via satellite hookup for the nation-wide unveiling of MLS, the new professional outdoor soccer league, a league that was a requirement for the United States to host the World Cup, a league that originally was expected to have its debut last spring but instead will get started almost two years after soccer's finest hour on American soil.

Some of the 10 MLS teams left Tuesday's gala with an actual player. Alas, your San Jose Clash was not one of them.[19]

But the names and logos were, to those covering them, the most puzzling aspects of the event. The *Tampa Tribune*, noting that the Mutiny name wasn't a surprise due to its having been leaked earlier in the month, observed, "What was surprising is that the Mutiny have nothing to do with a pirate walking the plank. This Mutiny, conjured up by artists at Nike, is a video-game inspired, high-tech creature resembling a bat. Another version of the logo mutates into something resembling a thorny-legged bug from outer space."[20]

And in a story headlined "Wiz GM Adjusts to Name," the *Kansas City Star* reported that "radio talk-show lines buzzed with criticism of the name Wiz" following the announcement, but Wiz general manager Tim Latta claimed that once people saw the name in context with the logo, they better understood the concept (or, at least, weren't so alarmed). As he put it, "We're probably now selling eight to 10 tickets for every knee-jerk reaction we received."[21]

Perhaps the best naming and branding story in the league involved the Columbus Crew. Had Columbus-based fast food chain White Castle had its way, the would have been named the Slyders after their signature hamburger, and had team organizers gone with their initial inclination, central Ohioans might have rallied behind the Eclipse.[22] Thankfully, the team allowed its pool of potential fans to contribute ideas for team names, and Colombian-born student Luis Orozco was one of thousands of Ohioans who contributed to the naming contest. Orozco was the sole person to come up with the Crew as a name; as he told *Eight by Eight* magazine, his vision played off Columbus sharing a name with Christopher Columbus, with the "crew" here being the sailors who helped the explorer sail the ocean blue in 1492. Orozco had even conceived a motto in line with the league's desire to help Americans seek out and find the world's game at home: "Christopher Columbus discovered America; come and discover us."

On October 17, 1995—the same day as MLS Unveiled—Orozco was announced as the winner of the contest, but the "crew" the team came up with was a far different crew than the one he'd imagined. To his disappointment—and, as it would turn out, the bewilderment and amusement of many—the team adopted a construction crew interpretation of the nickname, culminating in a shield-shaped logo in which "The Crew" topped a rendering of three alleged construction workers in very broad-brimmed hard hats.[23]

Even more remarkably, given that a number of teams made wholesale branding changes before the league reached ten years of age, the Crew retained its original logo until October 2014, when the team officially rebranded itself as Columbus Crew SC and replaced the hunky trio with a simple black-and-yellow circular logo made complex by a checkerboard, diagonal lines, and a shield with the number 96 inside it.

D.C. United, like the Crew, polled its potential fan base for a name, but ended up naming itself. As Payne recalls, he was having lunch with other US Soccer Partner team members, and he was talking about wanting a traditional name for the team. Someone in their employ not involved with the team efforts cracked, "Well, why don't you just call it United? That's what all the soccer teams are called." They ended up gravitating toward the name, even though other names were under consideration.

Payne recalls,

> It's not like we immediately adopted the name. There have been a few writers who took this story out of context and decided there was no thought put into it, that it was just blurted out in a meeting and that was that. We did spend time talking about it,

but the more we said it, the more we liked it. It did answer those two elements. It spoke to the soccer community, and we also thought it could speak to the DC community. Obviously, we needed to appeal to both. We didn't necessarily think that we could survive with just the soccer community in DC. We needed to get other people in DC interested in the team, and this seemed to be a name that would do that.

Like the uniforms, the ten team names taken together, even with D.C. United's European traditionalism factored in, represented a departure from traditional American sports and its predominantly plural animal team names. A FIFA feature on the league's impending debut in February 1996 made the departure seem especially extreme. The article aimed to highlight the "bright and distinctive" team names of the ten franchises, but with language that so clearly and fancifully departed from what Americans would expect a league to say about its teams, into something wonderfully pan-European and twinkly and sounding as if it were translated into English, that it demands a full cutting and pasting:

SAN JOSE CLASH
"Clash" is a favorite media word for an intense confrontation between close rivals, and the new Clash team hopes to play like a scorpion: quick and lethal, defending by attacking.

LOS ANGELES GALAXY
LA has long had its galaxy of stars in Hollywood and no doubt hopes the new MLS team will also sparkle; the energetic spinning logo should convey the pace of the city and of the game.

COLORADO RAPIDS
Colorado is a mountain State of rushing rivers in the Rockies, fast and free as no doubt the fans in Denver hope their team's football will be.

DALLAS BURN
The fire-breathing mustang shows raw horsepower and speed in the high-combustion Texan oilfield; "Burn" is a reference not only to Texas's most famous export but also to the effects of the summer sun.

KANSAS CITY WIZ

No real local connections, it seems, but instead a play on the name of the popular musical The Wizard of Oz—the rainbow strips coming from the musical's most famous song, Somewhere Over the Rainbow.

TAMPA BAY MUTINY

Despite Tampa Bay's ocean location and the nautical overtones of the new club name, the logo contains instead what its creators call a "cyber-mutant from the dark blue depths of space . . . soccer reaching the fourth dimension."

COLUMBUS CREW

Columbus Ohio has the image of a hard-working Middle American city and the name Crew, together with the three workers in hard-hats, reflect these demographics; the Crew aims to be the hardest working team in the new league.

D.C. UNITED

The only traditional football team name in the MLS, as the team from the federal capital aims for international and community appeal not least through the eagle, a symbol of freedom and strength and of the United States itself.

NEW YORK METROSTARS

The logo aims to project the non-stop activity of a big city that never sleeps, the skyscraper metropolis stretching from home-town New York out to New Jersey and the site of the Giants Stadium.

NEW ENGLAND REVOLUTION

A tribute to the crucial role played in the American Revolutionary War, 220 years ago, by this patriotic part of the United States.[24]

Ultimately the branding appeared rooted in a desire to appeal to youth, or at the very least, what Nike and its competitors imagined young soccer fans were looking for in team names and jerseys. Abbott judiciously observes, "I think there was a debate about it at the time that has now been clarified. I think at that point in time, a lot of people believed that the primary opportunity were youth opportunities. People said that for a long time about soccer, and that was a lot of the thinking about the branding at that particular time. What we've seen over time is that really a change, where while youth market support is always going to be important, the depth of the soccer market in the United States goes way beyond that."

The perceptions of the U.S. soccer market, and how MLS would reach it, extended beyond uniforms and into how the game would be played on the field. The league adopted two significant changes from soccer as the rest of the world played it. First, game clocks in stadiums would count down from forty-five minutes to zero, opposite to the customary count up from zero, with referees monitoring the time and determining when each half ends. Second, if a game was tied after ninety minutes, MLS would use a penalty shootout system to decide a winner. For a while, there was even serious discussion of widening the goals to provide for more daring shot attempts, more acrobatic goalkeeping, and (probably) more scoring.

Even with its imperfections, its jerseys accented in celery green and Kenyan gold, its countdown clock and other assorted variances bordering on jingoism, and its inception borne of a condition for the United States to host a World Cup, Rothenberg, Abbott, the sponsors, the investor-owners, and in no small part, the fans both old and new who found something rekindled within them via the World Cup all worked tirelessly to bring a new professional soccer league from a promise to reality. So it came to be that a spring day in a college football stadium in Northern California in 1996, professional soccer returned to a nation that, if it didn't necessarily want it or need it, was at least promised it.

Chapter 2

THE KICKOFF

In which the first game goes eighty-seven minutes
without a goal but then disaster is averted and
a successful inaugural season ensues.

Not a scoreless tie. Anything but that.

That's what pretty much everyone invested in the future of Major
League Soccer was thinking when the league finally launched on April 6,
1996, for its first-ever game between the San Jose Clash and D.C. United
in Spartan Stadium. Plenty had gone well leading up to the kickoff—the
game had sold out the nearly 32,000 seats available, and it was being nationally televised on ESPN. Though the game didn't feature the best soccer ever played, it was anyone's game heading into the second half. But
then, it just kept being anyone's game, right up the point where it seemed
that the game wouldn't have a winner at the end of regulation.

Of course, had the match gone to 0:00—for the countdown clock
was part of the MLS universe in 1996—the spectacle of the shootout
would have added to the opening-day pomp. Starting from thirty-five
yards out, a player would have five seconds to dribble and attempt to
place a ball past the goalie. Five players per team would take turns doing
this; it was a twist on the conventional penalty kick shootout that international soccer utilized when it was absolutely necessary to break a deadlock. Thanks to enough of a critical mass in the MLS offices concerning
the degree to which Americans abhorred ties, breaking them was considered an absolute necessity.

But, in the eighty-eighth minute, a miracle occurred. The Clash's Eric
Wynalda—a 1994 World Cup hero allocated to the Clash to become one

of the team's marquee players—dribbled through three United defenders and curled a wicked shot from just inside the left corner of the eighteen-yard line for a beautiful goal that was later named—for its historical significance as much as it aesthetic glory—the season's goal of the year.

Or, as the Associated Press's lead paragraph on the match cynically had it, "The latest effort to create a major outdoor pro soccer league in the United States kicked off with fireworks and balloons tonight, and, after 87 frustrating minutes, there was even a goal."[1]

As Wynalda remembers,

> I'd be lying if I said I didn't think about it during the game, what a disaster it would be if it went to 0–0 and we had to do that shootout thing. The reality was, I had two really good chances during the game. One was on a free kick that the goalie had an amazing save on, I thought it was in, and on another . . . I had a great pass in and was all alone and just pushed it wide. I was thinking I'm not gonna get another chance. I was hoping for it—but I think it served me well, because in the end, when I did get the ball the way the scenario played out, I was locked in and focus, because I knew this was my last shot at scoring. It worked out perfectly.

While Wynalda expresses some regret for beating U.S. national team-mate Jeff Agoos on the play, he also notes that because he played against him in practice, he knew his tendencies, which he was able to use in his favor.

Media roundups of the match were mixed: some found aspects to be critical of, now matter how tangential, and others legitimately looked to assess how MLS's brand of soccer—albeit only one game old—fared in comparison to that of the rest of the world.

Contra Costa Times writer Gary Peterson called attention to the pregame "obligatory skydiver," who stumbled and wrestled with his chute as he made a hard landing on the field, and who then appeared confused as he looked for a dignitary to accept the commemorative soccer ball he was holding, eventually wandering over to "a group of very self-important people conducting the 3- or 4,000th pregame ceremony of the evening." Peterson then asked, "Could there have been a more tidy or symbolic portrait of Major League Soccer?"[2]

Mark Ziegler, in a *San Diego Union-Tribune* article that generally skewed positive, noted that the game had featured "a first half of uneventful and unimaginative soccer, and a second half of blown chances—the residue of new players and new teams and new coaches, all squeezed by a painfully narrow field (63 yards instead of the usual 70) and the tension of a momentous occasion." He also was impressed enough by the sale of English bangers at the concession stand to mention it twice.[3]

Grahame L. Jones, in his postmatch wrap-up in the *Los Angeles Times*, asked, "Will the quality of play in MLS live up to all the hype?" He answered himself by saying "yes and no," and despite lauding several San Jose players, added, "There was also ample evidence that MLS has signed several players who do not belong at this level. Too many late tackles, too many crude fouls and sloppy passing kept the game from rising to any great height. But despite the lack of goals, there was drama and tension, and most important, enough entertaining soccer played to probably bring the crowds back. At least, that's what MLS is counting on."[4]

The American mainstream media was predictably guarded about how the new league might fare given the NASL's demise a decade prior. Ross Atkin's *Christian Science Monitor* article, published the day before the season opener, provided a series of concerns about the league's chances for success, using soccer commentator Seamus Malin as the primary yea-sayer to counter the criticism. Atkin brought up the end of the NASL, then countered that notion with Malin's observation that "the NASL enjoyed 'tremendous success' before it flamed out, attracting large crowds in a number of cities."

Atkin also noted that when the league delayed its launch to 1996, "[a]nxiety grew about the failure to capitalize on World Cup momentum and diminished interest in major league baseball" before noting that that "the delays have been advantageous," as, according to Malin, "they distanced the U.S. public from the euphoria and excitement that surrounded the month-long World Cup."[5] Which was, of course, exactly how MLS chairman Alan Rothenberg had wanted it.

Rothenberg and other league officials were publicly buoyed by the first match—especially its ending. "I don't think we could have written a script with a better ending," he told the media after the game. "To end up with a dramatic goal by the leading goal-scorer in American soccer history before a home crowd—what else could you ask for? I wouldn't have dared to write a script that had that kind of a corny ending."[6]

"I don't think if it had been a zero-zero tie that anybody would have believed that it was an exciting game and a great (inaugural) weekend," Sunil Gulati told the media. "What they would have written was that it was zero-zero (at the World Cup final between Italy and Brazil) in 1994, and two years later, it was zero-zero again, and that nothing has changed."[7]

Mark Abbott also felt a certain satisfaction, given the work he'd been doing for three years prior to get the league to this point. "There was a sense of collective excitement that here we'd been working on this for a long time and it had arrived," he notes. "And it arrived in a way that was really successful—it had sold out, it had a good television rating. It was just a really joyous occasion where we realized we really had something here."

The opening Clash–United match was a stand-alone game on the schedule, with the league's other eight teams debuting the following weekend. That same weekend also featured the very scenario league officials and proponents had been dreading in the opener: a game went to a shootout. The Clash traveled to Dallas, and their scoreless tie switched to a win, 2–1, by the Burn. Wynalda, the first player up in the shootout, wasn't even able to get his shot off before the requisite five seconds.

"I didn't particularly like it—it was odd," Wynalda recalls of the shootout system, which he notes was only familiar to those in the league who'd been around the NASL, which used shootouts to finish games. "We practiced them, and I tried to get as much feedback as I could from goalkeepers as to what they thought about it and what their plan was. It really came down to hitting it hard, slotting it to one side or the other, or chipping it. It really just came down to those three options."

The first full weekend also placed into motion something Gulati had said in the Atkin article on how to create the energized atmosphere that would come naturally with smaller, soccer-specific stadiums, but not in the larger stadiums that teams would play in before soccer-specific stadiums could be funded, built, or even conceived: "To generate a sense of excitement and intimacy with much smaller crowds, the league has adopted a novel strategy. Teams in nine cities will use colorful tarpaulins to cover vast expanses of empty seats, effectively downsizing football stadiums. 'To expand, we just have to roll back the tarps.'"[8]

This simple and elegant solution was employed perhaps earlier than anyone had anticipated. At the first Galaxy game at the Rose Bowl—a 2–1 win over the MetroStars—soccer fans made a pilgrimage to Pasadena that overwhelmed expectations.

Nick Green, a Los Angeles–based soccer writer who attended the first match, recalled,

> All week long the L.A. Times revised (upwards) the estimated attendance for the Galaxy's first game Saturday against the New York–New Jersey MetroStars: 25,000, then 35,000, 45,000 and then somewhere north of 50,000.
>
> I drove down from Ventura with my wife in our 1983 Oldsmobile Omega, which had a habit of overheating and certainly didn't disappoint, grinding to a vapor-spewing, volcanic halt in bumper-to-bumper traffic en route. We finally got to the vast stadium, negotiated the grassy oceans of [the nearby golf course that doubled as a parking lot] and got in a huge line for tickets (the first and last time I bought tickets the day of the game).
>
> It was around half time before we got in. It was impossible to find your seat. People sat and stood anywhere. I didn't care. Football was back.[9]

The opening day crowd of 69,255—still the all-time record for an MLS regular-season game—was largely the result of what Green depicts as a multiethnic city starved for soccer.

Green notes that there was a significant Mexican American contingent in the crowd—entire families coming out to celebrate soccer, tailgating in the golf course/parking lot before making their way to the actual game.

Rick Lawes, then a *USA Today* soccer reporter, but today the MLS's resident historian, noted the Rose Bowl game provided the exact hypothetical regarding the tarp plan he'd asked Kevin Payne about before the first season started. He figured as soon as the next people found their way to a game in a stadium that had reached capacity, the team in question would likely "find a way to take their money and not turn them away."

Thanks to that stellar opening day turnout—as well as a Father's Day doubleheader on June 16, 1996, bringing more than 92,000 to see the Galaxy versus the Mutiny and the United States versus Mexico—the Galaxy led the league in attendance, with nearly 29,000 per game filling the Rose Bowl (albeit a stadium that can seat about 100,000). While numbers varied from stadium to stadium, only the Clash regularly saw its stadium more than half full—with its 17,232 average attendance, fifth among teams, comparatively testing the limits of Spartan Stadium's 30,456.

Some of the teams did not test their tarps all season. The MetroStars averaged nearly 24,000 in Giants Stadium, which held more than 80,000. The Revolution averaged just over 19,000 for a stadium holding just over 60,000. The Crew's nearly 19,000 was respectable for Columbus, but dwarfed in "The Horseshoe," Ohio State University's 102,000-plus-seat stadium. Some of the lowest-drawing teams also played in some the league's largest stadiums—Colorado drew just more than 10,000 fans a game to a Mile High Stadium that could house more than 76,000; the Mutiny drew nearly 12,000 to the 74,000-plus Houlihan's Stadium; and the Wiz had nearly 13,000 attending games at mammoth Arrowhead Stadium, which could house more than 81,000 fans.[10]

On the field, the Tampa Bay Mutiny was arguably the most dominant regular-season team, and that dominance went beyond its league-leading 20–12 record. Carlos Valderrama, one of the all-time best-known and best-loved Colombian players—partly for his talent, partly for his impressive and distinctive blond mane—entered the league as a thirty-four-year-old rookie and emerged as the league's first MVP.

Teammate Roy Lassiter, a Washington, DC–born striker who came to MLS via the unlikely route of North Carolina State University and

Costa Rica's Primera Division, banged in twenty-seven goals and added four assists, playing in thirty of the team's thirty-two regular-season games, to win the league's first scoring title. (Though Chris Wondolowski and Bradley Wright-Phillips both tied the record in the thirty-four-game 2012 season and thirty-six-game 2014 season, respectively, no one's ever broken the record.)

Midfielder Steve Ralston won Rookie of the Year honors. (Though technically everyone who played in 1996 was an MLS rookie, MLS gives the award to a player with no prior professional experience, and Ralston, just off his college career at Florida International University, definitely qualified.) Thomas Rongen, a Dutch NASL veteran who started his coaching career at a South Florida high school and elevated to the Fort Lauderdale Strikers of the American Soccer League and the American Premier Soccer League, was named Coach of the Year for his work with the new team.[11]

And yet, D.C. United—which lost six of its first seven games, and only began flirting with the .500 mark in the last third of the season—reinvented themselves, made the MLS playoffs (eight of the league's ten teams made the postseason), and proved formidable when it mattered.

Payne was confident from the get-go; he told the media, following the post–MLS Unveiled event, "The very first-line item in our budget is for championship rings. That's something we intend to do—bring home the championship in the first year."[12]

Payne attributes the team's early season woes to several factors. Coach Bruce Arena and assistant coach Bob Bradley were stretched in the early part of the season due to their U.S. Olympic team duties; the United moved their preseason training to Southern California to be closer to the U.S. team headquarters where the coaches were based. And, heading into the season's start, the team needed to acquire some players that better fit with what it wanted to do. They made acquisitions throughout the season, bringing in five key players that Payne feels made a difference in the play-off run, including Mark Simpson, who brought stability in goal, and Jaime Moreno, a skilled forward who brought out the best in the talented Marco Etcheverry, who was still hobbled from a World Cup knee injury.

Part of D.C. United's success had to do with working within the MLS system to acquire players—a system that confounded a number of their compatriots around the league. Payne comments, "I think we had success because instead of complaining and throwing our hands up, we tried to figure out ways to work within the league rules. Billy Hicks [the Burn's first general manager] used to call us Loophole United. I never thought of it that way. Loophole has sort of a negative connotation. We just spent the time to really understand the rules, and then figure out how to accomplish what we wanted to within the rules."

Payne also understood the importance of creating a proper home atmosphere within RFK Stadium, and as someone who embraced soccer traditions, was intrigued rather than frightened when he was contacted in the summer of 1995 by two soccer fans looking to create supporters' groups for the nascent team—Matt Mathai, who founded the Screaming Eagles, and Oscar Zambrano, who founded Barra Brava. Though both groups still dispute who was first, Payne recalls that he first received an e-mail from Mathai, but that Zambrano called him shortly after. Zambrano, a native Bolivian, was inspired by South American supporters' groups and wanted to create something similar for the team, whereas Mathai had been part of Sam's Army, a core group of fans going to USMNT matches, and had been following soccer in DC since the NASL's Washington Diplomats were active.

Payne says of the fledgling supporters' groups, "It was kind of a nobrainer to support this. Of course we wanted to create a raucous environment in the stadium. We went out of our way to encourage those groups." This included advocating for the groups when stadium officials said they'd restrict flags, drums, and other musical instruments. "We spent a lot of time with the stadium on that. Luckily, we were dealing with reasonable people who ran the stadium. We convinced them that we could police the fan clubs, and that this would help us be more successful. And they bought into it. Right from the beginning, we were able to do things that most of the stadiums didn't allow."

Lawes understood the advantage immediately. He recalls, in particular, that a number of supporters in the Barra Brava section were on portable metal stands, moved around RFK to fit both the stadium's baseball and football configurations:

It didn't take long for the Barra Brava to figure out when they'd jump up and down, those seats would start jumping up and down. So, even in the first years of the league, there would be these wonderful visuals of that entire set of stands, packed, with people wearing black and red and white, all jumping up and down and the seats going up and down. We maybe didn't have the tifo, the big huge banners, but they did have banners that they'd display along the front railing, and that people would hold up, and it was 1996, but it was really the first. They were really the forerunners, and there wasn't really anything like that anywhere else. There were certainly places that had good crowds, and big crowds, and people going to their games, and people supporting them, but what you look at now, as far as the MLS supporter culture, DC was it. It was really pretty awesome. Poor RFK gets beat up these days, and it seems like it's going to fall down at any stretch, but the architecture of the place, with the roof covering up all the seats, was such that if you had 25,000 people in there, it was a rock concert.

Payne involved the groups early on. Mathai created a webpage on his personal site that would eventually morph into the official Screaming Eagles site, and when Payne's team was mulling over the team name, Mathai created an online poll to allow fans to vote. Mathai recalls that the team took out an ad in the *Washington Post* directing fans to vote, pointing them to his website.

Sotoudeh recounts, "The three names were Justice, Force, and Spies . . . Matt looked at those and said, 'Eww, those are awful.' A couple of weeks later, Kevin called Matt and said, 'You know, I've been talking to folks, and what do you think of the name D.C. United?' And Matt breathed a sigh of relief, and said, 'That sounds great.'"

Once United was an option, Mathai explains, "I did everything I could to drum up votes for it. I strong-armed everyone I knew into voting for it. Family, friends, kids, everyone. I didn't resurrect people from the dead to vote, but I was tempted to. D.C. United won in a landslide."

Though the assumption was that Barra Brava drew a Latino fan base and the Screaming Eagles drew an Anglo fan base, representatives from both groups insist that the groups were ethnically diverse from the outset; Sotoudeh goes as far as to say, "Barra Brava had chants in Spanish, but the Eagles had Spanish chants, too—we just did them with more white people!"

Jay Igiel, a longtime Barra Brava member, notes that from the outset two stylistically differences distinguished Barra Brava from the Screaming Eagles: first, "A large number of our songs and chants are in Spanish, and are adaptations of songs sung in South or Central America," and second, "through the atmosphere of really continuous singing, jumping, the involvement of the drums," which he characterizes as "more organic, free-flowing and lasting than the English style, which is more start and stop."

The United (if not yet entirely united) support helped propel the team to second in the East, and, thanks to the league's playoff plan, the opportunity to witness a plethora of playoff matches.

After a regular season that concluded on September 22—with only the Revolution and Rapids failing to make the first-ever MLS playoffs—the league embarked on a playoff schedule wedging a potential six matches per team into a tight window leading up to the first MLS Cup on October 20.

The eight-team playoffs incorporated a best-of-three format; the team with the better record hosted games two and three. Each of the four conference semifinals went to three games—with the series between D.C. United and the New York–New Jersey MetroStars providing particular drama and helping to foment the rivalry's contentious nature.

The rivalry was aided, in part, by the MetroStars having their own supporters' group, the Empire Supporters Club. Like the Screaming Eagles, the group was started before the league launched, with Sam's Army veterans in leadership positions.

Mark Fishkin, part of the original group of MetroStars fans in 1996, recalls meeting with many of the original members, who were interested in joining the Empire Supporters Club but also interested in seeing it expand beyond the core fifty members—a goal not necessarily paramount to the group in its first years.

"They were very funny and clever and even snarky," he said. One favorite early anti-United chant, "Sos Cagon Washington" (based on a taunting chant Argentine club River Plate directed at their Boca Junior rivals) name-checked their rival supporters' groups, including the lines, "Screaming Eagles are posers, they sing for the TV" and "Your Barra is quiet whenever you're losing." Ribbing other teams has remained part of their routine throughout their evolution; they would go on to welcome Houston to the league by calling them "just a street in Manhattan," and give an American welcome to Toronto by informing them, "You can be State 51."

D.C. United lost the series opener to the MetroStars via shootout after giving up a tying goal in the seventy-fifth minute; as a Jeff Bradley article on the MLS site noted, MetroStars sub Giovanni Savarese "[tugged] the shirt of rookie defender Eddie Pope to gain just enough space to touch the ball into the net from close range." The shootout went eleven players deep and involved controversy. As Bradley later recalled, "The MetroStars appeared to be out of shooters because (Peter) Vermes had injured his shin during the game and was not on their original list of shooters. When he stepped up to take his turn, D.C. claimed he was shooting out of order and, therefore, a miss should be recorded. Chaos ensued on the field before Vermes limped out to take his shot, which he made."[13]

The United, however, won game 2, with a score of 1–0, and in thrilling fashion won the deciding game 3, giving up a tying goal in the eighty-sixth minute, and nearly giving up a tie-breaking goal a minute later, only to win a penalty in the eighty-ninth minute and convert.

The other three conference semifinals had their own moments of drama. In the East, the Mutiny won on the road, 2–0, to open its series against the Crew, then lost 2–1 in the first match in Tampa, but then won 4–1 in the deciding match—with Lassiter scoring five of the Mutiny's seven goals in the series. In the West, the Galaxy lost the opener against the Clash in San Jose, 1–0, and then won a pair of 2–0 matches in the Rose Bowl to close out the series—though that makes it sound easier than it was, given that the game 2 goals came in the eighty-fourth and ninetieth minutes.

The other semifinal in the West was also the hardest one to say with a straight face: the Wiz and Burn went to a shootout in the deciding game 3, after each team won a home match by one goal. In the shootout, Frank Klopas, Preki, and Paul Wright made their goals to lead the Burn to a 3–2 win.

The conference finals weren't as suspenseful in that they were both 2–0 sweeps. Kansas City did take Los Angeles to a shootout at home in game 2, after the Galaxy beat the Wiz, 2–1, at home in the opener, but the Wiz were bested 3–1 in the shootout. The Eastern Conference finals between the United and the Mutiny became the Raul Diaz Arce show— he scored a hat trick in the 4–1 opener in DC, and then scored a late winner in the second game to propel D.C. United to the finals.

MLS adopted the Super Bowl/Final Four model of preselecting a site for its first finals, and apparently did not consult the *Farmer's Almanac* before selecting Foxboro Stadium just outside Boston. A torrential rainstorm, accompanied by winds of up to fifty miles per hour and temperatures in the low fifties, made the field borderline unplayable. But as the *Christian Science Monitor* pointed out, the league's willingness to play the game—and the willingness of nearly 35,000 fans to witness it—said something about the hardiness of soccer folk:

> The same nor'easter that wreaked havoc here had made a mockery of any attempt to hold Game 1 of the World Series in New York the night before, dropping four inches of rain on Yankee Stadium. But MLS was out to show it was of tougher stock, and the opportunity for a little one-upsmanship was not lost on MLS Commissioner Doug Logan.
>
> "There was never any doubt in our minds that we were going to play this game," Mr. Logan declared in the press tent over the sound of flapping canvas and smacking rain. "And there was never any doubt that we stood in juxtaposition to some sports that don't play in the rain."[14]

The Galaxy went up 1–0 in the fifth minute on a goal by Eduardo Hurtado, nicknamed El Tanque (the Tank) and responsible for a team-leading twenty-one goals during the regular season. Chris Armas would make it 2–0 in the fifty-sixth minute, and as the rain continued to pour down and the minutes ticked down toward a Galaxy victory, the United dramatically rallied. On a seventy-third-minute corner kick, Etcheverry lofted a corner kick to the back post that found a leaping Tony Sanneh for a deftly headed goal.

Mathai recalls that Payne left the executive box to stand with the Screaming Eagles in the downpour during the second half; for a 2011 MLSSoccer.com article, Mathai remembered the moment Sanneh's goal went in: "I screamed and as Kevin and I hugged, we fell over onto the people standing in the row in front of us. Thank God they were there—I could have killed our president."[15]

D.C. United wasn't done. With eight minutes left and Etcheverry free-kicking from a dangerous area, substitute Shawn Medved was in perfect position to settle an ill-advised Campos punchout to force extra time.

And, less than four minutes into extra time, Eddie Pope headed home an Etcheverry corner kick that would be his third assist of the day, evoking a wild celebration. Etcheverry recalled, for MLSSoccer.com,

> After we scored, I saw everyone celebrating and euphoric and I only thought it was because we were up in the score.
>
> I didn't think the game was over. That's one of the memories I had. I thought it was our third goal but there was a lot of celebration. And I celebrated with them. But when I saw no one was getting ready to kick off again, I realized the game was over.[16]

In the cleverly titled "Galaxy Go Thud in Mud," Kevin Acee of the *Los Angeles Daily News* described the Galaxy's postmatch deflation:

> Exhausted, hurting and so wet and cold their internal organs were shivering, the Galaxy players marched quickly off the marsh that used to be the Foxboro Stadium field.
>
> It was more than not wanting to watch the Washington D.C. United skip around in the mud while accepting the trophy they were certain was theirs. They were simply in a trance.
>
> Having a two-goal lead yanked from you in the final 17 minutes of the championship game will do that.[17]

Mathai almost didn't make the game—his flight from Washington to Boston was grounded in New Jersey, and he and fellow fans rented a car at the airport and drove the rest of the way. As he recalls of the match, "I've never felt an atmosphere like that before or since. The stadium was mostly DC fans, as you might expect given the opponent was LA, and it was loud. I have that match on my phone and I still watch it every month or so and it still gives me chills."

United fans were so moved by the win that they treated the players returning home to Washington to a postmatch celebration. An Associated Press article noted that nearly a thousand fans swarmed National Airport to laud the returning players, arriving an hour before the team was due to arrive:

> When the drums and chants of "Ole, Ole" started 20 minutes before the team's arrival, police bolstered security.
>
> After the first officer on the scene radioed that the "crowd was too big too handle," a group of officers ushered fans from the boarding area and down a level to the terminal's larger baggage claim concourse.
>
> The players, many weary after celebrating the MLS's inaugural title game, appeared startled by the size of the crowd.
>
> [John] Harkes and the other players were engulfed by a sea of singing fans in the team's red and black colors as they rode down the escalators to the baggage claim.[18]

To be successful in its first season, MLS had, first and foremost, to survive, and it decidedly did so. League officials had projected attendance numbers of 8,000 to 10,000, and with an average of over 17,000, had definitely underpromised and overdelivered.

All the franchises survived their inaugural season, though one team name—not surprisingly, the Wiz—didn't. New York City–based electronics retailer Nobody Beats the Wiz (whose unwieldy name doubled as a slogan, and was often abbreviated colloquially as just the Wiz) argued that Kansas City's team name infringed on their copyright, and the franchise opted to change its name from the Wiz to the Wizards, but still retained their rainbow color scheme.

At the start of the season, U.S. national coach Steve Sampson observed, regarding MLS's future, "The most important thing is stability. We shouldn't have such great expectations that we can hope to compete with the major sports in the U.S. right away. If we can establish slow growth, but consistent growth, in four to five years we'll probably have the fifth major sport in this country."[19]

To kick off the league's second season, Logan made the bold prediction that MLS attendance would rise appreciably from the first season, settling on the nice round number of 20,000.

This turned out to be an overly optimistic prediction; average game attendance for the 1997 season actually fell to under 15,000, and some playoff games ebbed into four-digit territory. Logan, to his credit, owned the misstep in predicting such a significant increase. At a press conference preceding the 1997 All-Star Game at Giants Stadium, he addressed the then average of 15,500, saying, "Fifteen-thousand-five-hundred is very credible, except for the fact that this idiot went out and said his goal was 20,000. By comparison it pales."

He also said, in an odd metaphor to contrast the first and second seasons, "We had this infant baby sitting in a cradle. Everyone had taken great delight in the birth. As with newborn babies, nothing goes wrong. Everything is terrific. Everyone overlooks even the soiled diapers. In a very real way, we're administering to a league that's going through its terrible twos."[20]

Back in the league offices, the 20,000 comment was merely seen as Logan being positive about MLS rather than making a bold promise the league was incapable of delivering on. "He was the leader of an organization trying to be optimistic," Abbott remembers. "He was thinking, let's set a goal, and some people really wigged out about that. Here we are twenty years later, and guess what? We're not hurt by the fact that someone twenty years ago said we'd be averaging 20,000 in our second season."

Yet some expressed concern about the proclamation. Payne notes, "He was trying to be bullish and optimistic. It ended up being a millstone around our necks. And for years, every MLS game story started out, in the first paragraph, there was always a mention of the attendance. And that didn't happen in the NHL—the Washington Capitals were drawing six thousand people a game! But it was always part of the story about MLS games. It took us a long time to lose that."

Lawes adds, "It certainly brought everything to bear on that attendance number that second year and beyond," noting that while the National Basketball Association had established from the inception of the Women's National Basketball Association that attendance was not a barometer for the league's success, Logan had invited the media to use attendance to calibrate the league's performance.

MLS was decidedly making strides ahead of its initial season in providing soccer worth watching. In a *New York Times* article assessing the midseason status of the league's sophomore year, Harkes noted, "The product has increased on the field. Foreign players have settled in, and the young American players are starting to lift their level of play. Last year, some of them were nervous and panicked a little. Now they're more confident."[21]

Fans were making strides as well; the Screaming Eagles were embarking on well-organized road trips of the variety that Sotoudeh said made for comprehensive fan support—one example of this being a trip billed the Northeast Invasion, in which a busload of fans from Washington, DC, was able to root for the United against the MetroStars on a Saturday before proceeding to Foxboro Stadium for a U.S.–Mexico and Mutiny–Revolution doubleheader the next day, returning on a Monday.

"I don't think you can't call yourself a fan group if you're not traveling," Sotoudeh explains. "It's expected. Around the world, away days are a huge part of being a fan—the idea that you'll always be there for your club. From a purely organization-building perspective, those kinds of trips, especially the overnight trips, really build camaraderie." He also points out that new chants would be practiced on the bus, tested out in away stadiums, with the ones proving satisfactory brought back to RFK.

The Screaming Eagles also helped bring about a change in how supporters' groups partnered with their clubs to fill seats, stemming from Mathai's wishes to move to a different part of the stadium. In the inaugural season, Barra Brava was in section 135 of the stadium—visible to TV audiences on the right side of the field—while the Screaming Eagles were across from them in section 113, above the dugout where the players would come out. Mathai wanted to move the Screaming Eagles into section 134—in part to be seen, and in part to help the two supporters' groups seem like one massed, unified front. Mathai talked to Fred Matthes, the United's director of ticket sales, about wanting to move there but, as Mathai explains,

> He refused, saying that those seats were too valuable and would sell easily. David Goodwin [a good friend and the current Screaming Eagles president] convinced me to take over section 134. We spent all but one thousand dollars of our money and bought the front row of 134. We figured that as season-ticket holders, they couldn't kick us out. We've been there since the start of 1997 and have since completely sold out 134 as well as a couple of sections on either side and other blocks around the stadium. I almost bankrupted us by commissioning a large sign to be put up in front of our section at RFK. It was huge and ultravisible. Most importantly, it would be in plain sight every time the TV camera passed the midfield line. I figured that people would see the sign and the group and want to come out and join the fun. It worked.
>
> Ticketing was a pregame nightmare. We'd man a ticket window and the team would have to shuttle us more tickets as we sold our stock. We didn't have the time, and the team didn't have the resources, to devote to shuttling back and forth on game day to give us more tickets to sell. Fred and I came upon an arrangement that the team would hold aside an entire section of tickets and turn them over to us. At the end of the day we'd hand over the unsold tickets and the money. Additionally, we'd get the tickets at a discount, allowing us to give our members a price break and keep some cash off each ticket in addition. It's a classic win-win. The team doesn't have to worry about selling three to four sections in the stadium while we get discounted tickets for our members.
>
> The trust came in time. I always insisted that we obey the team rules to the letter. We'd always ask before doing anything. By doing that and establishing ourselves as "good citizens," we

laid the groundwork to be able to ask for more stuff down the road since the team knew we would stick to any arrangement we made.

Our arrangement with the team was unique for the time and pretty revolutionary. Fred used to tell me about the league meetings he'd attend where he'd be asked by other league executives how he could just turn blocks of tickets over to us.

The league's 1997 story ended in much the same way the 1996 season did—namely, with D.C. United holding the MLS Cup on a waterlogged field. As in 1996, eight of the league's ten teams advanced to the playoffs, with teams advancing in their conferences via a best-of-three series.

D.C. United's route to the finals involved series sweeps. Against the Revolution, they dominated their opener, 4–1, and then won a shootout match on the road to close out the series. In the conference finals, they edged the Crew 3–2 and 1–0 to advance to the MLS Cup, which just happened to be in their home stadium.

The Western Conference also involved sweeps, though from an unlikely candidate. The Colorado Rapids—the league's worst team in 1996—also finished the 1997 season with a losing record again, but it was good enough to finish fourth in the West and win a date with Kansas City, whom the Rapids dispatched via a shocking 3–0 win at Arrowhead Stadium, followed by a 3–2 win at home.

The Burn got past the favored Galaxy on the other side of the bracket with a shootout victory (following a scoreless regulation) and then a 3–0 drubbing at home. The Rapids won its first match, 1–0, in Dallas, and then closed out the series at home in a 2–1 match that saw both sides trade goals in the first five minutes, followed by a tense, scoreless eighty-two minutes, broken when Chris Henderson bicycle-kicked the Rapids into the finals.

Sanneh, who sparked the 1996 comeback, was the outright hero of the 1997 finals, assisting Moreno on his opening thirty-seventh-minute goal and capturing the lead on a sixty-eighth-minute strike. Though the Rapids' Adrian Paz would score in the seventy-fifth minute to mount the start of a potential flashback-inducing comeback, they'd get no closer than 2–1, and United fans—by virtue of MLS selecting RFK as the "neutral site" location for the 1997 Cup—got to relive the rainy trophy presentation of 1996 in their own home stadium.

MLS officials spent the day after the finals congregating in a Washington, DC, hotel to contemplate the future. Associated Press reporter Joseph White noted that they were looking to reverse a "16 percent decline in regular season attendance and 14 percent dip in cable television ratings" as well as contemplating the end of the shootout and perhaps replacing it with overtime. Logan expressed concern with overtime fitting into the allotted two-hour TV time slot for a game; one proposal floated the possibility of an eight-minute overtime period that could fit within a telecast.

Logan struck a decidedly more cautious tone than he did before the 1997 season started, saying, "We have the patience to wait this thing out until we get it great and right. And we're going to take those small steps, and we're going to resist trying to create instant answers for anything," terming the 1997 MLS Cup "another step along the way."[22]

Payne, in a *Washington Post* article looking at the future of the league, said, "This whole league has been built from the beginning on a long-term vision. We didn't want to be a flash in the pan."[23]

And yet, the league would embark upon something ambitious the following year—bringing in two expansion teams for its third season, and going head-to-head with the quadrennial event that helped give birth to the league in the first place. For those invested in the league, 1998 would be important in gauging its solvency.

Chapter 3

THE FIRE AND THE FUSION

In which one team enters the league and has instant
success on many levels, and another team enters
the league in South Florida.

In 1998, THE STILL FLEDGLING MAJOR LEAGUE SOCCER PUSHED TO EXPAND
to twelve teams, which involved two cities that are, in a number of important ways, quite similar. Both are among the United States' most populous TV markets, serve as anchor cities for geographically sprawling regions, are home to sports franchises that have writ themselves into the annals of their respective sports, and—perhaps more important to a league entering its third season—have large and diverse multinational and multiethnic communities—important for MLS's strategy of appealing to fans already familiar with and hungry for soccer.

But, from the get-go, in choosing Chicago and Miami, MLS set the franchises upon divergent paths. The Chicago Fire made the best possible journey for a franchise in its debut year, winning both the MLS Cup and the U.S. Open Cup en route to becoming firmly entrenched as an MLS franchise. The Miami Fusion, on the other hand, would be out of the league within four years, a reminder of the fragility of fledgling soccer franchises, which invested observers knew all too well from the NASL's swan song. Fortunately for MLS, Miami was an anomaly rather than an omen of additional folding franchises.

The league announced both teams jointly in April 1997; Phil Anschutz would exercise his option for a second team from the initial investor operator meetings to launch the Chicago team, while Cellular One co-founder Ken Horowitz, based in South Florida, would own the Miami franchise. As Grahame L. Jones wrote in his *Los Angeles Times* article covering the announcement, Horowitz "paid $20 million for an MLS franchise that two years ago would have fetched a quarter of that price."[1]

Peter Wilt, who became the Chicago team's GM in July 1997, recalls, "The first thing I did was visit every other MLS team, to do a best practices tour. And, as it turned out, it ended up being a worst practices tour. I learned what not to do from virtually every team in the league except for D.C. United."

One memorable moment in Wilt's tour took place in Kansas City; there he noticed Wizards GM Tim Latta getting on a walkie-talkie to instruct security to throw several fans out of the stadium. They'd been tossing confetti, and as Latta told Wilt, "Our agreement here with the stadium is that we have to pay for cleanup, and it's so expensive to clean up after the games."

"That's obviously an extreme example," Wilt notes, "but it kind of encapsulates the relationship between the front office and supporters in the early days of MLS. They saw the supporters as a nuisance, maybe a necessary evil."

In Washington, DC, however, Wilt saw the one team that wasn't afraid of supporters' culture, and it made an impression on him. "They had three strong supporters' groups there, they created a culture in the organization that was in some ways driven by the fans. That was something that I thought was authentic, and we tried to replicate it in Chicago."

The team staged an event in October 1997 at Chicago's famed Navy Pier to announce the team name; as *Chicago Tribune* writer Bonnie DeSimone pointed out in her article on the launch, the team's decision to hold it on October 8, the anniversary of the infamous Chicago Fire of 1871, "dropped a broad hint" as to what the team would be called. And, yet, as DeSimone's article notes,

> An entirely different name, the Rhythm, was all but set in stone earlier this year when MLS announced its expansion into Chicago for 1998. It had been conceived by sportswear monolith Nike, which held the first option to be the team apparel supplier,

and approved by the league office. The Rhythm logo and colors, a coiled cobra in red, yellow and black, already had appeared on merchandise in soccer catalogues.

But there was one small glitch. The Colorado-based ownership balked at the name. Early this summer, the team backers dug their heels in and so did Nike. And while the situation eventually was smoothed out and Nike stayed in the fold, the struggle points up the high stakes involved in naming pro sports teams in today's market.

DeSimone pointed out that after rejecting the Rhythm, team president Bob Sanderman and Wilt went about test-driving other possibilities; Blues and Wind were considered and rejected in favor of Fire, even though the name had been used once before, by a mid-1970s franchise in the now defunct World Football League.[2]

Wilt's concern heading into the launch event was how it would translate into selling season tickets the next day. The Fire followed the event with a traditional media campaign: full-page ads in the city's two major newspapers, and TV ads featuring Jimi Hendrix's "Fire" playing over a montage of top MLS players (which, as Wilt described them, "were probably seen then as really cool and cutting-edge, but when you look back on them now, you were almost embarrassed at how rudimentary they were").

First and foremost, Wilt wanted the season-ticket sales numbers for Soldier Field to surpass two thousand—the number that the Colorado Rapids had sold so far for 1998. Competition with the Rapids, in fact, was something that drove the Fire's young front office. Looking back, Wilt says, "I think early on in MLS, people thought having single ownership [of multiple teams] would result in teams colluding with each other. We were competitive, on and off the field. I mean, we shared best practices, but we cared more about outdrawing Colorado than New York or DC or LA. We wanted Mr. Anschutz to like us best."

But there was more to the Fire's strategy than what Wilt termed the "outbound, external approach"—he also sought to encourage the supporters' culture that gave D.C. United its home-field advantage. As he recalls, "We connected with the group that became the Barn Burners. Even before we had a name and they had a name, they were online, on a listserv. I communicated with Don Crafts, who was the leader of that group and ended up being the first president of the Barn Burners, and gave them credibility and recognition as legit, and to an extent, inside information as to what was going on. I gave them an opportunity to look at Soldier Field and pick where they wanted to stand during games. They felt a connection to the team and were able to organically grow."

Wilt cheekily observes that building fan culture wasn't the only aspect of D.C. United that Chicago wanted to replicate. The Fire did, after all, hire Bob Bradley away from the United to become the Fire's first head coach three weeks after announcing the Fire name. And they were also taking notes on United's player acquisitions; when Wilt was overseeing the Minnesota Thunder in 1996, United was the only MLS team to inquire about Tony Sanneh. "He turned out to be an okay player," Wilt laughs, marveling. "He's playing in the second division of America and there's only one team that's trying to sign him?"

"D.C. United was an outlier in the early years of MLS, in that they did not rely exclusively on Sunil and the league office to provide players," Wilt continues. "I don't think any team relied 100 percent on the league, but D.C. United, more than any other team, was out pounding the pavement, using their networks, scouting and working lower divisions."

The Fire built a team with two aspirations in mind: gathering good players who would function together as a cohesive team, and signing players that would appeal to Chicago's diverse demographics—particularly, as it turned out, its Polish contingent. Polish national team captain Piotr Nowak, along with Jerzy Podbrozny and Roman Kosecki, became pillars of the new team. Another Eastern European player, defender Lubos Kubik from the Czech Republic, rounded out a so-called Eastern bloc. Greek forward Frank Klopas was acquired from the Columbus Crew in a trade; Wilt contends that the Wizards "tried to bury him in Columbus" by trading him to the Crew just prior to the 1997 MLS expansion draft, which allowed the Fire and Fusion to draft unprotected players from the league's other teams. Another trade, with the Galaxy, brought Jorge Campos and Chris Armas to the Fire; despite Campos's high profile, Wilt felt that Armas was the key player in the deal.

Like D.C. United before them, the Fire had two high-profile fan groups that helped create atmosphere in Soldier Field, and like Kevin Payne before him, Wilt knew it would help create stadium atmosphere to coordinate efforts with supporters' groups rather than ignore them or work against them.

The Barn Burners 1871 were created shortly after the announcement of the team coming to Chicago in 1997, under the working title of the Chicago Ultras, officially taking a Great Chicago Fire–themed name soon after the Fire made its initial arrhythmic name announcement. Group founder Don Crafts reached out to Anschutz's group in Denver soon after MLS announced a team was coming to Chicago, and was directed to the recently hired Wilt. Crafts found Wilt to be incredibly receptive; he remembers, "He hooked me up with everything we could hope for. He gave us information, he let us know it was going to be at Soldier Field, he asked where we wanted to sit in the stadium—which was fantastic." Wilt, in fact, proposed section 8 for its having cheap seats near where cameras would capture shots on goals, corner kicks, and other game action.

"He also hooked us up with being able to have banners and drums, and other things regular fans couldn't bring in," Crafts adds, noting that the Fire issued the team special laminate badges to get through certain doors and, eventually, allowed the Barn Burners to store gear in the stadium.

Crafts had also reached out to Matt Mathai early in his process of starting the Barn Burners to learn more about how to start a supporters' group. Mathai sent samples of what the Screaming Eagles gave to members and fielded Crafts' questions.

The Barn Burners, like the Screaming Eagles, started via online communications among soccer fans initially, but then graduated to meetings in conjunction with Premier League game showings at Chicago-area bars. The group initially started with about fifty people—by Crafts' characterization, split between urban and suburban twenty-somethings, with Craft being one of the few thirty-somethings involved—but by the middle of the first season, its ranks had swelled to over three hundred, thanks in large part to tailgate parties they were hosting.

"Personally I came to it with a punk rock, DIY ethic," Crafts explains. "We didn't want a product presented to us. We needed to be an integral part of the club, not customers. We were all in, and wanted desperately to make this thing happen and make it amazing."

The Fire Ultras were founded in early 1998 by a group of about thirty Polish fans, some of whom had recently immigrated to the United States and drew experience from being at games in Europe. As founder Mirek Krupa (known to his fellow fans as Mike from Fire Ultras) explains, "I think our group was responsible for bringing to MLS something different. Back then, in my personal opinion, none of the MLS clubs could compete with us when it came to the soccer atmosphere and organized support at the stadium. We had plenty of respect for D.C. United, but they were not even close to us back then. When I watch MLS now I'm proud of most things I see in the stadium: the atmosphere, the flags, banners, supporting sections; everything looks pretty good, and I think it is going in the right direction."

He also cheekily describes the Fire Ultras' specialty as "getting in trouble," and notes, "I was banned from the games many times. The police and security did not know how to deal with us, and we were in constant conflict with them. They were giving us trouble for everything but, believe it or not, they gave us everything that we wanted: a reputation as bad boys, and that's exactly what we wanted. The bad boy rep made our group extremely popular and we grew in numbers exponentially"—to an estimated eight hundred by the end of the first season.

Liam Murtaugh, an original Barn Burner, remembers that the Fire Ultras' style of standing for the entire game "was pretty novel for everyone involved, including security, who repeatedly pulled down anyone who tried to stand up in front of everyone. This was '98, this was old Soldier Field, and it's a certain kind of security. They'd never seen anything like this before in their lives."

Though the Barn Burners and Fire Ultras were the most prominent of the supporters' groups, Wilt notes that the Fire drew such a diverse contingent of fans—including a great number of Latino fans—that public address announcements were made in English, Polish, and Spanish.

"The very first game, there were more than 36,000 people there," remembers Ben Burton, part of the first season's Barn Burners, "and I'd estimate that 60 percent of the crowd, if not more, were non–white bread U.S. men's fans. They were fans from all over, and they brought a different flavor. Different styles, different methods of supporting; so there were clashes for sure, in the way that people did everything. It was a cacophony, and quite chaotic, but it was beautiful at the same time."

Chicago, in its first year, certainly bore out Burton's assertion that "you can't really have a major sports league in the U.S. without Chicago."

In Miami, Horowitz was discovering that MLS ownership was perhaps more challenging than he'd first anticipated.

Logan's announcement of the Miami franchise included mention of a ten-year deal in place with the Orange Bowl, but according to Horowitz, Miami mayor Joe Carollo "changed the deal" on the team in the summer of 1997. A *Miami Herald* article on the troubled negotiations reported, "The future of Miami's expansion Major League Soccer team was left in doubt . . . because of an acrimonious lease disagreement that boiled over—of all places—in the men's restroom at Miami City Hall." There Horowitz told Miami commissioner Tomás Regolado that he was ruling out the Fusion playing at the Orange Bowl—in part because the city was insisting on a ten-year lease, whereas Horowitz sought "a three-year or five-year lease, with an out clause after three years if average attendance finishes below 16,000."[3]

The article detailed Horowitz's predicament: other area stadiums didn't meet the league's minimum capacity, and the franchise couldn't be moved from South Florida without league approval. But the article hadn't factored in what Horowitz planned in order to move forward: take an existing stadium (in this case, Fort Lauderdale's Lockhart Stadium, a 7,800-seat facility operated by Broward County Public Schools), and completely renovate it to be a soccer stadium with a capacity of over 20,000.

Within weeks, the "courtship," as the *Miami Herald* characterized it, was underway, with one Broward County School Board member reasoning that the expanded capacity would, at the very least, allow the stadium to host high school football championships.[4]

Horowitz remembers, "We had a season coming up . . . I had no choice. We said, 'Let's build the stadium,' we hired a design firm, and we did it." While not disclosing the exact amount he personally spent to finance the stadium renovations, Horowitz said it was definitely in seven-figure territory and approaching $10 million, though MLS's website puts it at closer to $5 million.[5] The renovations included redoing the field, expanding the stands to accommodate three times what they once held and putting in new lighting, an electronic scoreboard with video capabilities, broadcasting facilities, and offices for the team's game-day operations.

A number of league officials and historians credit the Columbus Crew SC (and Lamar Hunt's ownership group) with building the league's first soccer-specific stadium in 1999. Although Lockhart wasn't "built" in the strictest sense of the term, Horowitz contends that Lockhart was the league's first soccer-specific facility, even noting that Hunt came to Fort Lauderdale and scouted Lockhart as he was planning the stadium. Horowitz boasts that Lockhart was transformed into "the best soccer field in the country—brand-new stands, broadcast lighting, beautiful field, the seats were right up at the field. It was a gorgeous stadium. People went on and on about how great it was."

Jeff Rusnak, in an October 12, 2008, *Sun-Sentinel* article, remembers, "When the Fusion debuted at Lockhart a decade ago . . . MLS teams were secondary tenants in football stadiums that were too big, often too narrow, and never truly home; Horowitz took the first step in changing all that when he abandoned plans to play at the Orange Bowl and instead expanded Lockhart to seat 20,000 fans. The Fusion lost to D.C. United in its opening game, but it wasn't the result that stuck. Instead, it was the sight and sound of 20,450 people packed into an intimate, almost claustrophobic stadium that had a pulse rarely seen in larger MLS sites."[6]

Horowitz, who moved to West Palm Beach in 1989, was aware of both the opportunities and frustrations of operating a sports franchise in South Florida. On the one hand, he was operating a team in a media market with nearly five million people, with a significant Latino population, a smaller but still significant European ex-pat population, and an NASL legacy in the Miami Gatos and then Toros, which rebranded (more successfully) as the Fort Lauderdale Strikers for seven seasons.

But on the other hand, it *was* a sports franchise in South Florida. As Horowitz recalls,

> Everyone wanted to see Florida work. There was a lot of discussion—the league was actually split on whether Florida was going to be successful. There was a lot of concern about whether Florida would make it. And Tampa was not doing well—it was an iffy situation.
>
> The big concern was the track record of sports in general in Florida. I got to consult with everyone—from Wayne Huizenga on down, everyone who owned a team in Florida—and we talked about the pros and cons. One of the real problems, the concerns we had, and there was nothing we could do about it, was the weather. It was very hot and humid, game nights would typically be Saturday nights. By the time eight o'clock rolled around, there would be thunderstorms, and it was hot. And you'd think about getting into your car and going to a game, and the weather was just really bad.

Horowitz even remembers at least one instance of dealing with Florida weather at its most extreme: having to disassemble the tents behind one of the goals, used for VIP receptions, because of an incoming hurricane.

Kevin Payne was one of the most vocally concerned observers within the board of governors about the Miami franchise, for the same concerns that Horowitz had about consistent support from a notoriously fickle fan base.

"I've always felt bad for Ken, because Ken bought the option for the team in Miami in 1998 really on the back of the '96 season, when we'd had a great deal of success," Payne reflects. "It's too bad, because if Ken had waited until the '97 season, maybe he would have done things differently, or paid less money for his team. I did, and I do have grave reservations about the Miami market. If David Beckham called me up tomorrow and asked me if he should move forward with this team in Miami, I would probably say no. The Miami market doesn't support any professional sports teams well."

Gabe Gabor, now part of MLS's front office as its Miami-based senior international communications consultant for Spanish-language media, said he instantly became a fan when it was announced that the team was coming to soccer-starved South Florida, and then was hired early in 1998 to be part of the front office frantically readying itself for the launch.

He recalls, "They brought the bulk of the front office in January 1998. If you compare that to now, with a team like Atlanta, which is getting a two-and-a-half-year head start, the people at the Fusion were getting a two-month head start. I had two months to put together a department, put together a plan for the opening of a revamped stadium, hire staff, do a media guide; we had to physically put that together from scratch. It was hard work!"

Gabor felt that Lockhart Stadium was a strong selling point for the team, and the work that had gone into it—especially the upgrades to the field itself and the seating—made it attractive. And yet, during his travels around the league during the first year, he noticed a distinct difference in the infrastructure between a Rose Bowl or an RFK Stadium when compared to Lockhart. "Other stadiums had tunnels for the team buses and permanent press boxes," Gabor remembers. "At Lockhart, the press box was essentially a giant trailer that they put on top. The existing press box that we used to use was the high school press box, so we had to build additional areas to accommodate press."

He notes that the evolution of the soccer-specific stadium over the last twenty years makes the league's newer facilities shine in comparison to Lockhart, yet feels that the stadium was important to the evolution of the league and the accumulation of knowledge in the making of new stadiums. "When I started traveling around the league, and getting the perspective of some of the venues other teams were playing in, then I felt there was a distinct advantage to playing in what was the first soccer-specific stadium," Gabor says. "While Columbus gets all the credit, Lockhart was the first stadium that was built on the idea of creating demand by having a 20,000-seat stadium."

But the Fusion would find it challenging to fill even a 20,000-seat stadium in its first year. "I remember telling Ken and the people who worked for him that the most important game for them was not their opening game," Payne explains. "That would do great. It would sell out. The most important game for them was their second game. They needed to be focused 100 percent on their second game. Unfortunately, the guys running the team there didn't do it that way. So the first game was a big success, and the second game, it dropped by 50 percent. And they were never able to get a consistent message across to that marketplace."

The team itself was good enough to secure a spot in the playoffs, and the front office accumulated a roster that still has some influence in the league today. The opening-day Fusion roster included one legendary player, Carlos Valderrama, who was moved from the Tampa Bay Mutiny in a trade that Horowitz said Logan helped shepherd in order to help draw fans (particularly, Colombian ones) to the team. Goalkeeper Jeff Cassar (today the Real Salt Lake head coach), plucked from the Dallas Burn as part of the expansion draft, would emerge as a critical member of the squad. Colombian forward Diego Serna and Argentine-born U.S. national player Pablo Mastroeni (today the Colorado Rapids head coach) would start their MLS careers with the 1998 Fusion.

The league opted to start the 1998 season at Lockhart, announcing in early January that Miami's March 15 game against D.C. United would be the stand-alone season opener, with Chicago coming to Miami to open its season the following week. But the announcement of the full season's schedule answered another pressing question going into the 1998 season: how the league would coexist with the upcoming World Cup in France. Whereas most professional leagues around the world opted for an August to May schedule to leave summer open for the World Cup (and other international tournaments more than happy to fill the vacuum in non–World Cup years), MLS was avoiding the bulk of the National Football League schedule in favor of a March to September regular season.

Logan was addressing the World Cup question as early as February 1997, even before the United States officially qualified for the tournament, saying during a media conference call, "In our first, formative years, we cannot afford to be out of sight, out of mind" for the month in which the World Cup dominates soccer consciousness.[7] And yet, MLS would ultimately have twenty-one of its most talented players, an average of nearly two per team, play in the 1998 World Cup.[8]

MLS ultimately struck a compromise: it would run its season con-
currently with the World Cup, but would scale back the schedule so each
MLS team would play three games or fewer during the World Cup's first
two weeks, when all the World Cup teams played in the group stage
games. (As it turned out, the U.S. team didn't last past the group stages
in 1998, which allowed players to return to their clubs just as the MLS
schedules were ramping back up.)

There was still an untamed, anything-goes approach to preparing
teams for the season and for the week-to-week grind. Rob Thomson,
now executive vice president for communications with Sporting Kansas
City, remembers being with the Wizards for their 1998 preseason tune-
up in Bradenton, Florida:

> We'd gotten a sponsorship with Olive Garden that year, which
> means that the team was eating every meal at Olive Garden,
> which as you can imagine, is not great for training. The night be-
> fore one of our training sessions there, three days before our first
> preseason game, we'd all stayed out really late. Coach [Ron]
> Newman wanted the team to do a two-mile run that day. The
> way those runs worked is that I'd be at the finish line, Coach
> Newman would call me when he started the run, and I'd start
> my stopwatch and then log their times as they'd reach the finish
> line. Before that day's run, Mo [Johnston] took me aside and
> said, "Some of us have had a rough night; maybe start the clock
> thirty seconds after we actually start." I'd intended to do that,
> but I actually started the clock three minutes after Coach told me
> to do so. And we had some really good times that day, and Coach
> was very excited by that, and thought we could play with an all-
> out attack formation in that game. Jake Dancy, who normally
> played left back, clocked in at 8:40, so all of a sudden he wanted
> to play him at striker.

Thomson noted that the Jake Dancy striker experiment was brief and,
sadly, not as fruitful as Newman had hoped.

Some players endured the other extreme of pregame preparation in
MLS's early years. Eric Wynalda recalls that the Clash's first coach—

English-born Laurie Calloway (who lasted all of 1996 and half of 1997)—ran grueling practices that Wynalda felt actually put players at a disadvantage. "This is going to sound horrible, but our coach was clueless," Wynalda comments. "He would run trainings too long, he had never really been in a professional outfit, he didn't know any better except maybe a '60s, '70s English-style thing where everybody runs for three and a half straight hours and runs to the pub and gets drunk, and comes back tomorrow and does it all over again."

Wynalda had a perspective that many of his teammates didn't have in that he'd been part of German practices playing with VfL Bochum. "In Germany, it's on a clock, seventy minutes long every day," he says. "It was completely explained to you, what you were going to do, minute by minute. And then if you had it in you that you wanted to do extra, you had to go to your coach with your hands behind your back and ask for permission to do more. The way they looked at this was the most important thing was taking care of your body. Your body was your capital."

By contrast, with Calloway, "There were some of days of training where we might as well have just taken off our socks and shoes and run through a field of glass and then just pick the glass out of our feet and come back the next day to see if we weren't limping. We practiced for four hours—it was horrible. It was the most unorganized mess I'd ever been part of."

One story in particular, from the inaugural season, highlighted an additional dynamic that put Wynalda and Calloway at odds—a league that was looking to promote a still largely unfamiliar sport by banking on its most marketable stars. Wynalda recalls the time the league decided to take a star player from Tampa to do a photo shoot, which neither Calloway nor Wynalda were particularly thrilled about:

I flew a red-eye flight after practice all the way to Tampa— I didn't get any sleep. They put me in a uniform, put some makeup on me, said juggle, laugh, say this, say that, you're done. And then I had some lady standing there saying, okay, we're going to take you back to the airport now . . . so I go back to the airport, flew through Dallas, fell asleep on the plane, and got

back to the airport, and I thought my wife was going to be there
to pick me up.

And it was my assistant coach with a bag with my gear, and
he told me we were going to the stadium and I was going to run
the stadium stairs because I missed practice. I looked at him and
said, "Are you serious?" I went up the stairs once, and came
down, and he said, "He wants you to do it ten times." I said,
"All right, that was ten, and I hope you enjoyed it." I walked off,
and I got fined one thousand dollars for that.

Alexi Lalas recalls training in the Rose Bowl parking lot as part of
their regimen. "Certainly when you talk about this generation of players
coming into MLS, they have no idea about what went on and off the field
in the early days. Nor should they. I'm actually proud of them being, for
the most part, oblivious to that."

The 1998 season brought some playoff surprises, even given that it
was an eight-team field that now represented two-thirds rather than four-
fifths of the league. Both expansion teams made the playoffs, and half
the bracket went into the playoffs with identical 15–17 losing records.

D.C. United once again led the Eastern Conference, though the
Columbus Crew had a strong showing to finish second in the East, in
large part due to newly acquired Trinidad and Tobago international Stern
John, who won MLS's scoring title with twenty-six goals and five assists
in twenty-seven games. The MetroStars finished third in the east, with
the Fusion edging its cross-state rivals by a single point to win the East's
final playoff spot.

In the West, the Los Angeles Galaxy won twenty-two of its thirty-
two matches outright and added another two shootout wins to capture
the most points in MLS with sixty-eight. The Fire finished second, with
the Rapids—finally reaching the .500 mark for a season—grabbing the
third spot in the West and the Burn grabbing the final playoff spot.

The Galaxy also became the first recipients of a newly created award,
the Supporters' Shield, born of a fan-led movement to honor the season's
best regular-season team. According to Kansas City soccer fan Sam Pierron, writing on a fan-created website detailing the Shield's origin story,

the suggestion came via the North American Soccer listserv, which Pierron described as "a large, sprawling list of nothing but emails back and forth among a few thousand subscribers that maintained a higher level of discourse than any forum for the discussion of the game in this country than any medium of any sort that existed before or since."

Pierron recalled that Mutiny fan Nick Lawrus, likely inspired by the Mutiny's stellar 1996 season and disappointing playoffs, proposed calling it the Supporters Scudetto, after the trophy given to the winner of Italy's Serie A. Pierron headed a committee composed of fans representing each team; Lawrus had a distinct vision of calling it a scudetto versus a shield and didn't want to count shootout wins, and when the committee disagreed with him on both points, he declined to continue, and the committee's enthusiasm waned.

But Pierron was able to revive interest in 1998. He cites a meeting with broadcaster Phil Schoen, himself a member of the listserv, as instrumental in moving the project forward; Schoen gave Pierron a five-hundred-dollar donation toward creation of the trophy. At the 1998 MLS Cup, fans from the listserv came together to hold the first-ever MLS Supporters' Summit—league officials were invited to attend a Q&A, accepted the invitation, and Pierron presented the idea along with sketches for his vision of what the trophy would look like.[9] Pierron notes that additional donations, including a significant one from Commissioner Logan, enabled them to create the shield (which cost about two thousand dollars to make) and award it to the Galaxy early in the 1999 season.

The committee decided—partly out of the practicality of not having to create a new trophy each year, and partly out of the romanticism attached to the Stanley Cup—that there would just be one Supporters' Shield traveling from winner to winner each year, and no replicas would be made for the winning team to keep in its trophy case after it left. A second, sturdier Supporters' Shield was made in 2013, which pays homage to the original trophy with an etched image at its center; Pierron said it is "five times the weight, and five times the price." (Pierron promised the original trophy will be donated to the new National Soccer Hall of Fame when it opens at Toyota Stadium in Frisco, Texas, in 2017.)

The conference semifinals were all sweeps; D.C. United did need a shootout in game 2, however, to get past the Fusion, and the Crew similarly needed a game 2 shootout to get past the MetroStars. In the West, the Galaxy dominated the Burn with 6–1 and 3–2 wins to advance, while the Fire had a pair of one-goal triumphs over the Rapids.

In the conference finals, D.C. United made its third straight MLS Cup with a 3–0 game 3 win, after winning the 2–0 opener at home and losing 4–2 in Columbus, while in the West, the Fire beat the Galaxy in front of more than 25,000 in the Rose Bowl for game 1, and won a shootout before more than 32,000 Soldier Field faithful to punch its ticket to an MLS Cup that was—to Galaxy fans' dismay—in the Rose Bowl.

Unlike the previous two rain-swept MLS Cups, the game was played in partly cloudy, seventy-four-degree weather, and in what was probably correlation rather than causation, D.C. United did not win its third straight championship. The Fire, on the strength of stout defense the entire match, got a Podbrozny goal in the twenty-ninth minute with assists credited to Piotr Nowak and Ante Razov—which is all they'd need to win—and then added another goal just before halftime when a Nowak shot, probably going in on its own, deflected off Diego Gutiérrez.

Not everyone in Chicago was impressed with the championship, however. *Chicago Tribune* sports columnist Bernie Lincicome, in a day-of-finals preview titled "MLS Cup Runneth Over with Nonsense," poked fun at the league, saying the MLS Cup "sounded like a food additive" and the league name itself "sounded like a software program," and yet quoted Nowak's observation, "Michael Jordan said that the key to success is defense, and we have the best defense in the league," before concluding, "We may be the next champions in Chicago sports history."[10]

Fire fans, however, were buoyed—Murtaugh remembers watching the match with his father in one of a number of Chicago's Halsted Street bars airing the match, and celebrating after the final whistle in a post-match conga line down the street. The week after winning the MLS Cup, the Fire hosted the Crew in the U.S. Open Cup final, and the match served as both a celebration of the MLS Cup win and its own triumph—a 2–1 extra-time victory, allowing the Fire to do what D.C. United did in its first year: win a double.

It's perhaps simplistic to say that in the early years of MLS, D.C.

United seized upon the best formula for success—which included the hearty endorsements of fans who, in Crafts' words, wanted to be more than just customers, but results certainly bore this out, especially given that the Fire followed much of the United blueprint and parlayed it into instant success. The year 1999 would prove to be another for the team's dominance—but it would also be the start of MLS's most challenging era, in which the league would struggle for its very existence and bring in a new commissioner to help with just that project.

Chapter 4

THE TRADITIONAL

In which a new stadium and a new commissioner each
help American soccer to be like soccer elsewhere.

IF YOU'RE LOOKING AT MAJOR LEAGUE SOCCER FROM A PURE SPORTS NAR-
rative, the story of 1999 is fairly succinct: D.C. United won a third title
in four years and looked to be an unstoppable dynasty. (In reality, as a
cautionary tale as to how quickly an MLS team's fortunes can turn, D.C.
United was about to enter a barren, trophyless quadrennial, a return to
MLS Cup glory in 2004, and then, save for the occasional Supporters'
Shield or Open Cup triumph, relative anonymity in the annals of Which
Team Won.

But if you're looking at MLS from how fan culture has evolved, and
how the league moved from curiosity to relevance and apparent perma-
nence, 1999 was one of the most important years in the history of the
league, in large part due to two debuts: first, a new, built-from-the-
ground-up stadium that was conceived and created with soccer in mind
that is still standing; and second, a commissioner who would make initial,
difficult choices to improve the league and ultimately ensure its
longevity—and who is also still standing.

People following soccer and, specifically, the fortunes of MLS, knew
the stadium was coming. Now known as MAPFRE Stadium (for its sponsors, a Madrid-based insurance company with American offices based in
Webster, Massachusetts), Columbus Crew Stadium opened on May 15,
1999, and—despite Lockhart Stadium's debut a year earlier—is still regarded as the initial soccer-specific stadium of record. The soccer-specific
stadium was writ into the initial plans of the league, and Columbus Crew

Stadium bringing those plans to life was as important to soccer's development as stadiums like Baltimore's Camden Yards and Cleveland's Jacobs Field were to baseball earlier in the decade. Like those stadiums, Columbus Crew Stadium had the size and the sight lines to enhance the fan experience, and others—improving on the concept and looking to further enhance the fan experience—would come once the stadium in Ohio opened its doors.

A *Soccer America* article told the story of the stadium's birth:

> After one public vote in Franklin County and one city referendum in Dublin, Ohio to build a stadium both failed, MLS Investor-Operator Lamar Hunt decided to take matters into his own hands and privately finance a major league soccer-specific stadium in Columbus. Stadium construction began August 14, 1998, leaving just 10 months and one day before the new 22,500-seat facility would open its doors to Columbus and America's soccer community. Due to the May 15 opening date, MLS schedulemakers had Columbus on the road for the first seven games of the 1999 season. After winning just four road games in each of the last two seasons (Columbus was 4–12 on the road in both 1997 and 1998), the Crew has jumped out to a 5–2 record and leads the Eastern Conference with 11 points. "If we didn't have a new stadium I don't know if I'd want to go home," Columbus Head Coach Tom Fitzgerald said.[1]

Hunt was already one of the league's main proponents for soccer-specific stadiums, and knew one was especially needed in Columbus—to garner attention for a team far removed from one of the league's major markets, as well as to create a place to snugly, attractively house soccer.

Steve Sirk, an author of two books about Columbus Crew SC, saw the creation of the stadium as a logical extension of what the team was in the first place—evidence of "Columbus growing as a community and wanting to be more than just a college town." Regarding the team's inception he notes, "Ohio State totally dominated (and still does) the local consciousness, but as Columbus started to grow, there were more and more people who were transplants from other cities, meaning they weren't necessarily OSU-crazed. They craved pro sports. Plus, Columbus had long lived in the shadows of Cleveland and Cincinnati, so pro sports seemed to be a way of legitimizing Columbus' ascendency into a major city."

And yet, the Crew was still in the shadow of Ohio State University even while established as a pro team, because they were playing in the paradox that was Ohio Stadium: the largest-capacity stadium in the league, seating over 100,000, but the narrowest stadium in the league, shoehorning a sixty-two-yard wide field into a stadium that included a sizable running track. Sirk remembers,

> For the games where there were 20,000-plus people there, it looked okay because fans were crammed into the areas along the sidelines. In those instances, you didn't really notice the empty B and C decks, nor the empty closed end of the Horseshoe. But anything less than 20,000, and you'd become acutely aware of the enormity of the stadium.

> There were two other main problems. One was that the 'Shoe had a track at the time, so the playing field was far from the fans. The second main problem was that because of the track, the playing field was much too small. People likened it to a postage stamp or a bowling alley. It was only sixty-two yards wide. The first game I ever covered in 1998, the Crew beat D.C. United in a game that finished 10 versus 9 due to red cards. Afterward, D.C. coach Bruce Arena sarcastically theorized that the refs were under a mandate to get the game to 7 versus 7 on that field so actual soccer could be played.

The Clash's Eric Wynalda, who played home games at a similarly narrow Spartan Stadium, remarked on the difficulty of playing soccer on narrow fields: "The real fans were watching and saying, wow, it must be so hard to play out there. But the on-the-fence guy or the casual sports fan was saying, they're not very good, they keep turning it over, the passes are bad, it keeps going out of bounds, it doesn't look good. They were right." He felt that once soccer-specific stadiums came on, giving players the room to showcase their talent, "the soccer just got better."

Columbus Crew Stadium was built out of necessity, in part, because Ohio Stadium was set to undergo several years of extensive renovations, starting in 1998—on the Buckeyes' schedule rather than the Crew's. Dan Hunt, today the president of FC Dallas, asserts that "one of the critical moments in the growth of this league was the soccer-specific stadium, with my dad taking the plunge first, and that's what catapulted the league forward," and that's by and large how MLS leadership and proponents regard the stadium.

For fans, it definitely made a difference to have a home stadium built for soccer. Sirk notes, "The new stadium was received incredibly well. Columbus led MLS in attendance in 1999, and . . . showed that there was a benefit to staging games in a true soccer stadium instead of in cavernous football stadiums. It completely changed the way the game looked, played, and felt to those in the stands and watching on TV. This was Lamar Hunt's calculated gamble, and since his wager paid off so handsomely in Columbus, it sparked the soccer-specific stadium revolution across MLS. Even today, we're all still benefitting from Lamar Hunt's vision and his faith in Columbus."

The Crew, who entered the league on the strength of season-ticket pledges, sold an MLS-record number of season tickets (9,300, besting the mark the team set in 1996), and when the team put its final thousand seats for the home opener on sale, a month before the match, they sold out in eight minutes. Also, in the lead-up to the game, MLS determined that nearly forty publications wrote more than eighty articles on the opening of the stadium, reaching an audience of (as those doing the PR metrics would have it) over 40 million in the process. While the articles certainly didn't reach 40 million different people, the numbers do give a sense that the breadth of the coverage went beyond just central Ohio.

Sirk recalls that the first game at the stadium, a 2–0 win over the Revolution, included a number of MLS and United States Soccer Federation dignitaries, such as Michael Buffer stepping out of a limo to do his then still relatively fresh "Let's Get Ready to Rumble" routine, and a clearly joyous Lamar Hunt beaming broadly the entire night. Sirk also notes, "What I mostly remember was that the stadium was an incalculably better experience than the Horseshoe over at Ohio State. Instead of a running track that essentially served as a moat to keep the fans separated from the field, fans were seated just a few feet from the corner flags. You were right on top of the action."

The Crew would end up leading the league in attendance, with the new stadium placing them in the same rarified air as D.C. United and the Galaxy, with attendance of over 17,000. This would end up propping up the league average numbers, offsetting teams that were struggling; most notably, the Fusion and Wizards struggled the most attendance-wise, both below the 9,000 mark.

Thanks to Doug Logan's proclamation at the start of the 1997 season, attendance was still being used by the media as a barometer for the league's success. Michelle Kaufman, in her *Miami Herald* article covering Logan's season-opening press conference, elaborated on Logan's declaration that 1999 would be "the year of no excuses," listing:

> No excuse for lagging TV ratings.
>
> No excuse for dwindling attendance in six of 12 markets— New England, San Jose, Dallas, Kansas City, Los Angeles, and most damaging of all, New York.
>
> Closer to home, no excuse for 939 Fusion season-ticket holders, up from last season but still dismal in a soccer-rich market such as South Florida.

Kaufman went on to quote Logan as saying, "I don't think having 1,000 season tickets in Miami at this point is good. There's been a modest amount of improvement, and the Fusion is still in the throes of reorganization. It will come in Miami; it just takes time and hard work. Selling sports is not rocket science. I'm not saying they haven't worked hard; they just need to work smarter."[2]

Another representative start-of-the-season article—from the *San Diego Union-Tribune* and ominously titled "It Could Be Do or Die for MLS in '99"—noted, "It's easy to say that the most important season in the future of Major League Soccer is any current season. And there's some truth to that. But the season that begins Saturday is really the most important one. There was the novelty of the inaugural season in 1996. There was the inevitable sophomore slump of Year 2. There was expansion and the

World Cup in Year 3. Year 4 has none of that." The article went on to say, "Attendance has fallen from an opening-year average of 17,416 to 14,312. TV ratings fell slightly last season as well. If those key numbers don't improve, or at least hold steady, the league could be in trouble. If they fall, the league is really in trouble."

In the article Logan expressed "cautious optimism"—which worked its way into at least one headline—and added, "Am I a little nervous? Sure. But I've been nervous since the day I accepted the job."[3]

The final 1999 average attendance numbers would be just several hundred below 1998's—essentially, a three-year flatline after the roughly 20 percent dip between seasons 1 and 2—but Logan would not even be allowed to finish out the year he'd placed so much hope in. MLS would look to the National Football League for new leadership—specifically, in the form of Don Garber, the forty-one-year-old vice president of NFL International and overseer of NFL Europe—to help the league move out of its malaise.

Garber was named commissioner on August 4, 1999, in a press conference that commenced with Logan announcing his resignation; then Stuart Subotnick, in his role as MLS board of governors chair, introduced Garber. As Logan told the assembled media, "Yesterday I was an 'is.' Today I'm a 'was.' Tomorrow, I assure you, I'm going to be an 'is' again. There's no elegant way to say I was fired."[4]

Subotnick said, regarding Logan's "year of no excuses" pledge, "We took that seriously. We are at an OK level but not where we want to be in respect to revenue and fan participation." The league was switching commissioners in midseason, according to Subotnick, to reach out to potential sponsors for 2000 and beyond while there was still time. Rothenberg, quoted in a *Columbus Dispatch* article on the change, lauded Garber for his "great marketing skills" and "grass-roots effort."[5]

Garber's lack of soccer experience didn't bother those who brought him in. Mark Abbott recalls, "He had a lot of energy and a lot of enthusiasm for getting involved in the league. He had a lot of experience in the professional sports business, and he was someone who was really going to commit himself to helping the league achieve its potential. I was really struck by the energy that he brought to it. He was a young guy when he came. He's still young, but he was particularly young then. He really threw himself into it."

Garber came in with a good deal of optimism, as well as praise for the owners. Reflecting on what excited him about the league, Garber notes (projecting a bit into the future),

> There were changes afoot—there was every indication that America would rise as a soccer nation. There were shifting demographics with the growth of the Hispanic market, all these young people who were growing up playing were consumers and influencers, and the fact that digital media was beginning to transform the way we were consuming content so that somebody could [eventually] watch a Premier League game or could watch the World Cup on their iPhone or early on Sunday morning. I believe those things would drive our country to become passionate about the sport.
>
> I saw enormous growth. It clearly was a start-up in the epic sense—it was only a couple of years old, and floundering when I came in.
>
> Most importantly, you had Robert Kraft, Lamar Hunt, and Phil Anschutz, three of the great sports industrialists of our time, who were really "long" on soccer. They were deeply committed to MLS—philosophically, spiritually—and I knew we would be able to get through some tough waters with those guys.

Despite Garber's optimism, though, he did have concerns. "The first couple of years were really rough," he acknowledges. "Attendance was dropping, our television ratings were struggling, we had a difficult time attracting sponsors, we were paying to get our games on television."

Kevin Payne says of Garber, "I think Don got it pretty early, even though Don was not a soccer guy. But he admitted that, and he tried his best to listen to what the soccer community was saying."

One thing that Garber instantly got, according to Abbott, was that MLS's "opportunity" lay in "authentic" soccer, stripped of the embellishments some of the early decision makers felt were necessary to sell the game to a hypothetical audience of youths and soccer moms with an American frame of reference.

"We'd had some rules that were Americanized," Abbott explains, "and we had been debating those, and he came down clearly and said the opportunity is to align ourselves with the international game, and very quickly ended the debate and said, this is the way we're going to go. Although he did not have a background in the game, he clearly understood where our opportunity was."

In particular, the shootout and the countdown clock were negatively impacting MLS's credibility as a league abroad, and angering American fans who wanted the game to be more closely aligned with world soccer.

Payne recalls a board of governors meeting in 1999 in which Garber asked, "Why are we doing this? This is pissing off the very people that we need to be the backbone of our fan base." Payne summarizes, "The players didn't like it. The coaches didn't like it. The serious fans didn't like it. So Don was asking the logical question of why were we doing this." It would be a question that Garber and the league would address head-on at the conclusion of the 1999 season.

One of the most important changes of 1999 involved a fan base rather than a team. The season started with the defending champions drawing an average of 16,000-plus fans to Soldier Field, with its two separate but spirited fan groups setting a tone that was sometimes a little too spirited.

The Barn Burners and Polish Ultras came together to form what is now known as Section 8 Chicago—a marriage arranged by Peter Wilt in the middle of the 1999 season. Security concerns, stemming from what was happening in the stadium's section 9, drove the discussion. Liam Murtaugh remembers a June 1999 "friendly" between the Fire and the Polish club Legia Warsaw, in which the Fire Ultras were "lighting flares, fighting, and sort-of supporting both teams," as a catalyst for the club to ponder options. It was, ultimately, a move that allowed the Fire to unify and strengthen the two most vocal factions of Fire fans.

Wilt recalls,

A lot of the Polish Ultras were young, first-generation immigrants who brought with them to Chicago an aggressive style of support from Eastern Europe. That aggressive style of support sometimes meant treating opposing fans poorly, and even on occasion, their fellow fans. By that I mean violence. We had to have additional security for fans, unlike anything MLS had seen prior, and we had to mediate and bring the two groups together in a way that they would not be competing and fighting with each other. I think that was an important watershed moment in fan culture in MLS history. It was in the second half of the second season—I scheduled a meeting with the leadership. Well, first I met with the leadership of the Polish Ultras at a soccer pub on the north side of Chicago, and got to know them. That, I think, was a big step, in that before they were maybe seeing us as a faceless organization, but once they were able to put a face to the team, they didn't want to cause as much trouble, I think.

So we set up a meeting with the leadership of Barn Burners, Polish Ultras, Soldier Field, and the security company in the bowels of Soldier Field on a non-game day, and had a come-to-Jesus meeting, and at the end of the meeting, the Polish Ultras agreed they would close down their section 9 and would relocate to section 8 and integrate with the Barn Burners.

From an operational standpoint, up to that point, the Barn Burners had the greater numbers, but Polish Ultras had the chants, the songs, the capos, the culture of supporting a team. So, when they combined, it was magical. It made the atmosphere in Soldier Field like none other—in my opinion—in sports in the United States.

Section 8 Chicago's website characterizes the merger as the Polish Ultras "choosing" to move into section 8, but they do agree with Wilt that the effect was galvanic. The site notes the melding of the two groups, "in a way that could only happen in Chicago sports," created "a completely new, vibrant, and infectious blend."

Don Crafts felt the Fire Ultras worked well in the newly configured section 8, in large part because

they just didn't stop. From before the game started to the end, they were just always on, whereas our group was all just learning this and making it up, so we didn't have that insane intensity. We were writing songs to sing and copying English songs, that were always really long and nobody knew the words. They just simplified it down to a few simple words and chanting, and everybody could follow along within the first thirty seconds of it starting. That helped. The one everyone went home singing went "Lo-lo-lo-lo-lo-lo, Fire go!" It was really simple, but it was really catchy.

Mike Krupa says of the merger, "Barn Burners were a bigger group than us, and there were a lot of good people in that group, but we had this energy in us that they lacked. They were a well-organized group when it came to Internet forums, barbecues, selling T-shirts, or organizing large events." He says that comparing the two groups was like "comparing one hundred cats to five tigers," yet ultimately he feels that "each group brought something to the table and it worked out well."

Today, Section 8 Chicago has evolved into more than just a group of soccer fans, and certainly beyond what its founders initially envisioned: it's a registered 501(c)7 organization with an elected board of directors and an operating budget of more than $200,000, paying for everything from road trip funding, to tifo, to platinum-level charitable donations, to the club's Fire Foundation.[6]

The 1999 season saw both Florida teams—even with losing records—join the dominant United and Crew in the East bracket, whereas in the West, the Galaxy grabbed the top playoff spot, with the Burn (benefitting from Jason Kreis's MVP season), the Fire, and the Rapids following.

In the East playoffs, D.C. United made easy work of the Fusion, winning 2–0 at RFK Stadium and closing out the series with a shootout win (after a scoreless game) at Lockhart. The Crew blanked the Mutiny with two identical 2–0 outcomes to advance to the Eastern finals. In the wild Eastern Conference finals, D.C. United won a 2–1 opener, lost 5–1 in Columbus (going up 1–0 and then giving up five straight goals, including a Stern John second-half hat trick), and then winning the deciding match 4–0.

In the West, the Galaxy was unscathed, sweeping the Rapids 3–0 and 2–0, while the literalist's dream matchup of Fire versus Burn went three games, including a game 3 in which the Fire jumped out to a 2–0 lead after five minutes yet gave up the equalizer and game-winner in the match's final six minutes of regulation to lose the series. The finals also went the distance; though the Burn was able to extend the series with a game 2 shootout win at home, the Galaxy won the series with a decisive 3–1 win in game 3.

So, the 1999 MLS Cup was déjà vu all over again: Galaxy versus United at Foxboro, though with much better weather conditions than the landmark 1996 match.

The *Boston Herald*'s Gus Martins led his postmatch article saying, "Even under difficult circumstances, D.C. United's unrivaled creativity and pride allows them to assert their personality."[7] But the Galaxy bore the brunt of difficult circumstances in the match—its MLS Defensive Player of the Year, Robin Fraser, was knocked out of the match in the ninth minute with a clavicle fracture, United's first goal came in a pinball sequence started when the Galaxy missed a chance to clear a ball sent into the goalbox, and United's second and final goal, just before halftime, was a true howler—goalkeeper Kevin Hartman badly misplayed a back-pass and ended up losing the ball outside the box, giving MLS Cup MVP Ben Olsen a clear path to a twenty-yard goal.

Jimmy Golen's Associated Press account of the game mused as to whether the United had achieved the dynastic status of comparable late-1990s teams like the New York Yankees and Chicago Bulls:

> Major League Soccer might soon have to ask itself whether D.C. United, which has never missed an MLS Cup while winning three titles, is hurting the sport by dominating the competition so completely.
>
> "I'm not worried about it," MLS Commissioner Don Garber said Sunday after D.C. won its third Cup in four years with a 2–0 victory over the Los Angeles Galaxy. "But I think that our fans would like to see another team give them a good run."
>
> So, it's not time to break up D.C., yet?
>
> "That's why they're called the United," Garber joked.[8]

If the third title in four seasons for D.C. United didn't provide enough drama for MLS fans, the U.S. Open Cup Finals certainly did. The Open

Cup, an annual competition held since 1914, was a single-elimination tournament involving amateur and professional soccer teams throughout the United States. Whereas the NASL teams before them opted out of the Cup competition, MLS teams competed in the tournament, and won the first three finals, timed to be played just after the MLS Cup. Results almost exactly paralleled what happened in MLS—United won the 1996 MLS Cup and U.S. Open Cup, and the Fire won the 1998 MLS Cup and U.S. Open Cup, and while the Dallas Burn won the 1997 U.S. Open Cup, it was via penalty kicks against United after a scoreless match.

But the 1999 finals (the first in which teams were playing for the newly named Lamar Hunt U.S. Open Cup trophy) featured the Colorado Rapids, who were marginally playoff-bound, against the A-League's Rochester Raging Rhinos. As a Dave Zeitlin article for MLSSoccer.com noted,

> The 1999 Rochester Raging Rhinos weren't a merry band of underdog misfits like in those clichéd sports movies. There were a lot of talented and experienced players on the team, some of whom could have played in MLS and a couple of others who later did.
>
> They usually played in front of at least 10,000 fans in their home stadium, nestled in an upstate New York community rich with soccer history. They were a dominant force in what was then called the A-League (now the USL PRO), capturing titles in 1998, 2000 and 2001. And in the franchise's inaugural season in 1996, they stormed to the US Open Cup final before losing to D.C. United.
>
> But let's also be clear about one more thing: as good as the Rhinos were and as young as Major League Soccer was at that time, Rochester still weren't expected to beat any MLS teams during their magical 1999 US Open Cup run, let alone four of them in succession.[9]

In the September 13 finals—for once, not held the week after the MLS Cup, but rather a month before the playoffs started—the Rhinos beat the Rapids 2–0, at Columbus Crew Stadium, to conclude a tournament in which they beat the Fire, Burn, and Crew on their way to the finals.

Zeitlin pointed out, "Back in 1999, one could argue the A-League was a serious contender with MLS, at least in terms of fan support. The Rhinos were such a thriving franchise that they made a serious push to join Major League Soccer." He added that the Rhinos fans' chanted, "If you can't join 'em, beat 'em" throughout their U.S. Open Cup run.[10]

But for Garber, witnessing his first U.S. Open Cup as commissioner, on his first visit to Columbus Crew Stadium, it was a bit startling to see an A-League team win—even one that could have functioned as a franchise in the 1999 edition of the league. "Our Colorado team lost to a [lower-division] team. I remember going in there and going, 'Man, what's up with this?' Here we have an MLS team losing to a minor league team?" It would turn out to be the last time that a non-MLS team won the U.S. Open Cup.

The week of MLS Cup 1999, Garber announced the rule changes that players and more traditional fans had been awaiting for to bring the game more in line with how the great majority of nations played it. The countdown clock was eliminated in favor of referees keeping time on the field (with the scoreboard clock now starting at 0:00 and going up), and as Garber boldly declared, "Beginning with the season of 2000, the shootout will be dead." There were a few other substantive changes made—the actual season was to be shortened by two months, and the league was divided into three four-team divisions (West, Central, East)—as the *New York Times* pointed out, "to create more interest in playoff races and, perhaps, will make it easier to allocate teams if the league expands."

The *Times* article noted, "Changes were made to comply with the wishes of the some 60 million people in the United States who considered themselves soccer fans. One of the first things Garber did when he took over for Doug Logan three months ago was to conduct a survey of soccer fans about their feelings for the shootout. The research showed much more than a mere dislike for it."

As Garber told the media via conference call, "There was a negativity buzzing among the hardest-core fans. It took a couple years to figure out you can't conclude a basketball game with foul shots." The ultimate message from Garber was, "We have to go back and shore up our existence with the core soccer fan."[11]

Wynalda, who was a vocal critic of the shootout process even before he was injured in a 1998 shootout collision with then Dallas Burn goalkeeper Garth Lagerwey, applauded the decision. "I think it was for the betterment of the game," he says. "I'd said before, when it comes to stuff like this, you kind of get tired about being right about stuff like this ten years too late. A lot of torture and stupidity and a lot of trial and error that really wasn't necessary in the early days of this league. We really did things in a maverick way, trying to be American if you will, and all we did was confuse the hell out of people." He adds, by way of explanation, "This league was founded by a bunch of NFL guys who were trying to make things more exciting."

The 2000 season would commence with more traditional rules, as well as with a resolution to a legal case that might have significantly impacted MLS had the ruling gone against them. In April 2000, a Massachusetts District Court ruled on the *Fraser v. Major League Soccer* lawsuit —filed by eight MLS players in the fall of 1996, contending that the league and the United States Soccer Federation were conspiring to monopolize the professional soccer market in the United States. The judge ruled that the league, as a single entity, could not violate section 1 of the Sherman Antitrust Act. Though it took until 2002 for the case to be fully resolved in the First Circuit Court of Appeals, the initial ruling and the subsequent appellate decision reinforced the league's position.

As Elizabeth Cotignola, a Montreal-based lawyer and devoted soccer fan who writes on legal issues pertaining to soccer, observes, "*Fraser* was significant for MLS, obviously, because it validated the League's single-entity status (and all that that implies) in the eyes of the law. From a broader legal perspective, *Fraser* is significant because it serves as judicial precedent in the assessment of how economic co-venturers with disparate economic interests should be treated under antitrust law, which could have a considerable effect on both traditionally organized leagues and nonsports joint ventures that require cooperation among economic competitors."

"The fact that MLS won this case allowed them to continue as a league," explains veteran soccer journalist Grant Wahl, currently with both *Sports Illustrated* and Fox Sports. "I have a hard time thinking that the owners would have continued had they lost. The reason so many of them got into the league was it was designed with the single-entity structure in mind. There's only so much tolerance these owners would have for losing money, and if the lawsuit created a situation where they couldn't continue as a single-entity league, I think they would have pulled the plug on it."

The season itself held one major surprise—not only was D.C. United unable to defend its championship, it wasn't even involved in the finals, even though RFK did host the 2000 MLS Cup. The Kansas City Wizards, who'd finished last in the Western Conference two years running, won the Supporters' Shield in the newly configured three-conference league, and won its first-ever MLS Cup.

Defender Peter Vermes, who came over from Colorado in the offseason to become the league's Defender of the Year, was seen by those close to the team as the key acquisition. Though Tony Meola was the league's MVP as well as its Goalkeeper of the Year, and served as the team's titular captain, the team was responsive to Vermes's leadership.

"Peter has no ego," Thomson says. "And he was the key to the championship team. In '99, we were 8–24, we were terrible, we had no leadership. Peter was the final piece to the puzzle. Tony Meola was the captain, but people knew Peter was really the captain. He didn't have to wear the C. He knew he was the leader."

"The team that we had in 2000 was very much a team," recalls Chris Klein, now president of the Los Angeles Galaxy, who started his lengthy MLS career with the Wizards in 1998. He noted that the mix of veteran leaders and younger players—himself included in the latter group—allowed for a cohesion that helped the team create an identity as a collective rather than a group of individuals. "That was a different group from the beginning. It was a group that had maturity, that had personality, that knew how to win. And we saw very early on that this was going to be a team that was difficult to beat, and a team that could definitely win the championship."

Even though the 2000 Wizards were a success on the field from the get-go, winning ten of their first twelve on the way to the league's best record, the team still struggled to bring in fans.

"We were embraced by a small amount of people," Thomson remembers. "There wasn't a rush to get tickets, because who can't get tickets for a 79,000-seat stadium? We were partnered with the Chiefs, and the corporate sales team was for both the Chiefs and the Wizards, so when it came to sponsors, we were throw-ins. From that perspective, there wasn't that much value to the club. People would come to the games, and enjoyed it, the kids would be running around and enjoying themselves, but if you asked them the next day who won, they wouldn't know."

As the number 1 seed in the eight-team playoffs, the Wizards were on the opposite side of the bracket as the number 2 seed, the Central Division–winning Fire, and the number 3 seed, the East Division–winning MetroStars. D.C. United was conspicuously absent in the 2000 playoff picture, having finished eleventh, just one point above the league-worst Earthquakes in the table.

Playoff excitement did not help the Wizards' attendance woes. For the Wizards' quarterfinal series against the Colorado Rapids, fewer than 9,000 people came out to Arrowhead for the initial game, and just over 4,000 saw the third and decisive game. (To be fair, this wasn't just a Kansas City problem: The lone Rapids game drew barely a hundred more than the first Kansas City game.)

In the semis, a more respectable gathering of nearly 12,000 attended the first match against the Los Angeles Galaxy, who'd gotten past the Mutiny, and the Wizards got to play the third, decisive game in front of more than 8,000. But the Galaxy, in its one Rose Bowl appearance in the three-game series, drew more fans than in both Wizards-hosted games combined.

The series demonstrated just how convoluted the MLS playoff system had become, and how not all of the early Garber-era rule changes were easy to understand. In the first game of the best-of-three series (with three points awarded for a win, and one for a draw), the teams played to a 0–0 draw. In the second game, the teams tied 1–1 in regulation, and then in the third minute of added time, the Galaxy's Danny Califf scored to give the team the win. The Wizards scored the third game's lone goal in the twenty-second minute to bring the series to a 4–4 tie on points.

Because this was a "first-to-five" series, with three points awarded for a win and one for a tie, the series went to a sudden-death overtime period, lasting all of five minutes and change before postseason hero Miklos Molnar scored the winning goal.

In the finals, which drew nearly 40,000 to RFK Stadium, Molnar scored an eleventh-minute goal, which would be enough for the victory, especially with league MVP Meola making ten saves to render the Fire's 20–6 shot advantage moot. Yet the postmatch coverage from the Associated Press marveled that Lamar Hunt chose to attend the MLS Cup over the Chiefs–Raiders game, and made reference to the league as "money-losing MLS," including Hunt comparing the MLS Cup to the early Super Bowl years the Chiefs were so instrumental in. As Hunt noted, "The battle here is against the bill collector. Here, the battle is to sell tickets."[12]

There were end-of-year reports, fueled by an *ESPN the Magazine* article running the last week in December, that one or two teams could be contracted in the new year to help offset operating costs after the league had lost an astonishing $250 million in its first five years. Papers in the Bay Area and Tampa Bay tailored a Steven Goff–penned *Washington Post* article to reflect that the Quakes and the Mutiny, respectively, were one of the teams rumored to be in danger of being folded.[13]

Michelle Kaufman, in a New Year's Eve article for the *Miami Herald*, ominously noted that the Fusion was a candidate due to its league-low attendance of under 7,500 a game, adding, "Garber has said he was disappointed in the Fusion's attendance, and it is no secret the team's future in South Florida is contingent on improved gate receipts. A Winston-Salem, N.C., group interested in building a soccer stadium already has inquired about the possibility of the Fusion relocating."[14]

Even the new league champions were being murmured about, given their five years of low attendance numbers. Yet, as Klein notes, the team didn't have to worry about its future in MLS as long as Hunt was involved in ownership. "Our league was built on strong ownership, more than anything else," he asserts. "We were owned by one of the greatest owners in sports. There was never that fear."

For other teams, however, that fear was very real. The year started with doomsday fervor for the nation and much of the planet in the form of Y2K, and it seemed the league was on a collision course with its own version of end-times hysteria. MLS would, ultimately, enter 2001 unchanged from the year before—with twelve teams and three divisions, playing soccer with rules in concordance with the rest of the world. But 2001 would prove to be MLS's most challenging year yet—and, indeed, ever.

Chapter 5

THE BRINK

In which the league nearly folds, loses Florida,
and somehow survives.

THERE WAS A VERY REAL POSSIBILITY, TO HEAR THOSE CLOSEST TO THE DISCUS-
sions of late 2001 and early 2002 tell it, that the story of Major League
Soccer would end with this chapter. People close to MLS call these the
dark times or the low point, and if not for the sheer will of a few of the
key people in the negotiations, 2001's behind-the-scenes discussions
about the future of MLS would have been not only the tipping point
leading to the league shutting down but perhaps even the centerpiece of
a once-and-for-all declaration that soccer and America were mutually
exclusive.

The year 2001 was already a very nervous one for those rooting for
MLS to succeed, even before its regular season was prematurely ended—
and thrown into the existential crisis that all American sports were
thrown into—by the September 11 terrorist attacks in New York and
Washington, DC. The more established National Football League took
a week off, and its return was billed as an essential part of what the
American zeitgeist positioned as a return to normalcy: essentially, serving
as proof to Americans that terrorists from a very different part of the
world could not take away the quintessential American ritual of pro football, and therefore, could not take away our spirit.

Soccer in 2001 was not even remotely close to American ritual, and
unlike NFL football, was at the ending rather than the beginning of its
season. The decision to cancel the ten remaining regular-season games—
which came from the league office on September 13—was prudent to be

sure, but still left teams to begin the playoffs on September 20, under the staggering gravity of fresh national tragedy.[1]

Had it been a normal year—in which fans were focused purely on the game, the players, and the jockeying of teams in the still unfamiliar three conferences and playoff format—2001 would have belonged to one of the most celebrated rookies in MLS history (but curiously, not the 2001 Rookie of the Year), Landon Donovan. Loaned from the Bundesliga team, which held his rights (Bayer Leverkusen), and allocated to the San Jose Earthquakes, Donovan spearheaded an incredible turnaround for the Quakes that culminated in a fantastic playoff run, and in the process, kicked off a career transforming our collective notions of American soccer players. The capacity for Americans to shine on the World Cup stage and the value of playing professional soccer in the United States versus the top European leagues weren't even debatable topics when Donovan first donned an Earthquakes jersey, but now they most definitely are.

Ultimately, though, 2001 was the year in which the mounting murmurings about the future of the league, fueled by mounting concerns about money, attendance figures, and the hard realities of coaxing American soccer to adulthood, would culminate in difficult, soul-searching discussions by year's end about whether MLS would live or die.

The simple answer as to what happened comes down to surgical analogy: MLS was a patient in grave danger, and Florida needed to be amputated.

The Dallas Burn and the Tampa Bay Mutiny were still, at the closing of the 2001 season, the two remaining league-owned and league-maintained teams; D.C. United was undergoing an ownership transition throughout the season to the Anschutz Entertainment Group (AEG).

However, the Burn had a better situation in that it made its home in the Cotton Bowl, which had its own sense of soccer history and World Cup tradition, and happened to be the only team in one of the nation's largest states, Texas.

The Mutiny spent its first three years in a truly ungainly football venue: Tampa Stadium, also known as Houlihan's Stadium, though often unofficially called the Big Sombrero for the undulating shape of its outer wall. Then, along with the NFL's Buccaneers, the Mutiny moved to Raymond James Stadium in 1999, and in what was perceived as a positive move, signed a five-year lease prior to the 2001 season that would keep the team there.

It's unfairly reductive to say that the Tampa Bay Mutiny were so bad that no one wanted to buy them. After all, they did have a promising 2000 season in which new acquisition Mamadou Diallo (awesomely nicknamed Big Mama) scored twenty-six goals, leading the Mutiny to a playoff spot (albeit with a first-round exit).

The 2001 edition of the Mutiny, however, showed no playoff prowess whatsoever. It had one of the worst records in the league's history, mustering only four wins and two ties in twenty-seven games. The number that perhaps mattered most, the attendance average, was next to the lowest in the league at just over 10,000.

Gabe Gabor remembers that Raymond James was better suited for soccer than some of the older football stadiums: "The new Tampa stadium was more modular, with decks, and a lot of different sections. I remember from pregame and postgame interviews on the field how loud it can get, even with ten or twelve thousand people. From the field, it feels way fuller because of your perspective."

He also notes, mischievously, "The team hotel for the visiting team was literally a stone's throw from Mons Venus, which is a very world-renowned adult club. I don't know if the team's intent was to distract [the opposing] players or not, but I thought that was interesting. It was close to the airport as well, and maybe they got the best deal there, but strategically, if you want to distract an opponent, not a bad idea."

Bill Manning served as general manager for the Mutiny's final two years in the league; Nick Sakiewicz, who initially came to MLS as part of the league's executive team, and who served as Mutiny team president from late 1996 to 1999, advised Manning on his way out, "Get an owner and build a stadium," for he thought Tampa could be a great market if it could just secure those two crucial elements.

Manning's principal issue was the inability to create supply and demand for season tickets in a 70,000-seat stadium: "The feedback we always got was, 'Well, if I feel like going, I'll just buy tickets the day of.' And so you literally couldn't create demand. It was a difficult situation trying to build a fan base of season-ticket holders who were really vested in the team." Manning claims that Sakiewicz was able to prop up the 1999 season-ticket numbers by selling blocks of as many as 500 to various corporations in the Tampa–St. Petersburg market under the auspices of "saving the team." But those companies didn't renew in 2000, telling Manning, "Well, you're here now, we don't need to save you anymore."

The Fusion, on the other hand, had a season that might have swayed the league that it was turning things around for the better—that is, if it had been a league-owned and league-operated team.

The irrepressible Ray Hudson, now a famously ebullient color commentator for beIN Sports, replaced Ivo Wortmann as manager in the middle of 2000, moving directly from the broadcasting booth (no, really), inserting life into the club as a decidedly player's manager. As he recalls,

> The Fusion had been a disaster for the first two and a half years, losing crowds with horrid football. Once the team was 1–8, 1–9, they'd said that was enough, there's not just a fire in the basement, the roof is on fire. They were desperate. [GM] Doug [Hamilton] was lining up [interim and eventual Revolution head coach] Stevie Nicol for the job, and I said, 'Tremendous. Great signing if you can get him.' I knew him as a player and a commentator, and I thought he was an inspired choice. And Doug said, 'Just take over the team for the first game; we should have it wrapped up pretty soon.' Then it went four games, and we kept on winning. We beat D.C. United in our first game, and then we won our next three. We were playing lights out. The team was rejuvenated. I took them to the beach every day and played tennis with them. I gave them days off in the midweek. They could go to Disney World, have a good time—go and see your girlfriends, take them to the beach, have a couple of beers, but you're gonna come back Thursday and work like you've never worked before. That was the structure!

On the field, the Fusion was the league's best team for the 2001 season, and arguably one of the best of all time. Alex Pineda Chacón was both the league MVP and scoring champion (with nineteen goals and nine assists).

Preki had come over to the Fusion (in his only non–Kansas City MLS year), contributing with eight goals and fourteen assists. Ian Bishop, another addition, contributed with thirteen assists. Diego Serna, a mainstay from earlier Fusion seasons, had a stellar fifteen-goal, fifteen-assist season.

Hudson credits Hamilton's acumen as GM—calling him a "magic man"—for bolstering the squad, but also notes he made some cavalier choices in fielding a strong starting XI. Hudson explains, "I put Pablo Mastroeni back in defense instead of midfield; Pablo didn't like it, I didn't care! It was inspirational for us. Nicky Rimando took the place of Jeff Cassar, he wasn't happy about that, I didn't care—Nicky Rimando turned out to be an absolutely Herculean player for us."

Rimando, who'd been drafted by the Fusion in 2000, had immediately emerged to challenge Cassar, starting more than half the games. Rimando started the majority of the 2001 games and was one of four Fusion players in the All-Star Game's East starting squad that year, though Rimando was to lose Goalkeeper of the Year honors to future fellow U.S. Men's National Team member Tim Howard.

Hudson might be overstating it when he says that the 2001 Fusion "played Barcelona football before Barcelona played it," but the team was decidedly the best in the league, and as Hudson accurately assessed, they did increase the gate by 50 percent—though the jump from 2000's woeful 7,460 to 2001's 11,177 still placed it in the bottom third of teams for 2001 attendance. By 2001 Gabor was just a fan rather than part of the organization, but still went to matches, recalling, "The atmosphere at Lockhart was electric. It was by far the best it had been those four years."

As Ken Horowitz tells it, the team was trying everything it could to market itself, including playing several midseason games in Miami's Orange Bowl as an experiment. Despite earlier friction between Horowitz and the city, leading to the exodus to Lockhart, Horowitz said the city was enthusiastic. He recalls, "The City Council of Miami lit up the buildings in our colors every time we had a game. The Miami skyline was lit up. People knew we had games, in our most successful season ever. People still didn't come. I was so sure that this was going to make a difference— you'd look out your window and wonder why are the colors like this. It was in the newspapers. We really were baffled."

Gabor notes that the team was getting better media support than other teams in the league, especially from the *Miami Herald*, which published stories about the Fusion three to four times a week. Horowitz knew, especially with Hamilton as GM, that the front office was skilled enough to put a good product on the field. Despite stories that Horowitz didn't want to spend money to market the team, he countered by saying the Fusion were outspending other teams on advertising and were getting guidance from the league on marketing. And, as he pointed out, he did spend literally millions of his own money to create a stadium for the team.

In my conversations with Horowitz, weather is a recurrent scapegoat, and indeed, players who toiled in the summer months were profoundly aware of its effects. Wynalda, recalling his time with the team in 2000, acknowledges that the weather did impact play as well as the fan experience, though it typically favored the players who trained in it: "In June and July, you could get dehydrated. Watching guys from Colorado, or New York, the West Coast . . . they'd get twenty minutes into a game, and they just became clock watchers, saying, God, I just want this game to be over with. Games were slower—and if you didn't know any better, it made for great soccer. It looked like great offense for us, whereas it was really just a guy too tired to defend."

Horowitz's mood that final year might best be described as bewilderment. Despite a great team, a popular coach, and a stadium that he invested heavily in, the team wasn't approaching the 14,000–15,000 in attendance that Horowitz and his investors assessed would be enough to generate the revenue needed to keep it going. And toward the end of 2001, when it was clear they still wouldn't hit that mark, Horowitz said he was ready to do the one thing he wasn't accustomed to doing in business. As he recalls,

> I came to the league. I finally said to the league, 'Unless somebody has an answer to this, this can't go on. We're bleeding.' It was financial. If you're running a business, and you can't fix it, no matter what you've tried, what do you do? It was me approaching the league saying this is enough.
>
> I started talking about it by telephone [toward the end of the

2001 season], and we decided we'd have an owners' meeting about it, what the ramifications would be if I went through with it. It was absolutely my decision. The league doesn't have the right to close a team—that's not in the bylaws, particularly when an owner pays a large amount to purchase a team.

Don't forget, the way the league worked, we shared revenues and expenses. So if there's a deficit, the league is sharing in this deficit. If there's a profit, they share a profit. So not only was I and my investor group losing money, the league wasn't making any money on the team, at the expense of the players. In Tampa, without an owner, the league was incurring all the losses for that team.

While Horowitz was talking to MLS's top officials privately about the very real possibility of folding the team, Hudson and an inspired group of players were on a collision course with another talented but troubled franchise in the Earthquakes.

The Quakes–Fusion series was one of the more dramatic offerings in the eight-team playoffs, again using the three-conference, first-to-five format that jumbled geography. In 2001, the Galaxy emerged from rounds that involved the MetroStars, Fire, and Burn to get to the all-California finals. The Quakes defeated the Crew in 3–1 and 3–0 matches, while it took the Fusion all three games to advance past the defending champion Wizards.

The third and deciding game between the Quakes and Fusion came down to extra time. Hudson was apoplectic about losing and recalls, "We got beat by Landon Donovan's stinkin' San Jose Earthquakes, on that Troy Dayak goal," referring to the defender's corner-kick header just three minutes into overtime for the match's only goal. "It was Landon. You don't need to say anything more about him—he was a one-man wrecking crew. That was the difference."

Hudson even goes as far as to intimate that the Quakes–Fusion series was a literal "loser leaves town" series, saying, "The rumor was at the time that whoever lost that semifinal was going to die. That was the heavy rumor. The players didn't know it, of course, but Doug had an indication that this might be it. That was hard to bear."

Others, however, saw hope in the narrow loss and the Fusion's stellar season. Greg Cote, putting an epitaph on the season (but not the Fusion itself), wrote in the *Miami Herald*,

> Hudson's band fashioned a season that stands as a hallmark in the almost 30-year and oft-mottled history of pro soccer in South Florida. This was the most inspired, attractive soccer we have seen since the old NASL Fort Lauderdale Strikers (led by a young British midfielder named Ray Hudson) made the same Lockhart rock. This was the most successful season, by the bottom line, since Hudson's Strikers lost in the 1980 Soccer Bowl title game.
>
> This was the season that saved the team, the sport down here.
>
> This was the season that made soccer begin to grow again.
>
> Oh how Hudson deserved to be the MLS coach of the year, not runner-up.
>
> The Fusion was on the brink of being moved, or folded, before Hudson assembled a bunch of discards and misfits and made them a magical team. Wednesday's robust crowd of 11,242 hints of the rejuvenation.
>
> Now the coach, even as he stanched tears after the loss, vowed to attack next season.
>
> "We will be ruthless," he said. "We'll get stronger. We'll get better. You ain't seen nothin' yet."[2]

The Earthquakes started 2001 with an incredible transition—in January of that year, Silicon Valley Sports & Entertainment, which managed the San Jose Sharks of the National Hockey League, took over as the Quakes operators from the Kraft Sports Group, which had been operating both New England and San Jose since 1999. Two days after taking over, the new owners fired coach Lothar Osiander, who'd led the Quakes to the worst record of 2000, and replaced him with Frank Yallop.

Dominic Kinnear, a former San Jose player who started 2001 thinking he would play for the Mutiny, retired and became Yallop's assistant while still recovering from abdominal wall surgery.

"During his five-year career in Major League Soccer," the *Tampa Tribune* recounted, "Kinnear underwent reconstructive knee surgery and surgery on his ankle, as well as a second-degree concussion, a serious sprain of his spine, and assorted hamstring, thigh and ankle contusions that forced him out of numerous matches."[3]

The most important improvement to the Quakes 2001 squad, in a busy offseason that included acquisitions of veteran defender Jeff Agoos, Canadian midfielder Dwayne De Rosario, and Danish standout Ronnie Ekelund, came in March, when Landon Donovan was loaned to San Jose.

The Quakes were able to come after Donovan by virtue of having the worst record in the 2000 MLS season and thereby receiving the league's first allocated player. Soccertimes.com—a soccer news site that still actively posts soccer news despite its retro, CSS-be-damned appearance—termed it "a complex deal in which he signed a four-year Major League Soccer contract, but is guaranteed to be with the team only for 2001."[4]

Donovan was initially supposed to circumvent MLS altogether. He had been signed to a six-year contract with Bundesliga club Bayer Leverkusen while just sixteen, and the plan was for him to develop within the Leverkusen system, earn his way onto the senior squad, and potentially become a landmark American player in gaining the success (read: attaining regular starting XI status with a Bundesliga side) that eluded generational players that came before him. But a little more than a year into his contract, they decided to loan Donovan to an American team, ostensibly with the hopes that he'd get experience in MLS that he could then take back to Germany and translate to success there.

When asked to contrast his experience between Bayern Leverkusen and the Earthquakes, Donovan simply says, "My fondest memories of San Jose were that I actually got to play professional soccer for the first time. MLS and the Bundesliga were vastly different in every way, but I loved being in San Jose and finally getting a chance to play."

After opening the season with a win over cross-state rivals the Galaxy, the Quakes lost their next two games—but then went undefeated in the next twelve games, bouncing back from an uncharacteristic loss with two more wins to head into the All-Star Game.

And then—in front of a home crowd at Spartan Stadium, with six Earthquakes on the West squad, Donovan scored a hat trick in the game's first nineteen minutes to kick off what was arguably the wildest All-Star

Game in MLS history. The West added a fourth goal in the twenty-sixth minute, conceded a goal two minutes later, let in two Brian McBride goals in the thirty-fourth and thirty-ninth minutes, conceded the tying goal just after halftime, regained the lead, conceded two goals at the eighty-fourth and eighty-seventh minute to go down 6–5, and then Donovan reemerged on the score sheet in the second minute of extra time for the final and tying goal, giving MLS its first All-Star Game draw ever.

Seeing that the league was on the precipice of folding immediately after the 2001 finals, that might have cast the Earthquakes' triumph as an ultimate Pyrrhic victory for the club.

But the victory did come—at the expense of the Galaxy, who'd made three appearances in five years of MLS Cups without once hoisting the trophy. Playing just four days after both California teams won overtime matches to get to the finals, the teams went to overtime again, after Galaxy standout and Mexican international striker Luis Hernández traded first-half goals with Donovan. De Rosario's ninety-sixth-minute goal earned him the match MVP trophy and the Quakes the crowning achievement in a worst-to-first season. The *San Francisco Chronicle* pointed out that with the Bay Area CyberRays recently winning the in-augural Women's United Soccer Association Championship—created, of course, to capitalize on the success of the 1999 Women's World Cup team, that the Bay Area was "the unofficial capital of American profes-sional soccer."[5]

And yet, while the drama of the MLS Cup was playing out on the field of what is now MAPFRE Stadium, a more significant drama was happening in other parts of Columbus around the MLS Cup.

As Kevin Payne notes, Horowitz's decision to fold the Fusion sent the MLS board of governors into a series of meetings about how to proceed with the future of the league. Without knowing it at the time, MetroStars goalkeeper Tim Howard might have saved the league with a well-timed, inspirational speech by virtue of being named Goalkeeper of the Year. Payne recalls,

> There was a board of governors meeting in Columbus around MLS Cup. That was a very, very difficult meeting. The business model was broken. There was not much consensus about how

to go forward. I've always believed that one of the things that saved the league, ultimately, was we met all day, and it kind of went nowhere. Then we broke to go the awards ceremony, which was in a theater-style setting. It's much more formal than what MLS does today. So I was sitting with Phil and Nancy [Anschutz], and Tim Howard won the Goalkeeper of the Year award, and he made this really beautiful speech about the struggles he had had growing up with Tourette's. And he talked about how big an influence the game had in his life, and how it helped him overcome his challenges. He expressed enormous gratitude to Major League Soccer. And as we walked out of the building, Phil turned to Nancy and to me and said, "We have to keep this league going for young men like that."

Payne knew Anschutz's commitment to the league was serious—he remembers talking to him at the 1998 World Cup, and asking him, "Why do you do this? You could be in any sport." And Payne recalls Anschutz saying, "I think I can help this sport a lot more than I can other sports, and I think it's a game that deserves an opportunity to succeed."

Yet there was no resolution by the time the board of governors left Columbus, and that's when the league's future was in its greatest jeopardy. Payne recalls a post–MLS Cup conference call so dismal that his group ended up getting off before it ended, followed by a meeting in New York where an actual decision was made to take the league into bankruptcy.

Dan Hunt, in an April 2016 interview for the *Soccer Today* radio show on ESPN Radio Dallas, recalled a slightly different timeline, but remembers being on the conference call where the decision was made to go into bankruptcy, with his father and brother in the Kansas City Chiefs' office, with this visceral level of alarm: "On my very first day on the job, it went out of business. They were preparing the documents and that was it. My brother looks over at me and in typical big brother fashion goes, 'Congratulations, you've been hired and fired on the same day' with a big smile, although it wasn't quite big enough because the situation was pretty grave. My dad was able to call everybody, get 'em back, and within 48 hours everybody was back all in."[6]

As Payne recalls, Anschutz followed through on what he'd said to him in Columbus, determined that the league could not yet fail:

> What ended up happening was Phil said, I'll step up and take responsibility for six teams, and he looked at Robert and Lamar, and said, can you guys stand up with me? Lamar said, yes, we'll do the two teams we have and we'll do Dallas. Which obviously made sense because that's where they lived. And then Robert said, we'll keep New England alive. And from there, we kind of reoriented the whole league. We adopted a very strict five-year spending plan. And the whole idea was to try to get the losses under control, to use some to build up commercial revenues.

Anschutz, who'd been operating D.C. United transitionally in tandem with the original ownership group, exercised his option to become sole investor-operator on the same day the Florida contractions were announced. He'd also coordinated a transition with Silicon Valley Sports & Entertainment to take over the Quakes—AEG would be its sole investor-operator by the end of 2002—adding to an empire that also included the Galaxy, Rapids, and Fire, as well as the MetroStars, which he'd purchased from Metromedia in November 2001.

"I think there was a recognition that the strategy we had been pursuing was not working, and that we continued to have an opportunity, but we needed to adjust, as all good businesses should," Mark Abbott remembers. "A few key decisions were made. One came from an insight that looks simple in retrospect, but which we hadn't had before, which was that there was a large market here for professional soccer, for capturing that, which led to the formation of Soccer United Marketing [SUM]. There were other aspects of the soccer business we could be involved with, that would allow us to generate revenue that would help the league, strategically, to help reach people who were potential fans of MLS."

Payne termed this a "doubling down" on the World Cup's potential to attract American fans. Indeed, a week before announcing that the Fusion and Mutiny would officially be contracted—even though there were already reports from media outlets speculating that the future was nigh for both teams—MLS sought to set the tone for 2002 via the public reveal of what would be SUM's centerpiece—the multiyear deal between ABC, ESPN, and MLS to air the 2002 and 2006 World Cups, the 2003 Women's World Cup, and MLS matches each year during the terms of the contract.[7]

But the league also recognized that more teams needed what Abbott termed "additional investment and infrastructure"—namely, more soccer-specific stadiums to follow what had been created for the Crew in 1999.

"We recognized early on that if the league was going to be successful, it needed its own stadiums, where its teams were primary tenants," Abbott explains. "What we learned when we went out and talked to potential investors in '94 and '95, they said, let's see if we can get the league up and going before we spend in what would become billions of dollars in stadiums. But by this point in time, there was clear recognition that we needed stadiums. We made some changes in the way expenses and revenues were allocated to further incentivize development of stadiums and I think that that helped. We also recognized that we needed to continue to invest in our product quality."

That had to do with the development of what Abbott called "MLS's media properties," which started with the new ABC/ESPN deal, as well as the questions "How do we get people to develop players?" and "What's the role of star players?"—which would eventually lead the league into the designated player rule and additional rules about how to attract marquee players to the league and how to allocate them to teams.

Garber characterizes the whole scheme as part of a plan B to make the league more attractive to new investors, summarizing it as "divesting the league-operated clubs, having Anschutz and [Lamar] Hunt take them over, making a commitment to build soccer stadiums—with the Home Depot Center being the first one to come out of that—and probably most importantly, it was a near hundred-million-dollar investment in the formation of Soccer United Marketing, which gave us a vehicle to capture the rise of the commercial value of soccer that was not necessarily dependent on what was a very long term growth plan for MLS, because SUM was invested in many non-MLS soccer properties that were doing very well."

Garber saw the contraction part of the plan as "part of a broader vision for MLS soccer." He adds, "While that is viewed as the most traumatic aspect of the new vision, ultimately we were able to come out of that with the blueprint for a better, stronger, more popular league, which ultimately is the league that we have today."

That frank matter-of-factness, which Garber maintains today, was evident in the Associated Press report on the Mutiny and Fusion contraction news in which Garber said, "The decision to leave both cities for the 2002 MLS season was extremely difficult. I can assure all of our fans that we worked tirelessly to find a plan that would have allowed us to remain in both markets. We simply could not find a solution that was economically feasible at this time, and we hope to return to the state of Florida when the league expands in future years."[8]

Ironically, the Mutiny had had its best financial year in 2001, according to Manning, and despite plans to upgrade the team while improving its financial status heading into the 2002 season, the lack of a buyer—despite the league's ongoing efforts to attract one—ultimately doomed the team to contraction.

"I got a phone call from Don saying, 'We've made a decision at the board level, and we're going to close the team down,'" Manning recalls. "It was literally twenty-four hours before the announcement. And I get it; they discussed several different options, and while they were doing so, they didn't want us to take our eye off the ball."

The *St. Petersburg Times* presented a rather sad epitaph for the Mutiny in its January 9, 2009, edition. Rodney Page began his article, "Mutiny employees showed up Tuesday morning at their office at Raymond James Stadium ready to work. By the afternoon, they were packing boxes and filling garbage bags with personal belongings, out of a job after Major League Soccer ceased operations of both the Mutiny and Miami Fusion."

The article noted that the league had spoken to "six to 12" potential owners since the league launched, with the Glazer family, which owned the Tampa Bay Buccaneers, being the closest to forging ahead. "We needed an owner in Tampa," Garber told the *Times*. "We spent an enormous amount of time trying to find that owner."[9]

Sakiewicz remembers an eight-month period in which he was trying to sell the franchise to the family for $5 million, and once he left Tampa for the MetroStars in 1999, encouraged Garber to pursue negotiations, believing that the Mutiny could succeed if the Glazers would step in.

Malcolm Glazer, quite famously, eventually did decide to invest in soccer—starting with a £9 million purchase to acquire 2.9 percent of Manchester United stock in March 2003,[10] with additional increases coming over the next two years until, in May 2005, he completed a £740 million (nearly $1.5 billion) bid to take control of the club.[11] Sakiewicz likens the process of going from the Mutiny to Manchester United to "walking into Macy's for a pair of socks and walking out of the store buying the whole franchise."

As far as the league was concerned, Tampa was welcome back—provided it could produce a soccer-specific stadium as well as an investor-operator ready to come on board.

For Fusion fans who'd had their hopes buoyed by their near story-book 2001 season, the news was particularly heartbreaking.

Hudson felt that the team could succeed there had the bookends of the first few games and few last games been consistent, but observes, in his inimitable fashion, that 1998's initial slide had sent the Fusion's fortunes "downhill like a giraffe on roller skates."

"The Fusion wasn't a failure in any way," Gabor maintains. "The team wasn't failing on the field. It was more of a situation between ownership and the league, and the direction the league was going, and the direction that ownership wanted to take."

As MLS headed into its sixth year, it had finally found investor-operator matches for all its teams, though it was obvious that the arrangement of one owner in charge of more than half the league's clubs was temporary.

Payne, in his new role, overseeing six teams, left soccer operations in the hands of general managers in each of the markets and worked from the D.C. United offices, sharing best practices and operating under a mandate "to do everything possible to reduce losses on the local level."

"Slowly and surely, we began to make progress," Payne notes of the postcontraction era. "The whole idea, when I was overseeing the six teams, was to try to show regular improvement in the bottom line of each of those teams, so we could potentially attract qualified buyers. Preferably, buyers who had an interest in the market. It took some years, but the process eventually worked."

And that process started the very next year—in large part, due to the gamble that MLS took on the World Cup.

Chapter 6

THE UNDERDOGS

In which an improbable World Cup run gives American soccer—both club and country—renewed hope.

THE 2002 WORLD CUP DIDN'T, AT FIRST GLANCE, APPEAR TO BE THE BEST possible World Cup to hook the SUM wagon to. South Korea and Japan, the first-ever Asian hosts of the worldwide tournament (and, as matters would develop, the only cohost nations ever) shared a time zone that happened to be thirteen to sixteen hours ahead of the four major American time zones. This led to the high hilarity of U.S. Soccer issuing a press release that sold the prowess of the team while glossing over the ghastly times during which new American soccer fans would need to tune in— 2:25 a.m. ET for its match against Korea, 4:55 a.m. ET for its match against Portugal, and 7:25 a.m. ET for its game against Poland.[1]

In addition to the insomniac start times to matches, the draw wasn't particularly friendly for a U.S. team whose 1998 campaign had been horrific. The Americans' first game would be against Portugal, led by a trio of world-class stars in Luis Figo, Rui Costa, and Nuni Gomes; the second game against the Korean cohosts; and the third against Poland. By the somewhat baffling rating system FIFA had in employ for 2002, the United States was actually the highest ranked of the four teams, but was still considered an underdog in the opening matchup.

In a 2014 retrospective on the 2002 World Cup team, Philly.com's Ed Farnsworth noted that U.S. coach Bruce Arena had used thirty-one different players in the sixteen qualifying matches for 2000–2001, increasingly relying upon a pair of twenty-year-olds—DaMarcus Beasley (who'd started his playing career in 2000 with the Chicago Fire while still just seventeen) and Landon Donovan (who'd had a pretty spectacular 2001 season)—who brought down the average age of the squad to twenty-nine. The team included eleven veterans from the 1998 World Cup and, interestingly enough, eleven Major League Soccer players (along with six players with English club teams and six from other European club teams). Arena was not terribly optimistic about how the Americans would fare. As Farnsworth noted, "We're not going to win [the World Cup] because we're not a good enough team. I don't think anyone is going to be damaged by us saying that. I mean, how many countries have won it? If we can get a point in the first game, it will put the whole group in chaos."[2]

"Bruce said those things publicly but, inside the team, we just prepared to play against a very good Portuguese team," Donovan recalls. "We knew they were better on paper. We also knew that we had the capability of beating good teams if we played well enough. I think the players really believed we had a chance to get something out of that game."

National Public Radio's Tom Goldman, in previewing the World Cup, declared, "Having qualified for its fourth straight World Cup, the United States still hasn't established a recognizable style," yet he also conversed with soccer historian David Wasser, who told Goldman he believed the United States was "on the cusp of finally adopting a national style" built around scrappiness, and speculated they could fight their way to an upset victory over Portugal.[3]

But that wasn't the only pre–World Cup coverage that concerned itself with American style. The *New York Times Magazine* ran a fashion photo spread a week before the start of the tournament, featuring what you might describe as provocative, even smoldering, photos of the U.S. national players in Prada and Tom Ford designer clothing with price tags in the hundreds and even thousands.[4] The clothing leaned toward the silky; Pablo Mastroeni's outfit, in particular, was edging into the Steven Tyler Zone.

Brian Phillips, in a hilarious 2013 send-up of the shoot, noted,

Need to drum up some publicity for your sports team in advance of its big event? *Of course* you sign them up for a *New York Times Magazine* style spread photographed by Dutch photographer and ex-Armani creative director Matthias Vriens. I mean, *of course* you do. What are the odds that the resulting photos, published in late May under the title "The Boys of Soccer," will be so tonally bewildering, such a steamy potpourri of sullenness and arch poses and billowing paisley and smothered rage, that they look like Mike Tyson's dreams the night after he first saw *The Muppet Show*? What could possibly go wrong?[5]

Nearly a decade and a half after first appearing, the photo of Donovan drinking from a water fountain remains an iconic image of the era that he hasn't entirely lived down. When a fan ribbed him about it on Twitter in 2015, he half joked that he wished that photo could be removed from the Internet forever, and when another Twitter user declared that the Donovan water fountain had been surpassed by a New York City Football Club promo photo of Frank Lampard, Andrea Pirlo, and David Villa in tank tops, uniform shorts, and with what appeared to be oiled triceps, Donovan responded, "I've been waiting for this day," and followed that with a series of hands-in-prayer emojis.)[6]

Once the soccer started, the United States was out to show that 2002 would not be the goal-bereft train wreck that 1998 was, and it didn't take long to do so.

In the fourth minute of its opening match, Brian McBride headed an Earnie Stewart corner kick toward goal, forcing Portugal goalie Victor Baia to dive to stop the shot. Baia got tangled up with one of his defenders while going to ground, and the resulting rebound fell to a lurking-at-the-far-post John O'Brien, who put the Americans up. In the thirtieth minute, Donovan intended to send a cross into McBride, who was being guarded closely by Jorge Costa; the ball struck Costa's shoulder and shockingly spiraled into the goal—Baia was taken off guard and too late to react. Donovan reacted with an expression that was part bewilderment and part, "Look what I just did!" In the thirty-sixth minute, McBride scored what might have been the game's first legitimately good goal—meeting a solid Tony Sanneh cross with a diving header that simply beat a prepared Baia with speed and placement.

Three minutes later, a poor O'Brien clearance, on a corner kick that devolved into pinball, found Beto's foot to slot past goalkeeper Brad

Friedel to make it 3–1. In the seventy-first minute, Agoos misplayed a Rui Costa cross, doing his best forward finishing impression on the wrong goal to bring it to 3–2. But the Americans had created enough of a cushion and displayed enough intestinal fortitude in the remaining minutes to beat one of the traditional soccer powers for its first World Cup win outside the United States since 1950.

In the second group match, the United States would tie the cohosts 1–1, with Clint Mathis scoring in the twenty-fourth minute, Brad Friedel saving a fortieth-minute penalty kick to temporarily preserve the lead, then making several memorable second-half saves, and Ahn Jung-Hwan heading in the seventy-eighth-minute equalizer, celebrating by imitating a speed skater, to remind the world of a speed skating controversy involving American and South Korean racers at the 2002 Winter Olympics in Salt Lake City that past February—which, at that point, was a controversy exclusively remembered by South Koreans.

After the match, Friedel said, "If someone had said we could have four points going into our final game, then I think we would have taken it,"[7] but they unfortunately stayed on four points following a lackluster showing against Poland in its final group match.

The United States seemingly returned to 1998 form, giving up two goals in the match's first five minutes. Nigerian-born striker Emmanuel Olisadebe won a header on a corner kick and then kicked in the resulting rebound to make it 1–0. It looked like Donovan had equalized a minute later, but was called for a foul on the play in which he'd headed the ball into the net, and on the ensuing play, forward Paweł Kryszałowicz beat Friedel with a well-assisted shot to make it 2–0.

Friedel made several brilliant saves to keep it 2–0, but the United States wasn't able to mount a successful attack, and in the sixty-sixth minute, substitute Marcin Żewłakow found an unmarked spot amid the frozen American defense to make it 3–0. The combination of a Friedel penalty save and a Donovan goal late in the game kept it a more respectable 3–1, but four points, under normal circumstances given this group's makeup, would not be enough to advance in the World Cup.

Fortunately for the Americans, this World Cup was not being played under normal circumstances. While the United States was losing, the Koreans were upstaging Portugal with a 1–0 victory perhaps most notable for the Europeans being reduced to nine men—a twenty-sixth-minute straight red for Joao Pinto, and a sixty-fifth-minute second yellow for Beto serving as preludes to Park Ji-Sung's seventieth-minute goal.

The Round of 16 was a gift from the soccer gods: the United States versus Mexico, the first time the fierce Confederation of North, Central American and Caribbean Association Football (CONCACAF) rivals had ever met in World Cup play. The United States won by the "dos a cero" scoreline that American fans have since come to favor, playing a cavalier 3–5–2 formation and riding an eighth-minute McBride strike and a Donovan header in the sixty-fifth minute to advance to the quarterfinals—already the U.S.'s best showing since its third-place finish in the 1930 World Cup—to face Germany.

The Americans' World Cup dream ended there, though they didn't go down easily. The game's lone goal came in the thirty-ninth minute, when Michael Ballack rose up in traffic on a set piece kick lofted into the penalty area for the successful header. But the game's definitive moment came in the forty-ninth minute—a shot by American fullback Gregg Berhalter appeared to bounce off goalkeeper Oliver Kahn, spin over the line for a brief second, and then connect with defender Torsten Frings's hand on the way out. Neither a goal nor a handball was called, and despite several other great chances from the Americans during the second half, the aforementioned hard-luck moment was the definitive one of the match, and Germany went through to dispatch South Korea 1–0 in the semifinals before losing 2–0 to Brazil in the finals.

The U.S. team had exceeded the expectations for its performance, beating one of the world's most respected soccer nations and their bitter rivals before giving one of the perennial best teams in the world all it could handle. They were doing this, unfortunately, in a time zone that was a direct affront to American TV viewers. According to Nielsen, the 1.4 broadcast rating and 0.7 cable rating (only counting English-language TV) was cumulatively down from the 2.6 broadcast rating and 0.5 cable rating that the previous World Cup had recorded. Just over an estimated 6 million Americans watched the finals, which was down from the 8.6 million watching in 1998, though the finals did air live at 6:30 a.m. ET on a Sunday morning, as compared to the midafternoon Sunday start time for the 1998 Finals.[8]

But the ultimate triumph of the 2002 World Cup, from an American soccer standpoint, was that it created a foundation for future World Cup cycles and the coverage that was to follow, making World Cup broadcasts more sellable to advertisers in future, more broadcast-friendly cycles. (And, when Nielsen would start factoring in Spanish-language broadcasts in 2006, it would reveal that half of more of the American audience for the World Cup was watching *en español*.) And for those Americans who were watching, the inspired and inspiring play was something to be excited about, creating a hope for the future of American soccer that the prior year's angst over MLS's fortunes had adversely affected.

For MLS, the performance was a double boon, as it not only provided a solid initial return on investment (excitement-wise, if not ratings-wise) for SUM's World Cup play but also helped raise the profile of players returning from the World Cup to MLS.

Mark Abbott recalls that, as a result of the Americans' World Cup success, "You have Landon Donovan and these players who are playing in the league who are all of a sudden known throughout the United States. That was a quick change from where we had been to what became people seeing what the future could be. And that was a real turning point. There was this decision made in 2001, and then with the success in the 2002 World Cup, a lot of people who had not been interested or engaging with the league became engaged. And that's what set the foundation for expansion."

Don Garber saw something in American fans' love of the game, through its team's incredible run, that gave him hope:

> I remember sitting in the stadium in Korea when the United States beat Portugal, and I remember looking a few rows behind me—where Lamar Hunt was sitting—and he was crying. And he said, "This could be the turning point for this sport"—the sport that he'd been committed to since the 1970s with the Dallas Tornado. It began to really resonate with people in America, getting up in the middle of the night watching in bars, the beginnings of these viewing parties and viewing events. I remember coming home from the final in Yokohama in Japan, and saying, "You know what?

There's something happening here. Americans really do love this game." You've gotta give 'em the right product. You've got to package it right. You've got to put it in their hometown. And you've got to celebrate it in ways that they were able to see the beauty of the game when they were watching the World Cup. That means great stadiums, great marketing, great quality of play.

While the 2002 World Cup did create an excitement about soccer that MLS was poised to capitalize on, it was also during a period in which the remaining teams were cost conscious and careful by choice. While not exactly a holding pattern period for the league, especially for the two California teams whose burgeoning rivalry was becoming one of the league's best story lines, the three seasons following contraction, if MLS were a movie, might be handled via montage to move the audience along to the next significant act.

The 2002 season was obviously a transitional one, not just for the league as an entity but also for many of its individual franchises. With MLS back down to ten teams, it reverted to two conferences from its short-lived three-division alignment, but still took the top eight teams into the playoffs regardless of conference affiliation; this resulted in the overachieving Western Conference getting all its teams into the playoffs, though both conference's top teams would find their way through the bracket into the finals.

Contraction, of course, allowed some (but definitely not all) Fusion and Mutiny players to find homes with other teams through a one-round allocation draft followed by a dispersal draft held just three days after the announcement. Though a number of teams were hamstrung by salary caps and passed on players in the dispersal, the Revolution found themselves with five All-Star caliber players after MLS Christmas, with Alex Pineda Chacón and Mamadou Diallo among them (though Diallo would go to the MetroStars that coming May in a six-player move, the biggest MLS trade to date, which also sent allocation-drafted Diego Serna to the Revs). Other notable dispersals included Pablo Mastroeni going to Colorado to be forever intertwined with that club's lore, Kyle Beckerman going to Colorado to mature into an oft-capped national team player and MLS mainstay, and the legendary Preki returning to Kansas City.[9]

Fusion coach Ray Hudson quickly landed on his feet, being named to D.C. United within an hour of the Fusion folding announcement. John Haydon's *Washington Times* article on the announcement noted that "the club's post-game news conferences will never again be the same" and noting,

> The colorful Hudson, known for his hilarious quote collection, didn't fail to please the crowd at the District's ESPN Zone. Hudson's audience included dozens of United fans and a number of United players.
>
> "This is not just big," said Hudson, still a little shell-shocked on acquiring the United job, "this is Anna Nicole Smith big . . . this eclipses every job in the league."
>
> Haydon also captured these thoughts from Hudson on the new D.C. United:
>
> "This will be a team with belief. They will be bursting out of their shorts. They will come out like jets and act like gladiators behind the bayonet . . . I'm going to let the players express themselves, to play free like lads in a sandlot. These lads will bloom under me."[10]

Despite those bold (and entertaining) predictions, and even with goalkeeper Nick Rimando rejoining Hudson at D.C. United via the allocation draft, the club finished dead last in the league, though they were in contention for a playoff spot heading into the final match.

The Chicago Fire faced perhaps the most challenging 2002 for any of the surviving teams. Soldier Field was closed for nearly two years of renovations in January 2002. Its primary tenant, the NFL's Bears, had found a temporary home downstate at the University of Illinois' mammoth football stadium in Champaign, but the Fire was also in need of a home, and suburban Naperville's Cardinal Stadium (after several may-you-live-in-interesting-times months for the Fire front office) emerged as the team's one viable option. As Peter Wilt recalls:

> At the end of the day, it ended up being play in Naperville or take a couple of years off. We'd even considered building a modular stadium quickly in Cicero, we considered playing at the horse

track in Cicero, building a soccer field on the infield. We also considered playing in Milwaukee. And we thought about Rockford, but I don't think we even looked at a specific site there. We were told by Mayor [Richard M.] Daley that Comiskey Park was going to be made available to us, but when I met with Jerry Reinsdorf, he said no. So we only had about ninety days to get a deal done.

We had businesses leaders there who didn't want us because they thought we might take away from their business, we had million dollar homes surrounding the stadium and the homeowners were NIMBYs, and understandably so. We met one-on-one with every alderman, often with the mayor, and then with the college; we had to make a financial deal with the college.

And then we had to expand the stadium—it was a 4,500-seat stadium. So, in those ninety days, we had to add 10,000 seats, we had to add portable concession stands, merchandise stands, restrooms. It was arguably the most rewarding accomplishment of my career, just getting that done.

The Fire ended up playing to 95 percent capacity crowds in their first season in Naperville, and Wilt was even named Naperville Person of the Year by the *Daily Herald*, the newspaper serving Chicago's western suburbs. But the Fire lost many of the Polish and Mexican fans during the Naperville years, only getting some of them back upon returning to Soldier Field. Diehards like Marek Krupa still made it out to games—the most remarkable time being when he was with his wife at a family member's wedding reception, told her he was going to the bathroom, and then disappeared for three hours to run out to a home game at the new stadium—but the trek proved difficult for some to make on a regular basis. On the bright side, though, the move allowed the team to tap into a young, suburban market that followed them to the City of the Big Shoulders once they returned there.

"It really did hurt support early on when we moved to Naperville," Ben Burton observes. "We picked up a new breed of people, though, who are still coming to games. It was a shift. But just being transient was very hard on people. Getting back to a solid home helped," he said, referring to the coming Toyota Park that would open in 2006.

The year 2002 was also the one in which the Galaxy would finally break through and hoist an MLS Cup. They rode two dominant wins in a best-of-three series with the Wizards, blanked the Rapids in the conference finals, and avoided the Earthquakes—who went to the Eastern half of the bracket and were bounced in the first round—altogether. The finals were at Foxboro, the very stadium where they'd lost to D.C. United in 1996 and 1999. And awaiting them there? The hometown Revolution, who'd reached its first MLS Cup by getting past the Fire and Crew in successive three-game series.

The match was scoreless throughout the first ninety minutes and well into the second half of extra time, but in the last MLS Cup to feature a golden-goal ending, Carlos Ruiz disappointed the partisan Revs crowd (which, at more than 61,000, was the largest ever to gather for a finals) in the 113th minute, allowing the Galaxy to capture its first title.

"With expectation often comes disappointment," wrote reporter and clearly jaded Boston sports fan Nate Thompson in the *Taunton Daily Gazette*. "New England's four other major professional sports franchises learned that the hard way and now so have the Revolution." He did also note, to momentarily accentuate the positive, that "the loss was just the Revolution's second since Aug. 18, a span of 13 games, but the outcome will do little to tarnish New England's best season since the team's inception seven years ago."[11] It would, indeed, mark the start of a new era for the Revolution; MLS Coach of the Year Steve Nicol, who was initially named interim coach in May, would guide the Revs to the playoffs in eight straight seasons; Nicol himself would be a fixture on the Revs sidelines for a decade.

Like the Fire before them, the 2003 edition of the Burn moved from its spacious, aging stadium (in this case, the Cotton Bowl) to a small, flawed, suburban stadium (in this case, Dragon Stadium in the northern Metroplex outpost of Southlake, where a nearly $20 million stadium was built in 2001 for perennial Texas high school football power Carroll High School).

Lamar Hunt had acquired the Burn from the league to help save the league, in part because he felt that the team in his hometown should have an investor-operator after going the first five years without one. According to Dan Hunt, now the team president for FC Dallas, the Hunts had two things in mind upon setting the purchase in motion (which would take until 2003 to finalize): rebranding the team, as the Burn moniker hadn't really ever been relevant to Dallas fans, and building their own soccer-specific stadium, as Lamar Hunt famously had in Columbus, to serve as a long-term home.

The rebrand was relatively easy to push forward. As Dan Hunt notes, "Dallas Burn is a little bit of an unusual name, and so we wanted something that had a more traditional feeling to it. We didn't get negative feedback about the Burn, but from a graphic standpoint it was a very difficult graphic to work with, it was very hard to get it right on uniforms, on branding stuff. It was a difficult logo to work with."

The Hunts acknowledged that any rebranding could be tough, but going with a traditional name was imperative, and FC Dallas was as simple, streamlined, and traditional as they could get. FC Dallas acquired its logo the same way another Hunt-owned team, the Kansas City Chiefs, did: according to Dan, his father sat in his kitchen and sketched out his vision for the FC Dallas logo by hand—a bull inside a shield, with a flame-shaped birthmark on the cow's forehead to show linkage to the fire-breathing horse that somehow had come to embody the Burn. While it wasn't quite the interlocking KC inside an arrowhead drawn on a napkin on a flight from Dallas to Kansas City, it did add a chapter to Lamar's innate skills in branding.

The elder Hunt had also brokered an agreement with the City of Frisco, Texas—announced in April 2003, with some of the salient details written out on a napkin during a meeting with the city manager—for the construction of a $65 million stadium to open in 2005, in concurrence with the official rebranding. But the team announced its move to Dragon Stadium in January 2003, before the move to Frisco was finalized, showing what might be construed as dismissal toward the Cotton Bowl before spinning Dragon Stadium as a preferential move:

"The Cotton Bowl has been a fine home for the Burn since 1996, however we feel this interim move to the Northern Perimeter of the Dallas–Ft. Worth Metroplex will be beneficial to our diverse soccer fan base in numerous ways," said Burn President and General Manager Andy Swift. "We will be able to create an intimate, high-energy atmosphere for the continued growth of the game. Burn home games will now be free of game scheduling conflicts which have in the past created problems related to dates, traffic and parking. Any change in venue inevitably becomes more convenient for some and less for others, however we believe that the evolving demographics and continued growth of the Northern Perimeter of the Metroplex make this shift appealing."

The release also went on to say that Dragon Stadium's artificial surface was "synthetic 'Field Turf' which has received high marks when tested by several groups of MLS players at other sites," helpfully adding, "'Field Turf' is a FIFA approved playing surface."[12]

The 2003 season went poorly for the Burn; they drew an MLS-low average of just under 8,000 (for a stadium the Burn themselves expanded to fit 12,000), and the team finished with an MLS-low 6–15–9 record, missing the playoffs for the first time in its league history. Fans expressed their disenchantment to such a degree that the club repaired its ties to the Cotton Bowl and signed a stopgap one-year deal for 2004 while its new stadium was being built. The club mea culpa'd by way of press release: "As an organization, we pride ourselves on maintaining open and direct communication with our fans and the marketplace," said new Burn President and General Manager Greg Elliott. "In this case, our fans spoke loud and clear and we listened. While we appreciate everything the Southlake community did for us last year, this move is the right thing for the Dallas Burn, its fans and our sponsors."[13]

"There was a lot of feedback," recalls Dan Hunt, laughing. "We still hear about that today." Though owning the one-year move to Southlake as an experiment they tried, he also notes that his belief that soccer should be played on grass made coming back to the Cotton Bowl for an interim year the right choice in the end.

The stadium debut of the season, however—and in many respects, the story of the season—was the debut of the Home Depot Center that June, transforming the idea of what a soccer-specific stadium could be.

What began as a $50–70 million soccer stadium morphed, according to Nick Green in his article on the opening, into a $150 million multi-sport complex (including track and field facilities, tennis courts, and a velodrome) endorsed by the U.S. Olympic Committee. The soccer stadium, with a Teflon-coated roof covering a percentage of its 27,000 seats and a grass berm at one end of the stadium serving as overflow seating for additional fans was, of course, the centerpiece of the complex.[14] While the initial opening on June 1 was for a track and field competition, the Galaxy staged its home opener there less than a week later. Pomp and circumstance included a gala dinner the night before with Pelé and FIFA president Sepp Blatter in keynote speaker roles, with President George W. Bush congratulating Phil Anschutz via taped message, and a live appearance at the match itself by Pelé, who handled pregame coin flip duties.[15]

"There's no doubt that if we didn't invest in stadiums, we wouldn't be where we are today," Garber says, attaching special significance to the Home Depot Center. He's not shy about using the nickname "the Cathedral of American Soccer" to refer to it, and though the nickname is self-assigned—deriving from the "Soccer's Cathedral" declaration on a Soccer America–produced advertising circular commissioned by U.S. Soccer and the Anschutz Entertainment Group (AEG)—the stadium has lived up to the lofty nickname. When compared to Columbus Crew Stadium, launched just four years earlier, it is a clear evolution, and even when compared to stadiums that opened in the years following, it's evident that it has endured in its first decade-plus as a well-conceived and well-executed stadium. It was certainly seen by its creators as a model for what other soccer-specific stadiums should be—the publication had AEG president and CEO Tim Leiweke predicting that "there could be 10 new MLS teams in the next five years all using the model of stadiums such as the Galaxy's new home."[16]

"I think it really celebrated the game for the first time in ways that rivaled the rest of the world," Garber notes. "It gave fans and the league a building a facility that was to the future of Major League Soccer what Lambeau Field was for the NFL, or Wrigley Field was for Major League Baseball. It wasn't just a building; it was a statement about what the future holds for us, if we're able to build hallowed ground for all our teams."

The league made sure to showcase the stadium right away; it was the site for both the 2003 All-Star Game, in which an MLS All-Star team beat Mexican powerhouse FC Guadalajara (a team about to be linked more intractably with MLS), and for the 2003 MLS Cup. Perhaps predictably, the West's fourth-place Galaxy drew the division-leading Earthquakes, setting up what became one of the greatest series in MLS history.

In 2003, MLS went to a two-leg aggregate playoff system for the first time ever for its conference semifinals, in which the lower-seeded team hosted the first match and the higher-seeded team hosted the second match, with ties broken via sudden-death extra time in the second game. The Galaxy, hosting the first match in their new "cathedral," won 2–0, and in the return leg in San Jose, went up 2–0 (and, most importantly, 4–0 on aggregate) after just thirteen minutes.

But the Quakes were ready to mount what many still regard as the greatest comeback in MLS history. As Dylan Hernandez reported for the *San Jose Mercury-News*,

> Earthquakes Coach Frank Yallop said it was the greatest game in which he had been involved. Landon Donovan said the same. And had they been given an opportunity to share their thoughts, many of the 14,145 fans at Spartan Stadium on Sunday night probably would have said they had never seen anything like it.
>
> What else could anyone say after the Earthquakes scored five consecutive goals in a 5–2 overtime victory over the Los Angeles Galaxy that vaulted them into the Western Conference final?
>
> San Jose had lost the first leg of this first-round, aggregate-goals series 2–0 and was trailing by the same score after 13 minutes on this night. It was a daunting mountain to climb but the Earthquakes did it, scoring four goals in regulation, the last in the ninetieth minute on a header by Chris Roner.
>
> That set up a sudden-death overtime, which ended after six minutes when substitute forward Rodrigo Faria put away a feed from Donovan. Faria's strike had the screaming crowd hopping as if on pogo sticks, waving their blue promotional rally towels.

"That crowd was more dynamic and louder than any of those at the World Cup games I was in," said Donovan, who scored the Earthquakes' second goal, in the 35th minute. "I would've loved to have had a ticket and been watching it."[17]

The Quakes met the Wizards in the conference finals—a Wizards team led by a rejuvenated (or maybe juvenated all along) Preki, who won an MVP at age forty with a twelve-goal, seventeen-assist season. It took the teams twenty-seven minutes of extra time, after a 2–2 deadlock, before Donovan scored the winning goal to put the Quakes into the finals in their rival's stadium, against a Fire team who had its own extra-time win against the Revolution, back in a newly renovated Soldier Field, to get to the finals.

In the finals, Ronnie Ekelund's fifth-minute goal on a free kick put the Quakes ahead, and Donovan doubled the lead in the thirty-eighth minute. Donovan's national teammate DaMarcus Beasley scored for the Fire to open up the second half, and after trading goals (a Quakes goal followed by a Quakes own goal), the Fire had the chance to equalize on a penalty kick but couldn't convert, and Donovan slotted his second goal in the seventy-first minute to preserve a 4–2 Quakes win—the team's second in three years.

The 2004 season was one that placed prior champions on a collision course, in the last year that MLS was a ten-team league. But it would be two rookies, both promising prospects when they came into the league, who would help define the season.

One was a twenty-one-year-old three-year college player who joined the Revolution, and one was a fourteen-year-old star-in-the-making who joined D.C. United. Both lasted three years with their initial clubs and eventually made their way overseas, but even by then were experiencing very different trajectories.

The Revolution's Clint Dempsey, who became the MLS Rookie of the Year in 2004, would move from the United States to enjoy great success with then Premier League side Fulham, peaking with a seventeen-goal, six-assist season in 2011–12 before moving across London to Tottenham Hotspur, and eventually back to MLS. United's Freddy Adu, who eventually ended his first U.S. era with a brief 2007 sojourn in Salt

Lake City, was signed by perennial Portugal power Benfica, but went on loans throughout Europe (including, at its most obscure, Turkish second-division team Caykur Rizespor), and attempted a 2011 comeback with the Union. After several years in Scandinavia, he found himself back in the United States by mid-2015 with the NASL's Tampa Bay Rowdies.

Hudson missed his window to coach Adu—he was fired and replaced by former Fire standout Piotr Nowak just before Adu was officially signed to the team—but he does remember workouts prior to the signing, when he was still at D.C. United's helm:

> He was a precocious young talent when he came in. We had two or three practice sessions where we invited Freddy in, and he was wonderful. It was twinkle-toes, he had a great light-it-up personality, he was wonderful with the ball. You could see the promise of magic.
>
> Whatever happened—it didn't work out with him under Nowak, and it just sort of spiraled from there. I don't know what happened. I can only speak for the few times I worked with him, at a young age. It was all there: the balance, the pace, the control, the touch, his inventiveness, his sharpness. The sky was the limit. That's why people were excited. There was something genuinely special there, but it just didn't pan out. They might have pinned that on me if I was still there.

In the short term, the team that signed Adu had a better 2004; D.C. United would make the playoffs (thanks in large part to prodigal son Jamie Moreno returning after a year with the MetroStars), would get past the Revolution in the Eastern Conference Finals (albeit on a 4–3 penalty kick shootout), and would defeat the Wizards 3–2 in the finals, despite losing Dema Kovalenko on the first-ever MLS Cup red card. Kovalenko was sent off for an intentional handball on a sure Wizards goal, and the Wizards' Josh Wolff converted the penalty to boot, but D.C. United returned to the winner's circle for the fourth time.

United hasn't held a trophy since the 2004 championship, but the win did harken back to the nascent days of the league—before the contraction, before 9/11, back when the 1994 World Cup was still a recent memory. And Nowak winning as coach gave him the unique distinction of winning the MLS Cup in both his first year as a player and his first year as a coach.

And yet, 2004 was more an end to a beginning. There were all kinds of new lying in wait: new teams to bring the league back to twelve teams, new owners with distinct visions about what their new teams could be, and—in one unfortunate case—a new city for an established team.

Chapter 7

THE EXPANSION

In which MLS brings more teams into the league, with a somewhat confounding international flair.

WHEN HISTORIANS OF MAJOR LEAGUE SOCCER PRAISE THOSE WHO KEPT the league alive in its time of need, Phil Anschutz, Don Garber, and Lamar Hunt are rightfully heralded. But there's another person deserving of praise—former National Basketball Association executive Dave Checketts, who fortuitously and successfully brought a team to his hometown of Salt Lake City despite the fact that Utah was not initially on MLS's radar as an expansion site.

For the 2005 season, Mexican powerhouse franchise Club Deportivo Guadalajara—known by its nickname Chivas (Goats)—proposed to launch a Los Angeles–based franchise named Chivas USA. This would be the first expansion team since the league's existential crisis following the 2001 season, and yet, just one expansion team seemed insufficient for a league that had just navigated contraction and a series of playoff changes for a ten-team league. Bumping up to eleven teams would have been odd in both senses of the word. Enter Checketts.

"Dave Checketts didn't want to come in [in 2005]," Kevin Payne recalls. "He wanted to wait another year or even two. He was hopeful to find a stadium solution before they started playing, and the league put a lot of pressure on him. To Dave's credit, he said, okay, I'll come in now. It would have been really awkward had we gone to just eleven teams. So Dave, over his own best judgment, agreed to come in early. And that was a really brave thing for him to do. And that was a really huge step."

Official league accounts have Chivas USA as MLS's eleventh team and Real Salt Lake as MLS's twelfth team, even though the Utah announcement preceded the Los Angeles announcement by about three weeks in the summer of 2004. The expansion would not only bring the league back to twelve teams, but would also send a message of solvency that countered the prior message of contraction.

And yet, the two-team expansion wasn't as cohesive as the 1998 expansion. Despite the reservations about trying to bring soccer to South Florida, the 1998 expansion had been aimed at putting the league in additional, large markets. The 2005 expansion, by contrast, would place a second team in an existing market (focusing on a Latino demographic that the Galaxy wasn't exclusively courting, yet was still attracting) and place a team in what is still—even a decade after entering it—the league's smallest media market.

Chivas USA represented an approach to MLS that hadn't been tried before—namely, the owner of a soccer club residing in another country, exporting its brand and even some of its players. The Mexican team was officially established in 1906, adopted its current name in 1908, and has been an enduring brand in Mexican soccer since.

Chivas USA initially tried to set a festive tone with a mariachi band, balloons, and streamers upon its announcement as the latest addition to the MLS family, according to Andrea Canales, a Los Angeles–based journalist now primarily covering Mexican soccer for ESPN FC (and called "Internet Girl" by colleagues early on because she wrote for Goal.com and four other soccer websites).

Chivas USA's 2005 season was not much of a party, however. It was, after all, a team that started out about as badly as a team could in its inaugural season—with a 4–22–6 record, switching head coaches midway through the first season, *twice*, and drawing just over 17,000 compared to the 24,000-plus the Galaxy were drawing to the exact same stadium.

But there was more. Canales noted that Chivas USA did not market themselves successfully to attract the Mexican American fans they sought, citing several key missteps: they populated the team with Mexican players from Chivas' reserve team, giving an impression of arrogance (or, as Canales put it, "we think your league is so pitiful that we can bring in our reserve players and win!"); they didn't do recruiting in Los Angeles to come up with potential "hidden gems"; and, perhaps most important, they aligned with a brand that was polarizing to supporters of Chivas's main Liga MX rival, Mexico City–based Club America.

Canales comments, "I realized from the beginning that their being wedded to the parent team was going to be problematic. It's not a concept that can translate well to the U.S. If it was maybe more that we wanted to honor the heritage of Chivas, and we want to be inspired by Latinos, kind of the more creative, dramatic flair that MLS needs, I think a lot of people would have been so on board with that. If it meant bringing, you know, more 'salsa,' more spice into this American league."

The Chivas–America rivalry and its potential to translate into a new crosstown rivalry wasn't lost on the Galaxy; Canales remembers a shirt soon after Chivas USA entered MLS in which the Galaxy's logo and color scheme was morphed into America's, so much so that Canales's reaction was, "Wow, there should be some copyright infringement there!"

But Chivas USA's branding problems went beyond that. Canales recalls,

> It wasn't just alienating the Club America fans. It was alienating every other fan base as well. Chivas had come into the league and said we want to represent all of Mexico. If they'd wanted to be the Liga MX club in MLS, I think other fans would have gotten on board. But by being so wedded to the Guadalajara brand, it became alienating to every other Liga MX team. Like León fans, for example; if León gets eliminated from the playoffs, then they'll cheer for Chivas—it becomes a nationalistic thing. But for Chivas to take its own brand to the league, to a different league, all alone, and to not even take the best . . . because it also became a joke as soon as Chivas started losing, it was so bad that a bunch of fans of Mexican soccer were horrified. They said, oh no, this is making us look bad, and making our league look bad. And then they became even more anti-Chivas USA. It was really obvious that it was hard for the brand to recover from that.

Canales does credit Antonio Cue, part of the original ownership group, for trying to inject some fun into a crosstown rivalry that Canales believes—had it been done right—the city might have embraced.

"Cue would do all sorts of fun bets," Canales comments. "Like, he promised to wash the car of [Galaxy president] Doug Hamilton if Chivas lost, or everyone in his office would have to wear a Galaxy outfit for one hour. He was really affable and putting up these silly bets—it added a really fun spirit to things. The Galaxy were winning all those games, so Cue was washing cars and wearing shirts. He was a good sport. He held up his end of every bet."

Just before the start of the 2006 season, Hamilton died of a heart attack while returning home from a trip to Costa Rica. Hamilton, a multiple winner of the MLS Executive of the Year award, was highly regarded for his work with the Fusion in its final years as well as with the Galaxy, and was beloved by many in MLS. His absence decidedly changed the tenor of the relationship between the teams.

"I don't want to say that Doug Hamilton ruined it because he died," Canales says. "I just think that Cue didn't feel right starting it with the new president. It just started things on a more somber note after, and then the Chivas USA [front office] infighting just sent them more downhill, and they didn't have any more of that playful spirit."

Bob Bradley was brought in to coach the squad in 2006, and he was able to work enough magic to immediately transform one of the historically worst teams in MLS history. While Chivas USA wouldn't ever be confused with the team it shared a stadium with, and though it would never make an MLS Cup in its decade of existence, it did something the Galaxy couldn't do in 2006: it made the playoffs.

The origin story for the league's other 2005 expansion team, in Salt Lake City, actually goes back to 2002, according to Trey Fitz-Gerald, who moved from MLS's top public relations post in 2004 to head up the new team's communications, in part to be able to be involved with a soccer team—or, as he put it, to "root for wins and losses instead of good attendance numbers and sponsors."

Checketts, a pro basketball player turned executive who'd seen soccer in Europe up close while managing NBA International, attended a conference for potential MLS investors in December of that year, which planted the seed for him. By June 2004 Checketts had committed to bringing the team to Salt Lake City with a $7.5 million investment and a pledge to make the University of Utah's Rice-Eccles Stadium a temporary home on the way to a soccer-specific stadium.

Fitz-Gerald points out that the demographics made sense: There was a young male "counterculture" element and "rebelling bishop's daughters with tattoos" who would embrace soccer but not the region's sports offerings; there were the two-thirds of Mormon missionaries who'd journeyed to soccer-loving countries in their formative years, and brought that love of soccer back with them; and there were Mormons from other countries who'd grown up with soccer and had specifically chosen, for religious reasons, to come to Utah. And Checketts knew how to successfully market sports in Utah—he'd become the Jazz's executive at age twenty-eight and helped engineer a turnaround from the initial rocky years following the franchise's move from New Orleans. According to Fitz-Gerald, Checketts thought—especially with his vision of a stadium on the fringes of downtown—that the team could "own the summer."

And Checketts also had designs on a name that would generate attention for its seeming incongruity: Real Salt Lake. "This name was not bestowed upon us by a Spanish king," Fitz-Gerald jokes. But it was a name that Checketts had in mind from the get-go. From his time in Europe, Checketts had gotten to know the Real Madrid front office, respected and admired them and their philosophy, and felt Real Salt Lake would be a fitting tribute. Though more than forty teams around the world use Real in their names, Checketts still felt it appropriate to ask their permission to use the name as a last step before officially announcing it. He reports they responded by saying, "You're going to be our sister team, go with our blessing."

"He wanted a name that was authentically soccer," Fitz-Gerald explains. Some of the first names floating around following the initial announcement came from former Salt Lake City–based soccer franchises, like Golden Spikers and Blitzz. But they didn't communicate soccer to Checketts in the way that a D.C. United did. (Plus, Blitzz featured that double z, instantly rendering it unworthy of consideration.)

Though Checketts was already heavily leaning toward the Real Salt Lake name, a Deseret News article that ran several weeks after the MLS announcement—and several weeks before the name announcement—

depicted a jovial Checketts turning the annual meeting of the Economic Development Corporation of Utah into a focus group on the new franchise's identity:

> "It's not going to be the Crickets, nor the Seagulls, nor the Pioneers, nor the Brine Shrimp. It's not going to be any of them," [Checketts] said during the lighthearted presentation.
>
> If Thursday's applause levels are any indication, the franchise may want to keep the name real rather than Real.
>
> Among the name options discussed Thursday, Real Salt Lake —patterned after European soccer power Real Madrid—drew the least-enthusiastic response. It prompted nothing but quizzical murmurs when Checketts first tossed it into the name mix.
>
> "Nobody will pronounce it properly," he said, explaining that "real" means "royalty" in Spanish. "That might be part of the appeal, don't you think?"

Other possibilities included the Glory, the Alliance, and the Highlanders, the latter inspiring Checketts to jest, "You like the kilts? That will bring the women in."

But, as Checketts helpfully explained to the gathering, "Names of soccer clubs are a little bit different than other teams . . . You want it to be known as a soccer club. You don't want any question that it might be an arena football team or remind you of an indoor lacrosse team. Soccer clubs are a little bit more traditional, when you think about the international names, they're a little bit more about tradition." He then proceeded to make a dig at the new cross-Rockies rivals, the Colorado Rapids, by saying their name sounded like an arena football team.[1]

As part of the process, Checketts did public polling via several different avenues, including a *Salt Lake Tribune* poll in which Highlanders triumphed with nearly 40 percent of the just more than 2,200 votes cast. In the *Tribune*'s poll, Real Salt Lake finished fourth, also trailing the Alliance and Glory.[2] But it wouldn't matter; Real Salt Lake won out, by one vote, in the only poll that ultimately mattered.

The actual name unveiling happened at Rice-Eccles in October 2004; *USA Today*'s coverage of the event, which included a pronunciation guide to Real in the lead, noted, "The event drew more than a thousand fans, who cheered the name when it was announced and began chanting 'Re-AL Salt Lake.' A huge banner with the team's crest was hung from the south bleachers, although it took several minutes to display the banner because the wind kept getting under it."[3]

"It didn't come off the tongue nearly as smoothly as it does now," Fitz-Gerald says of the name. "We still get people every week who come on our Twitter feed and tell us, this is stupid, you need to change your name. But we've embraced it, our fans have embraced it, and for all of us, it screams soccer in a way very few names would have."

Checketts sought to make the team one that everyone in the state could get behind—the team's color scheme purposefully mixed red and blue to unify both sides of the "Holy War," the keenly contentious rivalry between the University of Utah and Brigham Young University. It did also, unintentionally, dress a team inspired by Real Madrid in the home colors of its implacable Barcelona rivals.

Checketts remembers, "We had so much educating to do, that if someone came up to me and asked, 'Why'd you use the Real name with Barcelona colors?' I would have said, 'I'm so happy you know that.'"

In addition to readying the team for its arrival into the league, Checketts was also trying to deliver a new soccer stadium funded through a private-public partnership, so the new team wouldn't have to keep playing in a college football stadium. According to Checketts, the state legislature had earmarked hotel-motel tax money to fund the stadium, but the county wouldn't vote to release the funds.

It was a political battle so fraught and so challenging that the team began pursuing the option to move to another city. Checketts had actually gone as far as to secure an escape hatch sending the team to St. Louis, which, as Fitz-Gerald quipped, would have allowed the team "to at least be able to keep the RSL initials."

The battle between Checketts and the county culminated during several days in August 2006, when Real Salt Lake hosted Real Madrid for an exhibition match that highlighted their burgeoning relationship and their shared names. Checketts had learned about the county's latest downvote on the stadium money while on the way to a dinner with political leaders and the Real Madrid contingent the night before the match.

But rather than give up and move forward with plans to sell the team, he conferred with the Real Madrid contingent to see they'd help him announce the new stadium, and then used the dinner to declare a ground-breaking ceremony for ten o'clock the next morning—which would involve David Beckham, his Real Madrid teammates, and club officials. "So, literally overnight, we mowed this hayfield that had lain fallow in the middle of Sandy, Utah, for forty years, and put together a press event and ceremonial groundbreaking," Fitz-Gerald recalls. "It was the biggest leap of faith."

"I knew that that picture of David Beckham with the shovel would be all over the world," Checketts adds. "I knew that would put a lot of pressure on the county government. It was me playing some mischief, but it really worked. The news story was everywhere."

The *Deseret News* account of the ceremony quoted Checketts as saying that though details still had to be worked out, "sooner or later you have to make a go or no-go decision . . . I put my trust in our leaders that details will be worked out." The article noted that there were multiple suitors, seven in all, willing to buy the team and move it out of Utah. The story also included a quote from Sandy mayor Tom Dolan, who gushed, "Honestly, the emotions I'm feeling are similar to when my first son was born. I just want you to know that Dave Checketts is the man."[4]

But it would ultimately take more than a feel-good ceremony—namely, the intervention of Utah governor Jon Huntsman—to connect the dots necessary to unite all the parties and to make sure that Checketts's hayfield in Sandy would be transformed into what is now Rio Tinto Stadium.

While the presence of two expansion teams wouldn't directly affect the 2005 playoff race, a significant offseason move would. The Bundesliga experiment ended for Landon Donovan in early 2005—he decided to return to MLS, and because the Quakes had traded his rights away at the end of the 2004 season, he would be obtainable through MLS's allocation system. FC Dallas had the first pick, but the Galaxy traded Carlos Ruiz, its 2002 MLS Cup hero on the last year of his contract, for rights to the pick. The Galaxy, while cryptic about how they'd use the allocation when the trade was announced on March 30, were indeed involved with the press conference Donovan announced for the next day in Los Angeles where he said "everything would be decided."[5]

Donovan, who regards the Quakes–Galaxy rivalry to be the greatest of MLS rivalries, announced he'd be signing with the Galaxy, thus placing himself on both sides. Adam Serrano, who covers the team for the LA Galaxy Insider website, remembers,

> Landon was certainly not immediately welcomed when he arrived from Europe. The Galaxy–Quakes rivalry is the fiercest in Major League Soccer, and Galaxy fans were not eager to celebrate a player who had tormented them in the past. This reason is also why the acquisition was not viewed as a "victory" among Galaxy fans. LA supporters (and all soccer fans as a whole) are insanely territorial and wanted little to do with a player that had helped the Quakes succeed.
>
> The loss of Ruiz certainly stung among hard-core supporters because he'd quickly become a fan favorite after his heroics in the 2002 MLS Cup. In addition, he attracted a large Guatemalan fan base that still remains with the team to this day. Those fans soon flocked to Donovan once he started succeeding, but Ruiz remains a legend amongst Galaxy supporters.

The Quakes won the 2005 Supporters' Shield, but they again drew the Galaxy in the first round of the playoffs, losing 4–2 on aggregate, with the difference being Donovan's two goals in the Galaxy's 3–1 opening win. The Galaxy, in the one-match conference finals against the Rapids, won 2–0 on a Donovan brace. The Revolution, the number 1 seed in the East, led by MVP Taylor Twellman's seventeen goals, went down 2–0 on aggregate an hour into its second and deciding match with the MetroStars, and rallied with three goals in the remaining thirty minutes to make the conference finals, where Clint Dempsey's fourth-minute goal was all they needed to get past the Fire.

The 2005 MLS Cup, showcasing Frisco, Texas's new Pizza Hut Park, was scoreless for 105 minutes until Guillermo Ramirez struck from the eighteen-yard line to put the Galaxy ahead. Since MLS had dispensed with the golden goal, it wasn't quite a repeat of 2002's cruel end for the Revs, but they couldn't answer in the remaining fifteen minutes of extra time, and the Galaxy won their second title to equal the cup tally of their northern neighbors.

The offseason would bring one major change that further expanded the misery of Quakes fans, who'd just seen Donovan win an MLS Cup with his new team: the Anschutz Entertainment Group announced ten days before Christmas 2005 that the team would be leaving San Jose for Houston. While San Jose would retain the Earthquakes name and branding, to leave the door open for a Cleveland Browns–style reinvention, coach Dominic Kinnear and his players would find themselves moving from the Bay Area to—in more than one respect—its antithesis.

Alexi Lalas, the Quakes general manager at the time, notes that for the AEG, the lack of a soccer-specific stadium to replace Spartan Stadium—to be more specific, the inability for the AEG to get public funding to support a new stadium—was the key issue for a group concerned with keeping multiple teams afloat and the task of eventually selling some of those teams.

San Antonio was a rumored destination for the Quakes in the early part of 2005, when mayor Ed Garza was courting MLS by offering the 65,000-seat Alamodome as a home for an existing or expansion team. However, that May, Garza lost a reelection bid to Phil Hardberger, a relative political outsider whose first order of city business was to sever ties with MLS. Hardberger believed that a deal with MLS didn't make financial sense for the city, and was quoted as saying the only thing he would literally say to MLS was "good-bye," though MLS saved him the trouble by pulling out of negotiations with the city; Garber publicly declared, "This has been changed at the twelfth hour due to politics, and it is appalling."[6]

Houston would prove to be a more accommodating home for the Quakes, promising a soccer-specific stadium as well as a massive metro market accessible to dedicated fans in Austin and the newly neglected San Antonio (both closer to Houston than Dallas), and one closer to Mexico than any MLS franchise save for the two Los Angeles franchises.

Houston did, however, misstep immediately with its new identity. The original franchise name, Houston 1836, was announced in late January of 2007, intended as a nod to German franchises that included a year in the team name (most famously Hannover 96), and incorporating the year Houston was founded. However, 1836 was also the year that the famed Battle of the Alamo was fought. This was not the best way to engage Latinos, who then made up 40 percent of the Houston metro population and were largely weary of generations of Texas historians and even teachers framing the battle as one in which valiant whites protected themselves against Mexican aggressors.

Simon Romero, a Houston-based *New York Times* reporter covering the controversy, noted that the AEG appeared "to have upset some of the very soccer-crazy fans they were hoping to lure, after basing its venture in part on the crowds of Spanish-speaking fútbol aficionados who regularly fill stadiums here to attend the matches of visiting clubs from Mexico." Romero also quoted Houston-based Latino marketing expert Paco Bendaña, who dryly noted, "Clearly, not enough homework was put into this. Historically speaking, 1836 is not something we celebrate."[7]

Several weeks later, answering what the *Houston Chronicle* termed as the demands by numerous Mexican American corporate and political communities in Houston, the AEG announced a name change to the Houston Dynamo.[8] This was an inoffensive nod to the city's integral energy industry, it harkened back to MLS's history with abstract singular noun team names, and it capitalized on the European name trend that Real Salt Lake and FC Dallas had started; Dynamo was favored by a handful of Eastern European teams, most notably Dynamo Kyiv in Ukraine's capital and Dynamo Moscow in Russia. Houston also briefly had a soccer team (in 1984 and 1985) named the Dynamos, a member of the short-lived United Soccer League (not to be confused with the existing USL), assembled from remnants of the American Soccer League and the collapsing NASL.

Even though rumors had been swirling around the team for several years, the move still came as a shock to the team. As Brian Ching, who'd been with the Quakes since 2003, notes, there had been so many rumors that the players didn't put much stock in them: "We were shocked. We were told we'd be moving to a new city within a month, and for a lot of the team, with the salaries how they were, their wives were working. And I had January camp [for the national team], so I literally had fifteen days to move. I didn't know anything about Houston before I got here. I flew in, I had one day to go find a house. I walked into a place, said, okay, I'll take this, without not knowing too much about the city or where practice was going to be. We didn't really have too many people informing us about what parts of the city are best for what."

The promised soccer-specific stadium took until 2012 to manifest, in the form of BBVA Compass Stadium in downtown Houston. The WPA-built Robertson Stadium, which housed the University of Houston Cougars and went through renovations in the late 1990s to bring the stadium to near a 33,000 capacity,[9] served as the Dynamo's home for its first season (and far beyond), but it looked not unlike the Spartan Stadium the team had just left.

"To be honest, we thought our situation was pretty much the same, but just throw in 100-degree heat," Ching says. "We were still in a run-down college stadium, sometimes they had band practice out there, and sometimes there were college kids running around the track. There were times that our locker room lost AC. It wasn't ideal, but I think that's one of the things that made our team stronger on the field and attributed to our success. I think we were hardened by all the things we dealt with. It drew us closer as a team."

It wouldn't be long before San Jose got soccer back. In May 2006, Lew Wolff and John Fischer, principal owners of the Oakland Athletics, put forth a plan to revive the team that included a soccer-specific stadium.[10] To the relief of many Bay Area soccer fans, including a group that had created the Soccer Silicon Valley group in 2004 to lobby for a permanent stadium, the Earthquakes would return to MLS in 2008, though the stadium would be a little slower in coming.

In hindsight, Lalas and many others saw the move as a positive for both cities—especially for San Jose, which got a local ownership group occupied with just one MLS team and striving for a stadium. "I'm glad Houston got a team," he says, "but I'm also glad that, in a strange way, it made San Jose come back as a better version of itself."

But in a bittersweet development for Quakes fans, the Dynamo were instantly successful, winning two straight championships in 2006 and 2007 upon arriving in Texas. Both wins came at the expense of the New England Revolution, who'd made the MLS Cup in 2005 as well. The three straight losses, combined with the 2002 loss, cast them as the 1990s-era Buffalo Bills of MLS, making four of the past six championship games and losing them all.

The year 2006 brought another significant change; an MLS team was rebranded to share a name with an energy drink. That's the most reductive way to characterize the purchase and the subsequent name change, from MetroStars to Red Bulls. It's not as extreme as it might seem on its face: the MetroStars name is not so far afield from its Metromedia parent company, and Red Bull is a company who has notably branded other soccer teams worldwide, most famously Red Bull Salzburg (a top Austrian team). Given the lean toward Euro-styled names in this era, New York Red Bulls makes a certain sort of sense.

But still, for some observers, this close marriage of a product brand and a sports brand seemed a bridge too far.

The *New York Times* wasn't shy about using "a bracing jolt of Red Bull" as a metaphor for what the purchase of the team would do for a franchise it termed "terminally mediocre." Of course, the deal would bring with it the construction of a new soccer-specific stadium by 2008— one that would be more appropriately sized and more conveniently located than Giants Stadium, though still in New Jersey. But the front office also believed that the team was now poised to achieve greatness; Lalas told the *Times* to prepare for "America's first superclub," sounding very '90s when he added, "Red Bull is cutting edge and loves to push the envelope in everything they do. I hope everyone keeps an open mind because we are going to blow your mind."[11]

Nick Sakiewicz, who came to the MetroStars in 1999 from Tampa to head up that organization, was secretly involved in a prior rebranding effort; he notes, "For a couple of years, I tried really hard to acquire the Cosmos' IP and rights. I couldn't do it, so we ended up redoing the MetroStars logo before Red Bull eventually came to buy the team and change the name."

As Sakiewicz tells it, Red Bull's interest in buying the team hinged in part on the ability to rebrand, and even a name as revered as Cosmos might have not survived the purchase. MetroStars certainly wasn't going to endure as a brand.

"There were three real big triggers for the deal happening," Sakiewicz comments. "The first was getting the stadium done, so if I wasn't able to get that shovel in the ground when I did, Red Bull wouldn't have bought the team. Renaming the team Red Bull was a condition; there was really no option. That was part of the deal. And then the stadium and uniforms being Red Bull–branded was also a big condition. But the stadium was the biggest one. 20,000 people in an 80,000 capacity stadium with football lines all over the field did not work for us, and did not work for Red Bull."

Though fans should have been happy about a deal that got them out of a massive football stadium, the corporate name was going to be a roadblock for new fans who wanted to keep their sports as removed from commercial influence as possible—despite the slippery slope it was already on. A follow-up *New York Times* article recalled, "In 2004, a 'Spider-Man 2' promotion that would have placed ads on bases was shut within twenty-four hours after Major League Baseball heard from angry purists," and quoted one branding executive as saying, "No one's going to want to see the Coca-Cola Cowboys or the Kraft Singles," though it also included Lalas saying, regarding those disdainful of the Red Bull name, "The righteous indignation that people have about what this represents and the direction that this signifies is at times understandable, but also, I think, at times it's laughable."[12]

The sale of MetroStars to Red Bull was a quickly evolving sale of one of the teams the AEG was most eager to sell, a year after Anschutz sold his original team, the Rapids, to Kroenke Sports Enterprises to bring AEG holdings down to five teams.

"There was talk and concern about corporate 'sellout,'" Sakiewicz recalls. "But you have to remember what year it was. The league had just come out of a very difficult period. We were trying to get momentum. We needed partners like Red Bull. We needed to create strong partners, and you can't get much stronger than Red Bull as an organization and a brand. At the end of the day, I think the smart decision was made to make a good win-win deal with Red Bull."

"It came as a complete shock to us," says Mark Fishkin, speaking for the New York fans. "Not only was the team being completely rebranded, and for the first time in North American sports, for a consumer product, but we had no idea that the sale was happening until about forty-eight hours before. I know there were a few people for whom the name change was just too much, but of course, at the time, there was no other team to go to. They just said, 'Screw you, MLS,' and left."

"That day the team changed ownership and name was insane," explains Jeremy "Truman" Cadmus, an Empire Supporters Club member since 2005. "It was so close to the season starting, so it caught everyone off guard. For me, it was shocking that a company would rename a team after their product, but being a fan of the actual drink, I didn't flip out over it. A lot of people justifiably did."

"Ultimately, it ended up well," Lalas says, "but there was plenty of trepidation from the outside for how an energy drink was going to benefit MLS and benefit this particular team in the New York metropolitan area. For some people, the connotation was that this was just a marketing expense. When you're talking about sports, there's real emotion behind it, even though people understand it's a business, and there's a human element to it, be it the players or the supporters."

The year 2006 also brought another World Cup, and with Germany hosting, the tournament was more accessible to American TV viewers and to American producers overseas, with another Bruce Arena–coached team featuring twelve players from the 2002 World Cup squad, and a near fifty-fifty split among MLS players and overseas players.

It was not an easy draw for the allegedly fourth-in-the-world Americans, as they'd been placed into the tournament's Group of Death, matched with the second-place Czech Republic, eventual tournament winner Italy, and Ghana—a rising African power (and newly emerging American nemesis) despite its deceptively low FIFA ranking.

Michael Davies—today known to American soccer fans as half of Men in Blazers—blogged for ESPN's Page 2 in a series of columns that looked at the World Cup through a bemused, sometimes grumpy, but ultimately entertaining perspective that boldly claimed to be "unburdened by journalistic anything."

Covering the Americans' opening group match—a disheartening 3–0 loss to a superior Czech Republic side—Davies was critical of the team's defensive lapses and lack of width, but was also critical of the American fans who couldn't seem to be more imaginative in its "U-S-A, U-S-A" and "Ka-sey Kell-er" (in the familiar cadence of "Let's go, [team name]") in its chants and cheers. Noting the despondence of the team leaving the field at halftime, and the importance of fan support, Davies said, "At the World Cup you've got to sing, get up, shout, do whatever you can to lift your team—the U.S. fans are being dominated by the Czech fans more than the U.S. players are being dominated on the field."[13]

Ronald Blum's blunt assessment, writing for the Associated Press, was, "The United States looked like a bewildered World Cup newcomer again. The Americans didn't just lose Monday night, they were routed, roughed up and run over by the Czech Republic, a 3–0 crusher that put the Americans in danger of first-round elimination." An opening goal in the first five minutes by 6' 7-½" forward Jan Koller stunned the Americans, and Tomáš Rosický added thirty-sixth- and seventy-sixth-minute goals in a performance so lackluster that Arena criticized the team, specifically Donovan and DaMarcus Beasley, after the match.[14]

But according to Davies, both the team and the fans underwent a seismic transformation in the space of five days. The Americans played Italy and drew 1–1 in an ugly match that also drew blood—quite literally—when Daniele de Rossi viciously elbowed Brian McBride. That warranted the first of three red cards on the day. The Yanks, in turn, had two players sent off: Pablo Mastroeni for raking Andrea Pirlo's ankle, to which Mastroeni reacted postmatch, "I think that foul anywhere in the world is a yellow card," and Eddie Pope for a pair of yellow cards, the second coming just after halftime.

The *Guardian*'s Amy Lawrence asked in her postmatch report,

Is this the group nobody wants to win? Welcome to the group of fear, where at various stages so far all four teams have lost their nerve. The capacity for Italy and the USA to shoot themselves in the foot was liberally exposed here. The Italians started it with a gauche own goal and a nasty red card, only for the Americans to prick their own balloon with a dismissal either side of half time. More of the game was played with 10 men against nine than any other numerical formula and it made for an intense, overstretched encounter which was strangely compelling. Particularly as the USA were the more ambitious, more enthusiastic team by far.[15]

Davies, so critical of American fans earlier in the tournament, was full of praise after the draw, declaring the match "[a]n incomparable performance by the U.S. national team in the modern era. And listen to those fans. Football just arrived in America, I think. The players and fans played and cheered with the true passion of a footballing superpower. The U.S. may not win this World Cup, they may not even qualify for the next round, but this performance continues to lay the groundwork for the future. In fact, watching the performance of those players lifted in communion with their fans, I think they just completed the basement and the first five floors."[16]

Thanks in part to a controversial penalty at the end of the first half against their group stage closer with Ghana, the Americans lost 2–1 and would not advance—and yet there was optimism in the loss. Coach Arena, quoted in U.S. Soccer's official release about the bouncing, said, "U.S. Soccer has a bright future. I think in another group we would have had a better chance to advance. I think we were among the top half of the teams in this tournament. Despite the two losses, I think we demonstrated that we can play."[17]

Back in the States, D.C. United was winning a Supporters' Shield but couldn't get past the Revolution in the conference finals, with Taylor Twellman (like Clint Dempsey the year before) scoring a fourth-minute goal to get the team into its second straight finals. The Dynamo, formerly the Earthquakes, were almost undone by another Los Angeles team, Chivas USA, in the first round, but Ching scored a second-half stoppage time goal in the teams' second match to get the Dynamo through to the conference finals, where they took care of the Rapids.

The 2006 MLS Cup in Dallas rivaled the original MLS Cup (from ten years earlier) in drama. For 113 minutes there were no goals, and then there were two goals in quick succession, first from Twellman, then

from Ching, to deliver MLS's first-ever penalty kick shootout to determine the league champion.

"It was a pretty boring game heading into the last overtime," Ching
remembers, laughing. "There weren't a lot of opportunities. And then
once Taylor scored, it didn't take the air out of us—it was more like this
wasn't something we were going to accept, and fortunately, we had a little bit of time to rectify it. But our owner, Phil Anschutz, told me after
the game that he didn't even see my goal, because after they scored he
walked out of the suite, thinking we had lost."

After Brad Davis missed his fourth-round kick and Twellman converted his, the teams were tied 3–3. Ching converted his, and then Dynamo keeper Pat Onstad denied the Revs' Jay Heaps by diving to block
the final penalty kick.

"When it was time for me to take the kick," Ching remembers, "I
just thought, man, what a great year we've had, and it took the pressure
off, just thinking that it was great no matter what happened." Ching recalls looking up after the game and seeing a Texas sky that was a brilliant
Dynamo orange, and seeing his team's fans (who'd made the four-hour
drive up Interstate 45 en masse to see the match) in the stands. "I'm not
the kind of person to believe in destiny," he says, "but this was definitely
a case of things falling in place and going right."

The year 2007 brought expansion, with Canada joining the all-
American (up until then) MLS in the form of Toronto FC. Toronto had
been awarded an MLS franchise in October 2005, going with the simple
Toronto FC moniker rather than trying to wrest a nickname from
Toronto's confused NASL past. Toronto was represented for all but two
years of the NASL's fifteen-year history, fielding four different teams in
that time. The Toronto Falcons came into existence in 1967 to join the
National Premier Soccer League, became part of the NASL for the
league's inaugural season, and then promptly folded. In 1971 Toronto
received the Metros franchise, which bravely hung on through the 1974
season. Then, needing a cash infusion to stay afloat, the Metros sold 50
percent of the team to Toronto Croatia of the National Soccer League.
Fun While It Lasted, a website dedicated to failed franchises in multiple
sports, noted, that the newly merged Toronto Metros-Croatia was:

an anomaly within the North American Soccer League during the NASL's boom years of the mid-to-late 1970's. To the chagrin of league executives and observers, the merged club played up its ethnic identity, coming up with the awkward "Metros-Croatia" moniker and filling its management (entirely) and roster (largely) with ethnic Croats. In 1977, Tampa Bay Rowdies beat writer Ken Blankenship from *The St. Petersburg Times* published a long screed against the Metros-Croatia organization (and, by extension, the NASL for tolerating the club). Blankenship's hackles were raised by a miserable experience trying to cover a Rowdies road game in Toronto. The writer described the Metros-Croatia as essentially an insular "neighborhood soccer team" lacking the most basic professional standards of operation and promotion, and existing solely for the amusement of a tiny band of expatriate supporters.[18]

The team did have successes that were hard to ignore—namely, its 1976 Soccer Bowl triumph against the Minnesota Kicks in Seattle—but it was ultimately an iteration of the franchise that only lasted through the 1978 season. With the team's sale to the Global Television Network, the Toronto Croatia entity returned from whence it came (to the National Soccer League), and to the relief of many, the team was rebranded the Toronto Blizzard, hanging on until the league's demise after the 1984 season. In fact, the final NASL game was played in Toronto's Varsity Stadium, with the Blizzard losing the second and final game of the experimental Soccer Bowl best-of-three series to the Chicago Sting.

There was skepticism that the MLS would work in Canada—specifically, in Toronto—prior to the 2007 launch. "Before we launched," Mark Abbott recalls, "we were getting telephone calls saying, you don't know what you're doing, you're going to fail miserably there, the minor league team never drew more than a couple of thousand, you're crashing the league by going up there."

According to ESPN writer Doug McIntyre, the arrival of Toronto FC (and a fan base that understood what it was to be a proper soccer fan base) created an atmosphere that helped MLS move to a more cohesive, unified, and loud fan base—in other words, a fan base that seemed to effortlessly evolve from past to present generations in the major European leagues.

McIntyre remembers,

When I started noticing the fan culture of MLS changing was when Toronto FC came into the league in 2007. I knew there was a buzz around that team, and I had the opportunity to go to a few early games, and I said, "Wow, this is just a different opportunity than you see with other MLS teams." The other professional sports teams in Toronto were not very good, and here they have this nice little stadium right on the water, a team that was well branded, that did things right at the start. They marketed themselves well and sold a lot of season tickets. And that was really an authentic sort of soccer atmosphere. Around the league, up until that point, I think the league had mostly marketed to families, as opposed to a sort of young urban core. And it showed. So that was the only place in MLS that had a sort of intimidating venue where fans were singing and chanting, and it was young men drinking beer and yelling things. You had that in pockets in other MLS stadiums. You had the Barra Brava in DC, and even the MetroStars had a fan section, it was just very small behind the goal—the majority of the stadium was still soccer moms and their kids, by and large.

That was really where it exploded, and then two years later, with Seattle, you saw it go to another level. And so you were starting to see a change where MLS started changing the way it marketed itself. It did start trying to appeal more to young urban professionals. I think that was a big turning point for the league. They started attracting a different sort of fan—maybe fans who had watched soccer on TV.

The advent of soccer on TV changed things a lot. I think a lot of people were watching the Premier League on TV in the mornings, and really enjoying it, and wanted to experience that themselves, and go out to a stadium. People talk about going to a winter schedule in MLS, but I think one of the great things about MLS is that on a beautiful summer night, you can take a subway or a short drive to a beautiful, soccer-specific stadium that has a grass field, you have a beer in your hand, you're yelling for your favorite team—that experience can't be re-created on television. You can say whatever you want about the quality of play, but if you want to have that experience as a soccer fan, you can't get that watching a team on TV that plays three thousand miles away, no matter how good they are.

Abbott remembers the MLS executives' trip to Toronto FC's inaugural home opener, which included Toronto brass renting a streetcar to take them through downtown Toronto to the stadium: "I remember we go past this pub, and these people come out of the pub after watching the Premier League game that morning. And they have their TFC scarves on, and this one guy kisses his wife, who's got a baby in the stroller, and then he goes off with the other fans . . . it's like we're in Europe or something. And I'm thinking, *this* is a soccer fan base. That opened up a lot of people's eyes when they hit."

Mike Langevin, one of the original and still current leaders of Red Patch Boys (one of Toronto FC's primary supporters' groups), notes that the team's incredible diversity made Toronto soccer-ready without even its residents even realizing it. The main concern, at the outset, was reconciling the British, South American, and other Spanish-speaking styles of support into one cohesive, unified group. Langevin remembers,

It took a while to find a happy medium between these styles of support, which can often be in contrast to each other. Luckily the guys were all here to support the Reds, so we were generally happy to reach a compromise. I think a key factor we've always embraced is the desire to be inclusive, and to invite people to participate.

We sometimes see people yelling at the casual fans, demanding that they sing along, and that tends to backfire. Our policy has always been to sing the loudest and encourage people to get involved. Come paint banners, come practice songs. We just make a point of being open to outsiders, and welcoming to different opinions. That's how we grew so fast, by realizing that there's no right way to do it, and that imposing some old-world vision of what is a real supporter would probably keep a lot of great people on the sidelines.

Toronto FC had a successful inaugural year, with 14,000 season tickets sold, sellout crowds for all its home games, and finishing third in league attendance with over 20,000 per game. It is not entirely inaccurate to say that some MLS eyes were on Toronto in 2007, but thanks to one of the most famous players in the world—one known beyond soccer-loving households—many more eyes were on Los Angeles or, really, wherever David Beckham happened to be throughout the 2007 season.

Chapter 8

THE FIRST DESIGNATED PLAYER

In which one of the most famous players in the world
transforms the league and how the world views the league.

The Designated Player Rule—one of the most important, transformative rules in Major League Soccer history—will forever be identified with David Beckham, as he was the first player brought to MLS via the rule. Despite a recent wave of internationally known stars coming to play in America as career final acts and, increasingly, while still in their primes, Beckham may still be the best-known player to come via the Designated Player Rule through the entire decade of its existence.

Don Garber maintains that the rule "wasn't just dreamed up on a piece of paper as a mechanism to attract world-class players." He notes,

> It came out of a fairly significant consumer research study we did in 2006 after the World Cup, to try to get an understanding of what American soccer fans were really thinking about as they were becoming more and more engaged with the sport.
>
> They wanted to see more star players—more world-class players—and they wanted to see more American players who they watched compete for their country in the World Cup. We needed a mechanism to do that that would not break our system, and that mechanism was the Designated Player Rule, which gives teams the opportunity to sign outside the [salary] cap. That mechanism exists for all teams, which is part and parcel to our core equity. It's not like Real Madrid, who can just go out and sign whichever players they want. Each team has the same opportunity.

The idea of providing our teams the right and the opportunity to sign world-class players did not come from owners, and it didn't come from David Beckham. The DP concept came from a research study that told us the fans are looking for more players that they recognize. We then met as a league, utilizing the value of our single entity, and met to come up with a strategy that would allow us to do that and provide the opportunity to sign a player outside the budget.

Garber does admit, though, that the Galaxy were having conversations with Beckham about bringing him over to play during the latter half of 2006, when the league was looking at how to make this possible. In fact, according to Alexi Lalas, AEG had a relationship with Beckham dating back several years, tied to soccer camps he'd started in Los Angeles: "They understood that this was something that would change the LA Galaxy brand, change MLS, and change soccer. But you also needed a mechanism in order to do it, and MLS is very, very adept at creating mechanisms as need be."

The chance to bring in Beckham at age thirty-two was enough of a catalyst to make the Designated Player Rule a reality, and Beckham announced his move to Los Angeles on January 11 from London, on the eve of the MLS SuperDraft. The *New York Times* reported,

> Beckham's signing by the Galaxy, long-rumored, catapults the league into the global soccer spotlight. Up until last November, M.L.S. tightly controlled player salaries under its single-entity system, in which the league owned all player contracts and a team's salary budget could not exceed about $2 million a year, with only a few exceptions. The league's board of governors voted to relax that restriction and allow each team to sign one player for any amount, of which the league would pay only the first $400,000. They called it the designated player rule, but to soccer fans in the United States it has been referred to as the "Beckham Rule" since Day 1.[1]

Lalas says,

> I remember the moment we finally got the signed papers. I remember being at Christmas with my family and having to leave

the table to go over the Excel sheets to look over the numbers. We were paying a lot of money; it had to make sense about how we were going to monetize this off the field, with international tours, with jersey sales, with ticket sales. I'll never forget when I finally got the call that it was done and sending the e-mail out to my staff saying things are going to change now, from this moment on, in how we do our business. It's up to us to make sure that we monetize this and use this to better the Galaxy and MLS.

"I was surprised he was coming as early as he was," Grant Wahl remembers. "I thought he still had some time to play at the highest level in Europe. But I'd also written a column a few months before, looking at his situation in Madrid, and thought that maybe MLS should pursue him sooner rather than later."

Though some media outlets reported that Beckham's contract was a colossal $250 million over five years, ESPN Soccernet found that the annual salary was more in the neighborhood of $9 million a year, with the bulk of the $250 million coming through "endorsements and creative clauses." One rumor mentioned in the article was that "Adidas will be paying an additional $5 million to $6 million a year just to sponsor the Galaxy's jersey, ironic since they already manufacture them."[2] Soccer America's Paul Kennedy revealed, in a 2013 article, that one bonus in Beckham's contract was the right to purchase a MLS franchise for $25 million upon his retirement from playing, as long as the franchise was not in New York.[3] (But Miami, for instance, would be acceptable.)

The AEG (and MLS) plan for Beckham involved him playing out the rest of the season in Madrid, with a debut press release on July 13 preceding an exhibition match in which the Galaxy would play Chelsea on the July 21—a perfect time for a debut, provided the ankle he suffered in the later stages of the victorious 2006–7 Madrid campaign would heal in time for him to play.

The AEG's vision was for the introduction to be historic, and in Lalas's words, "a big, Los Angeles, epic event." It drew media from all over the world, and satisfied the AEG's expectations, while placing them squarely in what Lalas called "the hurricane of the Beckham effect."

Beckham was also unveiled at that year's MLS All-Star Game on July 19, at the newly opened Dick's Sporting Goods Park in Commerce City, Colorado, just east of Denver. The soccer-specific stadium, which Garber proclaimed "our newest soccer cathedral" in the press event announcing the 2007 All-Star Game location,[4] seemed a hybrid between FC Dallas's integration of academy-ready auxiliary fields within its footprint, and an aesthetically pleasing stadium owing to its older sibling in Carson, with a series of slanted roofs over the sideline seats evoking the nearby Rocky Mountain peaks.

Doug McIntyre recalls,

I was at his first game against Chelsea, and the amount of media there was just incredible. You had every outlet in England, and from as far away as Asia and Australia. They had to set up an auxiliary press box. It was a huge, huge game. It was on ESPN, it was marketed, I still remember the commercials. I remember the day he signed in early January, and the buzz in our office at *ESPN the Magazine* in New York. There weren't many soccer news stories that had everyone in the office talking, and that one absolutely did. It was just shocking, and it was the biggest story in U.S. sports for a day or two. Everyone was watching his games with Madrid leading up to him coming here, as he helped them win the title. He'd worked himself back in toward the end, and Madrid wanted to keep him. So he came in playing well. There was an awful lot of buzz.

Andrea Canales comments,

I myself was disappointed when Beckham came from Madrid. We knew that he'd been given Spanish lessons in Madrid. Occasionally, he'd make a few remarks. And the Spanish-language media in Los Angeles was excited to get him on camera to say a few things, even if it was just a little statement, "It was a good game" in Spanish, and he absolutely refused. He was shy about it. As a shy person I understand, but it was still a huge disappointment. The media here was dying for Beckham to do something in Spanish, and he didn't.

> We would have postgame press conferences and people would ask him about Tom Cruise. And it'd be frustrating because we'd be on deadline for an article on the game, and we can only ask a certain amount of questions, and someone's saying, "We saw Tom Cruise in your box watching the game; did that inspire you?" They were sending people from *People* magazine or *OK* or whatever tabloid, and those poor people had to ask those dumb questions. And we'd say, "You're going to come to our press conference to ask this?' On the other hand, we also knew he was the reason we were getting extra assignments.

The rise in website traffic for MLS's fledgling website, MLSnet.com, was even attributed to Beckham. A press release from London-based digital metrics company comScore attributed the July 2007 traffic, over one million unique visitors, to curiosity about Beckham, noting that in December 2006 the site only attracted 206,000 visitors, while in January 2007, the month Beckham announced the move to the Galaxy, traffic jumped nearly fourfold to 808,000, with more than 200,000 of those in Europe.[5]

Due to the ankle injury, Beckham only played sporadically in 2007, though his first start was about as memorable as a first could be. The August 18 game in Giants Stadium pitted the Galaxy against the Red Bulls, who had signed their own difference-making designated player—Colombian international Juan Pablo Angel, who'd previously played with Argentine giants River Plate and Premiere League stalwarts Aston Villa. The match exploded into action with a fourth-minute free kick goal by Angel, who sent the ball under three Galaxy players in the wall who chose to jump, but Beckham assisted on two goals before the ten-minute mark to pull the Galaxy ahead. The Red Bulls, though, would level the match just before halftime, two important national team players (Landon Donovan and a promising young striker named Jozy Altidore) would involve themselves in second half scoring, and Angel would score a game-winner, for a 5–4 final score, with less than ninety seconds remaining.

"That was one of the best advertisements for MLS we had seen to that point," McIntyre says of the match. "Everyone in that building walked away from that game thinking they had gotten their money's worth. It was exciting, it had star power, it had buzz, it had everything. It was back-page news in New York the next day, where they were saying Beckham was basically the king of New York for a day. For a regular-season match, we hadn't seen anything like that since Pelé's last game. It was easily the biggest game they'd had in their ten seasons, and possibly since."

Empire Supporters Club board member Jennifer Muller, who joined the group that day, remembers, "The atmosphere was definitely electric with the larger than normal crowd. But there was definitely an air of resentment among regulars toward those that just came out to the game because of Beckham."

Beckham brought much to the Galaxy, but he didn't bring instant success. The Galaxy ended the season eleventh out of thirteen teams, and wouldn't get to the playoffs until 2009. "We didn't have a great team until 2009 when Bruce [Arena] revamped the roster," Donovan says. "From 2006 through 2008, we had an average team and it showed in the standings. In soccer, more than any other sport, you need a group of players that achieve things together. You can't just do it with one player." He adds, "Once we got the right players into the team, Bruce was able to mold us into a champion"—though it would take longer than many anticipated.

Wahl, who'd flown out to Madrid that May to meet Beckham (in preparation for a July cover story to coincide with his American debut), remembers,

He seemed pretty at ease, at least in talking to me, about his decision to come over. It was a story that transcended sport; in fact, the soccer part of it wasn't important to anyone at the time. Off the field, it was successful—he'd obviously come here as an A-list celebrity. But he arrived injured, and on the field, it went poorly. I don't think people knew how to prepare for it exactly, and no one wanted to say no to Beckham. So that would result in situations where he played for England in Europe, got on a plane, and tried to play for the Galaxy less than twenty-four hours later in LA.

On August 30, in the final of the SuperLiga tournament involving Liga MX and MLS teams (which the Galaxy lost to Pachuca on penalty kicks), Beckham left partway through the match with a knee injury and would only return to action for the Galaxy's final match of the 2007 season as a sub. "It was clear with that injury he'd be out for a while," Wahl noted. "The lunacy stopped because it had to stop."

Though Beckham dominated MLS coverage in 2007 and beyond, that year was also remarkable for Chivas USA. The "other Los Angeles team" completed a worst-to-first transition, topping the West and just missing out on the Supporters' Shield to D.C. United. But both top seeds were bumped in the conference semifinals by the number 4 seeds—the Wizards were fifth in the East and slotted into the West's number 4 slot to face Chivas, whereas the East's number 4 Fire met the United. But it was the number 2 seeds that ultimately advanced to the MLS Cup—the first time that finalists repeated from the prior year.

The Revolution got off to a lead with a twentieth-minute goal from Taylor Twellman, but second half goals from Joseph Ngwenya and Dwayne De Rosario gave the Dynamo its second straight championship—a dynastic four in seven seasons, if you count what they did as the Quakes—while the Revs were continuing a Charlie-Brown-with-Lucy's-football existence with a 0-for-4 MLS Cup run.

The 2008 season brought an expansion Earthquakes team back to San Jose to rekindle its rivalry with the Galaxy, but they finished last in the league (though the Galaxy did tie them on points), with the Crew and Dynamo heading their conferences, but the playoffs held a bit of a surprise—the Red Bulls, finding their way to the MLS Cup as the West's number 4 seed, in a continuation of an MLS playoff conceit that was having fun with geography.

The Crew's success in 2008 had much to do with a player they'd secured the year before, who would be granted Designated Player status at the end of that year—Argentine forward Guillermo Barros Schelotto. As author Steve Sirk recalls,

> The signing of Schelotto was immensely important. I imagine I was probably like most people in Columbus when I say that I honestly didn't know much of anything about him prior to his arrival. I'm

sure there are some people who follow South American leagues, but most of the big names come from Europe or make their names in the World Cup. When Schelotto signed, his resume at Boca Juniors spoke for itself, but it's not like he was a well-known name to many Ohioans. That, of course, would soon change.

If you talk to players that played with Guille, they talk about how he simplified the game for them. Everybody knew their roles. He made so many players better. Schelotto was very good about coaching players on the field, especially the younger guys.

It wasn't just what he did on the field. Sirk notes,

He was committed to Columbus and really wanted to be just one of the guys. He cherished that he and his family could live a relatively normal life in Ohio, and he had zero of that superstar attitude. He got along with everyone on the team, regardless of age or nationality. An example of how he wanted to be one of the guys is that he would participate in Frankie Hejduk's NFL picks pool. Guille didn't know much about the NFL, but he studied hard and wanted to do well in the pool. After all, Guille is a competitor who wants to win. He was always asking questions and trying to learn. Learning English is another example. Learning a new language can be daunting and it risks embarrassment, but he embraced it. He was never afraid of making mistakes. He carried a little book around with him to write down what he learned and to correct any errors he made. A player of his stature could have done none of those things and nobody would have thought twice about it, but he was determined to be just one of the guys and to make the most of his American experience. I'm sure that went a long way toward the growth of the team as a unit, both on and off the field.

The league's regular-season MVP, Schelotto also became the MLS Cup MVP by assisting on all three goals in a 3–1 game that saw Columbus pull away in the second half, with a Chad Marshall goal two minutes after the Red Bull's John Wolyniec tied it. The match, in the Home Depot Center, featured two teams from the same conference for the first time, and featured two first-time finalists for the first time since, of course, the inaugural MLS Cup.

It would also show, perhaps unexpectedly, the power of the designated player (DP). While Schelotto wasn't made the Crew's first DP until immediately after delivering Columbus its first cup, he had the immediate, transformative, galvanic reaction that spoke keenly to the impact of a single player, even if Beckham didn't. Their 2008 MLS Cup opponents, the Red Bulls, had secured two DPs in Angel and Claudio Reyna, and upgrades improved a team that was appearing to shed its mediocrity along with the MetroStars moniker that led fans to react to its team's failings with a weary, "That's so Metro."

Even franchises that didn't launch themselves into the upper echelons of the playoffs found value in the designated player. The Fire, for instance, signed veteran Mexican striker Cuauhtémoc Blanco and reengaged a portion of the fan base they'd largely lost five years earlier when the team was exiled to Naperville. There was a mechanism in place to bring internationally known players to the league, even though the highest-profile players were coming to MLS for the final few years of their career, which didn't exactly help the image of the league's comparative competitiveness (though that perception would continue to evolve, and to be buoyed by future DP signings).

Beckham—to pick his story line back up—did play more in 2008, scoring five goals and adding ten assists, but at the conclusion of the season arranged a loan to Italian club AC Milan, which needed to be signed off on by both the Galaxy and MLS. The loan was presented as a means for Beckham to get more European seasoning in advance of the 2010 World Cup, meaning that he wouldn't sit idle while the Galaxy waited out the November–March period in which many of his English teammates, as well as on-the-bubble players competing for spots on the team, were in the thick of a Premier League season.

The loan was initially announced as spanning just two months, from the first week of 2009 to when training camp started, though Milan director Umberto Gandini did tell the media the loan was "for as long as David wishes."[6] But then Beckham decided to extend his loan through the end of the Serie A season; Milan and Beckham contributed jointly to what was termed a multimillion-dollar payment to the Galaxy in order to extend the loan.

This did not sit particularly well with some Galaxy fans. In a particularly ugly incident in July 2009, in Beckham's first start after returning from Milan (in which, incidentally, he tallied two of his three 2009 season assists), he was booed and jeered repeatedly and even got into an angry confrontation with several fans in the LA Riot Squad section. Fans also expressed themselves with banners that called him a "fraud" and a "part-time player," as well as asserting their Galaxy fandom as resolute "before, after, and despite" Beckham.

Bruce Arena responded to the incident in fatherly fashion, telling the media, "We regret the incident that happened at the end of the first half. While it is important that our fans remain free to voice their opinions, they must do so in an appropriate manner. We appreciate our players' and fans' passion for the team and the game, but we all must aim to hold ourselves to higher standards."[7]

Regarding the "part-time player" banner, Canales notes that it was

valid to a certain point. He was trying really hard to make the England national team, and [England coach Fabio] Capello was saying he didn't trust the level you're playing at in MLS. The England national team was always coming first to him, and he was doing what he needed to, to be on the team, only playing with Milan to get to England. But it was important for the fans to let him know, "You can't play half the season with another club and say you're committed to this club." I thought that it was important for fans to care enough about their club to show that point of view. That confrontation was probably needed from both sides, which ended in an *agree to disagree*.

And yet, there was no denying Beckham's importance despite the part-time status. As Lalas observed, "At the time, and to a certain extent, there is nobody else even to this day who is able to check all those boxes and bring more people into the tent. When you think about Major League Soccer [in its twentieth year], the first team you think about is the LA Galaxy. And we paid for that type of relevancy and perspective, and we got it. David Beckham gave us that relevancy."

The year 2009 was strong for the Galaxy, but was ultimately owned by Real Salt Lake, who'd created some buzz heading into the 2009 season by opening Rio Tinto Stadium in October 2008. Bill Manning, who was general manager for RSL, thought that the team should dot all i's and cross all t's before opening the new stadium to the public, and debut the stadium at the start of the 2009 season. Dave Checketts—who, remember, had scheduled a stadium groundbreaking on faith before a deal was finalized—thought the good people of Utah had waited long enough. Manning, like many who worked with Checketts, credited him with the vision to charge forward. "He knew they needed the stadium," Manning says, and the team rode a league-best home record into playoff contention.

As Trey Fitz-Gerald recalls, the 2009 regular season boiled down to a final-day situation in which five teams were in contention for the eighth and final playoff spot. "We were a sub-.500 team that got into the playoffs on the last day because five different results went our way," he says, laughing. In addition to RSL needing to beat its rival Rapids (which they did, 3–0), a number of other dominoes needed to fall, leading Fitz-Gerald and other fans to scoreboard-watch. Fitz-Gerald even created a flowchart—"my greatest professional achievement," he jokes—to help track the results that would deliver RSL to the playoffs, which included an improbable (but certainly welcome) 5–0 Toronto loss to the MetroStars.

RSL defeated Supporters' Shield winner and defending champs Columbus in the first round of the playoffs (as the East's number 4 team), and then relied on a shootout-savvy Rimando to get past the Fire in the Eastern Conference finals that went seven penalty kicks deep. Meanwhile, in the West, an improved Galaxy dispatched their crosstown rivals in the conference semifinals, and then knocked the Dynamo out with two extra-time goals—after a scoreless first 102 minutes—to advance to the finals. A year after two East teams played an MLS Cup in Los Angeles, two West teams would face off in Seattle for the championship.

The *Seattle Times* described the match as, in large part, a celebration of Sounders fandom: "A crowd of 46,011, mostly Sounders FC fans, turned out for one last match on their team's home pitch, and were treated to a classic between the two teams. Thousands of fans in rave green on hand to say goodbye to the inaugural season, part of the fourth-largest attendance for a Cup final, stood and made noise for much of the match. They witnessed RSL, a five-year-old franchise, capture its first-ever league MLS Cup and were in full throat during the penalty-kick phase."

As in the conference finals, the penalty kick sequence went seven shooters deep, with RSL winning 5–4, in part because a normally reliable Donovan pushed his shot over the bar, in part due to "tired legs."[8]

"The 2009 MLS Cup may be the greatest disappointment in the history of the LA Riot Squad," says Scott MacKay, the supporters' group president, adding, "In penalties, you never expect your three strikers to miss." Several hundred Galaxy supporters (from both the Riot Squad and the Angel City Brigade) made the trip up the coast; AEG president and CEO Tim Leiweke even dropped in to their pregame bar to buy drinks; MacKay recalls it was supposed to be for an hour, "but ended after about ten minutes and a massive bar tab."

The 2010 season—in a World Cup year that would be memorable for the Americans—would bring another first-time winner into the circle of MLS Cup holders in an even more bizarre playoff configuration than years past. MLS altered its eight-team bracket to only guarantee two spots per conference versus the three per conference of the prior few years. The underachieving Eastern Conference only produced two playoff teams. One was the Red Bulls, which bolstered its lineup by bringing in two DPs doubling as legendary fan-base motivators: French international striker Thierry Henry, who'd been revered during his stellar years at Arsenal and had most recently featured for Barcelona, and Mexican international Rafa Marquez, who'd spent the past seven seasons with Barcelona and who'd served as El Tri's captain since the 2002 World Cup. The other was Columbus, for which Schelotto was playing his final season.

The Galaxy won the Supporters' Shield, involving more team depth than before due to Donovan's and teammate Edson Buddle's involvement with the American team and what was supposed to be Beckham's return to England. Beckham's March 2010 injury—an Achilles tendon rupture suffered while on his second loan with Milan, keeping him sidelined until his September 2010 return to the Galaxy—ensured he wouldn't be play-

Lamar Hunt speaks at the groundbreaking for what would become Pizza Hut Park in Frisco on February 18, 2004. Dignitaries seated behind the podium include Hunt Sports Group chairman Clark Hunt and MLS Commissioner Don Garber. (Photo courtesy of FC Dallas)

"Timber Joey" Webber stands in front of the Timbers Army faithful in Providence Park's famed North End for a September 2015 home match.
(Photo courtesy of Steve Dykes, *USA TODAY Sports*)

DC United fans create a tifo of the District of Columbia flag prior to an RFK Stadium match in March 2013.　　　　　(Photo courtesy of Matt Mathai)

Carrying on a worldwide tradition of red vs. blue rivalries, Toronto FC's Sebastian Giovinco and Montreal Impact's Victor Cabrera battle during an August 2015 game in Toronto. (Photo courtesy of Nick Turchiaro, *USA TODAY Sports*)

Sporting KC goalkeeper Jimmy Nielsen raises the Philip F. Anschutz Cup with his team after winning the 2013 MLS Cup over Real Salt Lake at Sporting Park.
(Photo courtesy of Peter G. Aiken, *USA TODAY Sports*)

Landon Donovan addresses the crowd with a bullhorn, celebrating the LA Galaxy's 2014 MLS Cup victory over the New England Revolution.

(Photo courtesy of Gary A. Vasquez, *USA TODAY Sports*)

#TIFOSWEAT members gather in their warehouse in April 2016, preparing a tifo for an upcoming Columbus Crew SC match.   (Photo courtesy of TifoSWEAT)

Ray Hudson, the former Miami Fusion coach, and Phil Schoen, who called the first-ever MLS game for ESPN, now work together as beIN SPORTS commentators. (Photo courtesy of beIN SPORTS)

President George W. Bush with the MLS Cup–winning Houston Dynamo team for a White House reception on May 29, 2007. (Photo courtesy of Houston Dynamo)

The fan-created Supporters' Shield, awarded annually to the team with the best regular-season record, framed by a selection of scarves representing MLS supporters' groups. Scarves are typically brandished by fans in pre-game ceremonies and are de rigueur for any serious supporter. (Photo Credit: Sean Dane)

Houston Dynamo fans, in the new Zona Naranja section created by the team for its supporters, cheer on their team during an April 2016 match against the Seattle Sounders. (Photo credit: Phil West)

American Outlaws, the official supporters' group of the U.S. Men's and Women's National Teams. Founded in 2007, they helped raise awareness of American supporters' culture in the lead-up to the 2014 World Cup.

(Photo Credit: Will Leverett/American Outlaws)

ing in that summer's World Cup. The *Telegraph*'s Henry Winter, declaring it a "desperately sad development," prophesized that the severity of the injury plus Beckham's advancing age (thirty-four) meant he'd never be the same again, and would certainly not see national team action. "For all the celebrity circus around Beckham," Winter wrote, "he remains a remarkably humble individual obsessed with football and he will be devastated to miss the World Cup." Winter then looked into the future again, incorrectly predicting, "Beckham can still deliver for England in a World Cup but only as an ambassador, in winning the rights to host the 2018 tournament."[9]

The Galaxy couldn't get through to the finals, losing 3–0 to FC Dallas in the Western Conference finals. The Rapids, a wild card team that was seventh in the standings, beat the Earthquakes in the "define east" Eastern Conference finals to reach their first finals since 1997, and then would face the first-time finalists in the first MLS Cup hosted on Canadian soil.

The *Washington Post*'s Steven Goff was not impressed. His review of the finals began,

> Appropriately, an MLS Cup lacking artistry and losing the attention of a thinning crowd was decided by an own goal. And with the deflection in the 17th minute of overtime Sunday evening, the Colorado Rapids claimed their first league championship with a 2–1 victory over favored FC Dallas before an announced sellout of 21,700 at BMO Field.
>
> In front of thousands of empty seats, vacated by neutral observers escaping the late-night chill, reserve Macoumba Kandji settled Conor Casey's long diagonal ball just inside the penalty area. After toying with Jair Benitez, Kandji struck the ball an instant before Ugo Ihemelu's challenge.
>
> George John slid over to protect the near side, but with goalkeeper Kevin Hartman committed to the far end, the ball caromed off John and floated into the closest corner.[10]

Though certainly heartbreaking for FC Dallas, it was a breakthrough moment for a franchise that had, as the league's official website pointed out, had "overhauled nearly everything except their team name" since last appearing the finals—including five coaches, three logos, one color change, and, of course, one new stadium.[11] And with the victory, a Galaxy team entering its fifth season with Beckham was still without a title.

But that would change the following season. Finally, in 2011, Beckham's fifth year with the club, the Galaxy won its first title since 2005 with a 1–0 victory over the Dynamo. The game's lone goal, coming in the seventy-second minute, came on a play that intertwined all three of the Galaxy's designated players: Ireland national and Premier League veteran Robbie Keane, perhaps the final piece that the team was missing, combined with Beckham to assist on Donovan's goal. It was the culmination of a playoffs in which an unlikely hero emerged: Mike Magee, acquired via a trade with the Red Bulls in 2009, scored crucial goals in matches leading up to the Galaxy's Cup appearance.

The Galaxy had finally done what the front office had envisioned when they'd signed Beckham half a decade earlier, albeit with a third designated player completing their transformation from a team that couldn't quite win a championship to a team that looked like it could win many.

The five-year period between 2007 and 2011 in MLS was writ large with Beckham's presence and sometimes absence, but there were certainly other fascinating story lines during this era that saw the league grow from twelve to eighteen teams. One of the most fascinating ones doesn't even involve players or coaches but rather a group of soccer fans from Philadelphia who didn't have the heart or the stomach to support teams from natural rivals like New York or Washington, DC. So, rather than sit idly by and wait for MLS to come to Philadelphia, the fans decided to entice MLS to come to them.

Chapter 9

THE SONS OF BEN

In which the fans of the idea of a team help their
hometown get an actual real live team.

THE 2007 MLS CUP MIGHT BE BEST REMEMBERED FOR WHAT WAS HAPPEN-
ing in the stands rather than on the field.

A group of about a hundred fans, some with drums, all dressed in
light blue shirts, were visible and loud, yet weren't cheering for New England or Houston. Instead, they rhythmically chanted "Phil-a-delph-ia,"
and created songs around sentiments like "We don't have a team" that
they gleefully sang through the stadium. The Sons of Ben, rooting for a
Philadelphia-based Major League Soccer team they envisioned and hoped
for, brought fan support as performance art to MLS's biggest stage in
what ultimately was a successful endeavor like nothing the league—or
indeed, any sports league—had seen before.

When the Sons of Ben formed in Philadelphia in January 2007, they
weren't coming together to support a team—they were coming together
to support the *idea* of a team. The group's founders initially met through
the Big Soccer website, and according to founder Bryan James, he'd spent
2006 with other Philadelphia-area soccer fans, engaged in the same sort
of public lobbying efforts that Soccer Silicon Valley had used to inspire
a new ownership group to rekindle the Earthquakes.

"They were successful, so we'd wanted to emulate that," James remembers. "But what we'd done up to that point was yielding no tangible results, so I thought what might work better is giving Philadelphians
a chance to be fans of something rather than doing all of this background political wrangling, and I put out a call to anybody who might

be interested in creating a supporters' group for a team that didn't exist."

The idea started small. Six people came to the first meeting and became the de facto leaders, seized upon the Sons of Ben name (which had the added advantage of abbreviating to SoBs), chose the distinctive light blue and yellow colors of the city flag, created a logo, and set out to mobilize potential fans. Their first action was going out to a Philadelphia KiXX game to cheer on not the Major Indoor Soccer League team that had been active there since 1995 but the concept of a Philly-headquartered MLS team.

Good fortune struck them; they'd generated enough attention with the recruiting campaign that Steven Wells, an English ex-pat writer living in Philly, saw the Sons of Ben at the KiXX game and decided to write about them for *Four Four Two*, a revered yet irreverent English soccer magazine.

In a *Guardian* article recalling his visit, Wells wrote, "With their custom-made scarves, raucous chants and vigorously thumped bass drum, the 60 Sons made more noise than the rest of the arena put together. And they made particular sport of the Baltimore Blast keeper, Sagu. They got drowned out only once—when the 4,000 strong Girl Guide audience joined in with the SpongeBob SquarePants theme tune (something of a ritual at KiXX games). But then—in a flash of spontaneous genius that would have brought a smile to the face of the Kop—the Sons of Ben responded with a mournful 'Sagu SquarePants' And poor old Sagu visibly wilted."

Unable to resist a dig at David Beckham, Wells continued, "With the entire U.S. soccer press (such as it is) fixated on how Mr. Posh Spice is going to save American soccer (from what, exactly, nobody ever says) very little attention is being paid to the ongoing revolution in U.S. soccer fandom. Sick of the dull, pasteurised, one-size-fits-all, preprogrammed Disneyfied McFan experience that's all but got a deathgrip on U.S. pro sports, soccer fans have increasingly been doing it for themselves."

He went on to praise American supporters' culture by contrasting it to other pro sports, wherein "the majority of fans sit sipping pissy beer and munching tasteless hot dogs or nachos slathered in fake cheese while some blandroid on the PA makes all the noise. Which makes soccer's new breed of self-organised, scarfed-up, singing, chanting, banner-hoisting, flag-waving, noisy-as-hell ruffians the sport's clearest brand differential—and potentially its greatest asset."[1]

The group then arranged for a group of twenty-five to attend a Red Bulls game in June. "We had a section far away from the New York supporters," explains James, "but they knew we were there, and started singing 'Fuck Philadelphia' to the tune of 'La Donna e Mobile.' They were playing Kansas City, but they were focusing their hate on us, so it was good." In response, the Sons of Ben initiated a new chant: "We've won as many cups as you, and we don't have a team." That appearance led to *Sports Illustrated* featuring the group in its weekly "Faces in the Crowd" section for the issue covering the San Antonio Spurs' NBA finals victory against the LeBron James–led Cleveland Cavaliers, which further propelled their notoriety.

That was a victory in and of itself, but the Red Bulls game had been a test run for the ultimate goal: attending the 2007 MLS Cup at RFK Stadium in force to demonstrate to Don Garber and the many others watching that Philadelphia was serious about soccer. They were also meeting weekly, signing fans to petitions and season-ticket pledge lists, putting in their own money for scarves, tifo material, and room rentals, and continuing to contact political leaders who could help.

The group grew to fifteen hundred by the time the MLS Cup rolled around, and the Sons of Ben were able to send a group of a hundred to the match—as good luck would have it, right next to the Revolution fans whose team was representing the East. James remembers the reaction from other teams' fans to the group tailgating and then entering the stadium as a mix of incredulity and respect.

The Sons of Ben wouldn't be able to bring a team to Philadelphia on their own, of course. But even as they were putting together their first public appearances, Nick Sakiewicz was already at work, trying to put together the necessary elements to bring a team to Philadelphia, moving from the north to the south end of New Jersey.

As Sakiewicz explains,

I left New York right after I put the shovel in the ground on what would become Red Bull Arena. We wanted to do something at Rowan University, which is across the river from Philadelphia in South Jersey. We had gone down the line quite a bit in the development of six hundred acres at Rowan, with some real estate developers, that would include a soccer stadium. There was a small get that we needed, maybe five or eight million dollars of sewer and roadway infrastructure to be built. There was a change in governor in the middle of that—John Corzine became governor. And New Jersey was in about, I don't know, six billion dollars in debt, and Corzine put a screeching halt to any kind of spending in the state.

Knowing that stadium development was essential to attracting an MLS team to Philly, Sakiewicz took over those efforts. In concert with his initial efforts to secure a stadium, he also convinced real estate magnate Jay Sugarman to be the majority investor for an ownership group he was looking to coalesce.

Sakiewicz learned of the Sons of Ben via Wells's *Four Four Two* article, which he read while sitting on a plane in an Italian airport, returning home after a trip during which he had tried to interest AC Milan, the legendary Italian soccer club, in investing in MLS. "I read about this group and how they were lobbying for an MLS team, saw the names of the people in the group in the article, and decided to reach out to them," he explains. "I thought these guys could help me lobby for a stadium and for a team. We had some competition. Don Garber, at the time, was talking to a few other cities about expansion. Other cities were in the mix. I wanted a grassroots movement to help with my political lobbying and my lobbying with the league."

"Within a week or so of reading that article, [Sakiewicz] reached out to me for the first time," James remembers. "His vision made this happen. When he started reaching out, we got a little more direction to our pursuits—it's really how the hard work we'd been doing dovetailed into luck."

Sakiewicz and the Sons of Ben met and developed a plan to showcase their enthusiasm for soccer and to make that the public face of the soccer-to-Philly movement. "Those guys were awesome," Sakiewicz recalls. "They were really helpful in my efforts of credibility. When I went to Harrisburg to talk to the governor about how popular soccer was, they made it look like there were these thousands and thousands of people back in Philadelphia ready to support the team. They helped me create, really, in retrospect, an illusion of *thousands* of fans. It had really grown to maybe a couple of hundred by then, and eventually seven hundred, and then eventually to the thousands."

James recalls Sakiewicz being at the 2007 MLS Cup with a potential investor in Philly soccer, but it was also during a time in which he was interviewing for a job with the Los Angeles Dodgers. "He saw us across the way [in the stadium], and the fact that he could see us very clearly really solidified what he wanted to do. I believe that solidified the funding as much as anything."

Sakiewicz's meetings with governor Ed Rendell started in August 2006, and he labeled the initial discussions as "really speculative." By January 2008, however, he was able to negotiate enough money from the state of Pennsylvania, Delaware County, and the city of Chester to go forward with stadium plans.

"At the same time, I was meeting with whoever, talking to anybody and everybody trying to get investment into the league," Sakiewicz says, noting that at one point he'd talked to Merritt Paulson as part of the Philly investment group. "I didn't know he had his heart set on buying a minor league baseball team in Portland," he adds, laughing. That was Paulson's stepping-stone to launching an MLS team in the Rose City several years later. Though Sugarman was still committed to the project, Sakiewicz felt he needed additional investment from minority owners to get the team operational.

Sakiewicz and his group, buoyed by bringing in the stadium money package, did go ahead with the announcement that Philadelphia was getting an MLS team—the city's first Division I team since the NASL's Philadelphia Fury became the Montreal Manic at the end of the 1980 season.

The Sons of Ben were involved with that press conference, closing the event by presenting scarves to Philadelphia Union's ownership group.

According to James in an article for the Original Winger website, "The Sons of Ben, as a group, unofficially heard two days before the official announcement at an event we set up with the ownership group. Over 250 people crowded into The Dark Horse in Old City Philadelphia, and when Nick said, 'If you happen to come down to The Wharf Building in Chester at around 2 o'clock on Thursday, you wouldn't be wasting your time,' we could all finally celebrate."[2]

But behind the scenes, even with Philadelphia believing the team was coming, Sakiewicz was still working to get to the finish line, complicated by the recession—and, in particular, the stock market crash of October 2008. "It was crazy, crazy times," Sakiewicz remembers. "That project could have died a hundred times in these twenty-four months" between the announcement of the team and its 2010 home opener.

The Sons of Ben would be involved in subsequent franchise milestone events, including the stadium groundbreaking in late 2008 and the unveiling of the Union name at City Hall in May 2009, and were brought in to give input on features they'd like for the stadium, which included having teams come out in a tunnel directly below the Sons of Ben section. As James characterizes it, "The unexpected was becoming normal."

Sakiewicz is particularly proud about the process that brought about branding the Union, noting that even though he had been involved with management of both the Mutiny and the MetroStars, Philadelphia gave him an opportunity to build a brand from the ground up. He not only gave the Union a distinctive identity of its own but also nodded to the region's soccer history through the team's 2013 alternate uniforms (or, in soccer parlance, third kits). Those uniforms paid tribute to Bethlehem Steel FC, founded in 1907 and lasting until 1930, and revered by soccer historians and serious American soccer fans as one of the most successful teams of the early twentieth century, when soccer was gaining its first familiarity in the United States. (The Union's ownership group would go on in 2015 to create an affiliate team in Bethlehem, Pennsylvania, and brand it Bethlehem Steel FC to honor its forerunners.)

Current Sons of Ben leaders still look proudly on the efforts that brought the Union. "To say there was a well-thought-out plan would be a mischaracterization," explains Kenny Hanson, president of the group during its 2015 season. Yet, he boasts, "We were the only supporter group in American sports ever that created an organization from a bunch of fans."

"There were so many rollercoasters of emotion with this," adds current Sons of Ben president Ami Rivera. "There was never a definite that this was going to happen; when we finally got the announcement, it was just so relieving and validating and positive. People came out of the woodwork to congratulate each other. All these crazy things we had done finally made sense—and it became this really great story about how Philadelphia fans had done something positive, for MLS and everybody else."

In the aforementioned Original Winger article on the Sons of Ben's successful efforts, James said that Wells compared their group to the "South Seas Cargo Cultists [of Melanesia] who would build runways in hopes that the planes present during World War II would miraculously reappear and bring wealth to the island." He then added, "The difference in this case was that we got the plane to land."[3]

The opening day at PPL Park (today Talen Energy Stadium) was June 27, 2010—which ended up being the third rather than the first 2010 home game, due to delays in finishing the stadium. (The team used Lincoln Financial Field, where the NFL Eagles play, in the interim.) And yet, Sakiewicz—marveling that it'd taken him five years to solidify a stadium plan in New York, compared to just two years in Philadelphia—describes his mood at PPL's opening as "euphoric."

"We finally had a home of our own," he remembers. "Getting my second gold shovel was awesome, and actually building the stadium and opening it was an incredible trophy day for me and all the great people who built that. I'll never forget it."

"Major League Soccer, from its very first season, wanted to be in Philadelphia," explains Jonathan Tannenwald, a veteran Philadelphia-based soccer journalist. "But there was no suitable venue for it. There also was not a demonstrated demand for a team. Some person or entity had to be able to organize people to the point demand would be proven to have a team, and in turn invest in a stadium to house it. And that's what the Sons of Ben ultimately did, and they did it in a way that no other market in MLS's history has ever seen."

Soccer has unfortunately added to the hard-luck lore that has infused Philadelphia sports for decades. The Union has only made the playoffs once in its first six seasons, back in 2011, and though the team has made U.S. Open Cup Finals in 2014 and 2015, it's managed to lose both in heartbreaking fashion. In 2014, the Union took the Sounders to overtime before losing 3–1; the next year, they took Sporting Kansas City to *penalty kicks*, losing 7–6 in the shootout sequence.

The team also decided to usher in a post-Sakiewicz era at the end of 2015. This is how MLSSoccer.com's Dave Zeitlin characterized the Sugarman-Sakiewicz relationship and its end:

> In simplest terms, Sugarman provided the money and Sakiewicz the business savvy to drive the development of a new team and stadium—and both were equally instrumental in Philadelphia being awarded an expansion club for the 2010 season.
>
> But around this time last year, Sugarman, the franchise's chairman and majority owner, said he began to think about dissolving that long-standing partnership and forging a new direction without Sakiewicz as CEO.
>
> And on Friday, he made the decision to officially let him go, just two days after the Union dropped their second straight US Open Cup final at home.
>
> "I'm really appreciative of everything Nick put into this," Sugarman said in a conference call with reporters. "I think he gave this team his heart and soul. And I guess when his employment agreement ended last year, we really needed to take a step back and decide how we were going to move the ball forward and really build on all the good stuff that has taken place. I think the conclusion is that what we need now is perhaps different than what we needed then. There were some issues that just didn't seem to be getting resolved. This is not a decision that was made lightly, but I think it's the right decision for the team to move forward."

The article goes on to note that the team had "constant roster turnover" and two head coaching changes, as well as an admission by

Sugarman that "there were philosophical things that he and Sakiewicz did not see eye to eye on," though he didn't elaborate on specifics.[4]

Sakiewicz, elaborating on specifics, says, "Jay never really liked or bought into anything the club did. He was not a big fan of the senior staff I'd put together, he wasn't a big fan of the way we'd built the brand and constructed the brand together with the fans. He wasn't a big fan of bringing in key marquee players. He was very skeptical and I think continues to be skeptical of the academy development system that I set up with Rich Graham, who was another co-investor. I don't think he believes that to be money wisely spent. So, yes, I think there were a lot of philosophical differences between he and I in how I ran the club."

Sakiewicz also points to on-the-field and in-the-ledger successes the Union had toward the end of his tenure. For the former, he points to reaching the back-to-back U.S. Open Cup finals as an encouraging sign, reflecting a well-founded faith in head coach Jim Curtin, who Sakiewicz named as the team's interim head coach in June 2014 and its official head coach five months later. For the latter, he notes, "My last year there, we had the highest revenue we'd ever achieved in the history of the club. If that's an indictment on my business savvy, then I'll take it."

One particularly alarming harbinger of front office change came that May, when the Sons of Ben preceded a home match against D.C. United by protesting the front office's management of the team during a march to the stadium. As Tannenwald reported, the supporters' group "raised a banner which read 'UNION FANS DESERVE BETTER,' and carried a coffin whose interior depicted Sakiewicz with the inscription 'NICK SAKIEWICZ FRANCHISE SERIAL KILLER.'" Tannenwald's article goes on to report,

> The protest ended at the stadium gates, as the Sons of Ben had promised when it was first announced. In a statement Sunday morning on its Facebook page, the organization said: "Inside PPL is where we show support for our team. That support will not change—win, lose or draw."
>
> Still, it was a rare sign of organized dissent from a group that has long been among the Union's most fervent backers no matter the results.

"It was clear that this was something our membership wanted," Hanson told the Daily News at the group's pregame tailgate. "People are frustrated, but I think that a lot of our members still support this club, and they support the team that's on the pitch. We'll continue to support our team inside PPL Park."

One of my questions to Hanson was about whether there is any particular direction in which the Sons of Ben's members are casting blame. While the protest focused on Sakiewicz, Hanson told me that a lot of parties are in the crosshairs for criticism. "Some people are pissed at the players, some people are pissed at the coach, some people are pissed at Nick," he said. "Some people are pissed at the lack of investment that the investment group is willing to put in. So I think it depends on who you ask about where it went wrong."[5]

Sakiewicz acknowledged the protest the day after with an official statement that simply read, "We agree wholeheartedly with the Sons of Ben and we share the frustrations of all fans to the start of the season. We are committed to assisting [coach] Jim [Curtin] and his Staff in every way so we can get the team back on the right track."[6]

Rivera, in a November 2015 article on becoming the Sons of Ben's new president, recalled, "It's been a rough couple of years. The protest was probably the hardest I remember having it"—though she felt that having the protest outside the stadium and refusing to bring their signs, coffin, and invective toward the front office into the stadium was the best decision they could have made given their emotions.[7]

And yet the Sons of Ben, now boasting more than two thousand members, remain one of the most impressive supporters' groups in MLS, displaying a sense of humor that has helped them rise above the indignity of multiple losing seasons. Their numerous chants include "No one likes us" (originated by fans of the generally disliked English club Millwall) and a goal celebration song simply known as "DOOP" (#DOOP is a go-to hashtag for Union fans tweeting about the team).

For 2016, the group published a new chant on its website, imploring its members to "Learn it, live it, love it." Set to the tune of the Foundations' "Build Me Up Buttercup," it goes, "Why do you build me up, Philly U baby, just to let me down and mess me around? Then, worst of all (worst of all!), you never score, Union, like you say you will, but we love you still! We need U (we need U!) more than anyone, Union, you know that we have from the start! So build me up, Philly U; don't break my heart."[8]

And where is Sakiewicz now? After considering a departure from sports altogether, or at least a hiatus following his time with the Union, he seized upon an opportunity to help grow a sport even more at the margins of American awareness than soccer was in 1996. Since January 2016 Sakiewicz has been at the helm of the National Lacrosse League for its thirtieth anniversary season, seeking to grow lacrosse in the same way that he helped grow soccer for two decades.

Chapter 10

THE RIVALS

In which the most pristine and seemingly relaxed enclave of
North America reveals itself to be a fierce hotbed of hate.

THERE'S BEEN SOME RESISTANCE IN MAJOR LEAGUE SOCCER TO FRANCHISES
rekindling their old North American Soccer League nicknames for reap-
propriation in the new league. In part, that was to seek separation from
the former league, but it was also to avoid rekindling memories of the
failures of yesteryear. After all, this was a league trying to find its own
narrative rather than borrowing one authored by NASL.

And yet, one of the most successful regions in the league, now with
a three-team rivalry that sometime plays as three spirited siblings trying
to best one another, and sometimes plays out in a two-against-one dynamic, revels in its NASL history. Its teams proudly bear the names they
started with in the mid-1970s.

In 1974 the Seattle Sounders and Vancouver Whitecaps joined the
NASL and started hating each other, and by 1975 the Portland Timbers
joined suit. The team names all later became attached to United Soccer
League (USL) A-League franchises, once the A-League emerged to fill the
void for cities who were either waiting to be awarded MLS franchises or
weren't large enough to expect them.

Given that the Pacific Northwest was passionate about soccer and
intractably wound into NASL lore, you might expect that MLS would
have found its way to the region before the 2009 season. It wasn't for a
lack of trying—but in Seattle's case, initially, it was for lack of a proper
stadium.

The Sounders were the first of three professional sports franchises that brought about Seattle's great sports legitimization of the mid-1970s and charioted Seattle into a more defined national focus. Seattle did have since 1967 an established NBA franchise in the SuperSonics (a team that remained there until whisked away to Oklahoma City and renamed the Thunder in 2008), but the city wasn't fully embraced by the major leagues until the Seahawks joined the NFL in 1976, and a year later, the Mariners joined Major League Baseball to endure generations of futility (2016 will be the franchise's fortieth season, and the team has still never won an American League pennant).

The three new franchises had a common home—a domed concrete monstrosity, the Kingdome, which was shorthand for King County Domed Stadium rather than something more intentionally grand. The first sporting event in the stadium was soccer: a match between the Sounders and the New York Cosmos on April 9, 1976, brought 58,128 fans, making it the largest gathering to watch soccer in the United States to date. Pelé scored twice, the Cosmos won 3–1, and the Sounders found a nemesis that would haunt them throughout the entirety of their NASL stay.

The Kingdome served all of the major Seattle franchises—yes, even the Sonics—through the late 1970s and 1980s, but would barely survive the following decade so crucial to Seattle's national identity. There was growing dissatisfaction with the Kingdome from both the Mariners and Seahawks camps even before July 19, 1994, the day that four ceiling tiles fell from the stadium's roof, causing that evening's Mariners game to be cancelled. (This was followed by a monthlong exile to the road before the MLB players' strike prematurely ended the season.) By 1995, plans were underway for a baseball-specific stadium to be built next to the Kingdome, and Los Angeles—which lost both the Rams and Raiders that year—began courting the Seahawks.

As the *Guardian*'s Les Carpenter noted in a January 2015 article titled "How soccer saved the Seattle Seahawks," Microsoft cofounder Paul Allen offered to buy the team in 1997 and keep it in Seattle, but on one multitiered condition: "He wanted a new stadium to replace the dreary Kingdome, he wanted $300m of public money to help finance it and he wanted the financing to be approved in a statewide referendum that Allen would pay to hold." If the referendum failed, Allen would refuse to buy the team, allowing its owner to move the Seahawks to Southern California.

The pro-stadium campaign turned on a phone call from Seattle attorney Fred Mendoza to Allen's office, with the idea that the stadium could be marketed as both a football and soccer stadium. Mendoza claimed that 300,000 people in the Seattle metro area had some involvement in soccer (largely through its numerous youth leagues), and a number of them would vote for a stadium if an MLS franchise were to follow. Allen's team created blueprints for a stadium that would be able to showcase soccer as well as football, and Mendoza led efforts to engage area soccer fans in the project.

As Carpenter wrote, "A key moment came in the spring of 1997 when MLS Commissioner Doug Logan and NFL Commissioner Paul Tagliabue attended a city luncheon in support of the stadium. After the lunch, Logan said: 'You have our assurances that Major League Soccer will be here if the stadium is built.' Suddenly Seattle's soccer community had something tangible: a guarantee. People who hated the idea of helping to fund a stadium for Allen were campaigning to have it built." The referendum passed by a narrow margin—under 37,000 votes out of 1.6 million cast—and proponents of the stadium maintained that the soccer vote made the difference.[1]

Construction began in 2000, shortly after the Kingdome was (cathartically) imploded, and the stadium was ready for the Seahawks by the start of the 2002 season. MLS happened to be fighting for its very existence those years, and the promise Logan made to Seattleites in 1997 wouldn't be fulfilled for a full decade after he spoke it.

Frank McDonald, a Seattle soccer historian who'd been part of a committee working to bring a team to Seattle since the mid-1990s, notes,

> Once the new stadium was built, it seemed you also needed strong local ownership. It seemed like a moving target because initially the league had only a few owners, and not all of them were local. I wrote a guest editorial for The Seattle Times that effectively said, "MLS, keep your promise. We built it, now let's have our team."
>
> The effort to get an expansion team in 2005 was unsuccessful and relatively quick and low-key. However, we began to sense it

was just a matter of time. To be honest, perhaps it's best that we waited. By the time 2009 rolled around, MLS was much more mature and respected, because of [David] Beckham and the [Designated Player] rule, and because of the supporters' culture driving success in Toronto. When the team was awarded, the timing felt right.

The Sounders brand was a bit star-crossed—the final NASL year in 1983 was widely regarded as disastrous due to new ownership, a new coach, a new uniform scheme featuring pinstripes, and decidedly less enthusiasm from fans in response to all that new. McDonald remembers, "My biggest concern by the time the MLS franchise was awarded in 2007 was that the Sounders brand would be more closely associated with a second-tier product that averaged only around three to four thousand fans."

The club held a name vote in March 2008, and fans were allowed to choose among Seattle Alliance, Seattle FC, or Seattle Republic or to cast a write-in vote.[2] Of the 14,500 votes cast, nearly half were write-in votes, with nearly half of those being for some permutation of the Sounders' name. As the club's official press release noted, "Traditionally, write-in campaigns rarely have an impact on the final results but in this case the write-in name received over 20% more votes than the other choices."[3]

Ultimately the gravitation toward the Sounders name had much to do with the goodwill that the NASL edition of the Sounders fostered. "While it ended badly, fans held onto some great memories of those teams," McDonald recalls. "Particularly in the first few years, the team was so connected to the community. The players were friendly and served as true ambassadors of the game. Seattle didn't have the stars and championships of the Cosmos, but as the sign read at Memorial Stadium for Pelé's first visit in '75, 'Pelé, we'd be here even if you weren't.' The team played hard, played together and played attractive soccer. When the NASL era ended, the Sounders brand was still associated with some very good, very special times."

For the Timbers and Whitecaps, there was even less hesitation about adopting the NASL names as their own.

Timbers owner Merritt Paulson, who bought the USL version of the

Timbers in 2007 with an eye toward MLS, comments, "There was never a question about the name. There was so much brand equity built up— Portland's an anomaly in the American soccer landscape in that we have such a rich history here, forty years now. The wind was at our back from that perspective. Timbers is a name there from day one, in all the different iterations and leagues. There was absolutely no doubt—I would have been crucified if we'd changed the Timbers name, and for good reason. We actually tweaked the logo a bit and had tremendous amount of back-lash from that process."

Bob Lenarduzzi, who played with the Whitecaps for the team's entire eleven-year NASL history and now serves as the president of the MLS Whitecaps franchise, also didn't have questions about wanting to use the name; it was just a matter of legally being able to do so. One of the own-ers of the original NASL Whitecaps had trademarked the name and was guarded about selling it, and until the team's ownership group worked out a deal to purchase the name the new Vancouver team was simply an-nounced without a name. Lenarduzzi wasn't considering a second option; as he puts it, "There's a whole pile of history behind the name, and it seemed crazy to not want to capitalize on that."

Before the Cascadia teams, only the San Jose Earthquakes had harkened back to their NASL roots for a nickname, and the San Jose team was the Nike-coined Clash for its first four seasons before delving back into its own history. (According to current Quakes president Dave Kaval, there was even some concern expressed about the name by league officials as recently as 2011.)

But there were also those in MLS who also understood the incredible resonance the names had in their respective markets, and those voices ul-timately triumphed. Mark Abbott remembers, "There was a big debate about the Sounders when they came in, it was a traditional soccer name that had a forty-year history in that market. . . . There was a debate about whether they should have a more current versus traditional name. I think they made the right decision going with the one that had such a heritage in their marketplace. I think that wouldn't work everywhere, but I think in a number of markets, that brand was still so relevant from the success they had in the '70s."

And it helped that the three teams had kept the embers of their rivalry aglow by playing in the USL while they were waiting for versions of themselves to graduate to MLS. It was during the USL era that two of the best-known and most fiercely competitive supporters' groups—Emerald City Supporters and Timbers Army—were born.

Timbers Army, officially named in 2002, was an outgrowth of a group of fans calling themselves the Cascade Rangers (for the mountain range that gives Cascadia its name), joining with other supporters for pregame drinks at a nearby pub, and then to section 107 in the north end of what was then PGE Park.

The Timbers Army's official site notes,

> In 2002, Section 107 (the "Woodshed") was made general admission and became a place where fans relinquished their assigned seats in favor of a standing only, terrace-like atmosphere. Supporters made banners, waved flags and hung them from the baseball dugout located in front of the section, and lit smoke bombs and fireworks in fervent celebration of goals. Pickle buckets served as makeshift drums, creating a deafening cacophony accompanying the chants. Supporters spontaneously erupted onto the dugout after successful match results. The group embraced the now infamous chant "We are Timbers Army; We are mental and we're barmy; True supporters for-ever more," in the midst of the 2001 season. "Mental" and "barmy" seemed to aptly describe the heterogeneous mix of supporters when they abandoned their daytime personae as lawyers, ironworkers, carpenters, chefs or firefighters, and raised their voices in unison, singing the praises of the Timbers.[4]

Scott Swearingen, a founding member of the 107 Independent Supporters Trust (or 107ist) that oversees the Timbers Army's organizational needs, has been enamored of MLS since writing to the LA Galaxy for stickers in the league's inaugural season—while he was in grade school. While studying sports business at Oregon State University, he did coursework framed around the idea of bringing an MLS team to Portland, and met Timbers Army members upon arriving for graduate school in 2007, getting involved with them through games and through the Soccer City USA online message boards where a number of future Timbers Army members first congregated. He also jumped into work with the MLS to Portland website, which involved a number of Timbers Army members looking to engage beyond just rooting for their USL team in the stadium. After all, the USL's fortunes were in continual question, and Seattle was leaving it for the first-tier league.

"If Timbers Army is the party," Swearingen comments, "then the 107ist is the party planning organization." Using the Section 8 Chicago bylaws as a jumping-off point, they created a structure for a democratically elected board that would serve as a liaison to the front office and create a platform in which individual sections could have their own identity and creative expression, encouraging organic, authentic support while staying one unified group.

Swearingen feels that the group set themselves up for success by starting two years in advance to create its structure, and preparing to work with the front office on issues that mattered to them, which allowed them to have a say in how the MLS version of the north end would be. He asserts that Vancouver fans, by contrast, "partied until it came time for 2011 to start, and then got totally steamrolled by the front office, ticketing, and new faces, and they're still struggling to get unified now."

Paulson recalls, "When I got here, the prior ownership said, 'Stay away from those guys! It's dangerous over there—you don't want to be anywhere near there!'" Looking to get past the acrimony existing between the prior front office and the Timbers Army, Paulson met with the newly elected 107ist board members once every two weeks to involve them. "There was going to be mutual respect, and the communication lines were going to be open," he explains, noting that Timbers Army input shaped some key factors to the supporters' group experience: the move to a general admission model, the location of capo stands (where the capos, or yell leaders, would be positioned), and even the pricing of north end tickets.

The Emerald City Supporters (better known by their ECS initials) started in 2005, when the USL edition of the Sounders played in what was then known as Qwest Field, the new stadium that soccer supporters had helped vote in. One of the group's founders, Sean McConnell, recalls a formative 2004 Sounders–Timbers game he attended there. "They brought up a good fifty to one hundred guys, and in 2004, for a USL second-division team, that was a good number. In our supporter area, which wasn't really an organized group yet, there might have been twenty to thirty of us. And so we were definitely outnumbered by away fans in our home stadium. The Timbers Army always rubbed it in our faces in those days, how big they were and little we were."

That offseason, McConnell and several other supporters determined they could organize into a cohesive unit. The group's name came from a banner that a fan had brought to a 2002 game, and the group began recruiting members, aiming for a "continental" style of support owing to chants and imagery from Italian and German supporters, departing from the British style more familiar to the region's fans. Buoyed in part by the Sounders' 2005 USL Championship over the Richmond Kickers (which included a playoff series victory over the Timbers to get them there), the ECS ranks swelled to several hundred in the first year, and by the time of the 2006 season opener against the Timbers, the ECS matched the Timbers Army's numbers.

While the MLS announcement was exciting for fans, McConnell noted it also created concern for the ECS, as they weren't sure that the Sounders would field a USL team in the 2008 "gap year" predating the inaugural 2009 season. They ultimately did so, playing where they had played a number of 2007 games—at Starfire Soccer Complex in the southern suburb of Tukwila. The 2008 season allowed the ECS to continue its momentum into the inaugural MLS season—which brought, McConnell recalls, "thousands of people who were willing to be led by a capo."

Not everybody agreed with the continental style of support; McConnell recalls that some preferred the sort of organic chants that circulated in the terraces of England, but as he reasons, "I know the culture of this town, and I know people aren't just going to sing to sing. They want to be led, they want to have someone starting the songs and then join along. It lends to more powerful support. When you hear it in the terraces of Poland and Italy, and they're all on cue, it's the most powerful support in the world. And that's what I really wanted. Heavy, powerful support."

The Southsiders have been supporting the Whitecaps since 1999, when they were using the 86ers nickname, but as president Brett Bird notes, membership was down to several devoted dozens in the waning days of the team's involvement—though the Whitecaps' elevation to MLS in 2011 helped the group grow from about a hundred at the start of the season to eight hundred at season's end, in proportion to how the team's audience ballooned from several thousand in the final USL season to over 20,000 for its inaugural MLS season. The Southsiders, the largest of three Whitecaps' supporters' groups (alongside the Curva Collective and the Rain City Brigade), now claims more than two thousand members.

What's clear in talking to each supporters' group is there's respect (not even of the begrudging variety) and general accord between Timbers and Whitecaps supporters' group members, but they both vehemently hate Sounders supporters.

Perhaps Garrett Dittfurth of Timbers Army explains it best (or, at least, most bluntly) when he says, "I love Vancouver and I love their fans. You'll never meet a nicer set of people. We definitely enjoy ribbing one another about a win or a loss right after buying each other pints. Vancouver is a good-natured rivalry. I believe both the Timbers Army and Vancouver feel pretty much the same way about Seattle: if a meteor hit CenturyLink Field during a match, the world would be a better place. I dislike Seattle fans; they believe they invented fan support in MLS. In 2007, the ECS was quite literally forty fat guys and a fog machine."

Bird is a little more diplomatic in communicating his preference for Timbers fans over Sounders fans, merely saying that Sounders supporters "like to maintain this edge of disagreeability."

The rivalry has even evolved to where there's a Seattle-based Timbers supporters' group known at TA:CO (Timbers Army Covert Operations), formed in 2013 to provide Portland ex-pats and other Timbers fans in Seattle a place to coalesce. Though the group was initially seen as an outlet for Portland fans in Seattle to engage in some fun mischief-making (mostly, putting up Timbers stickers and logos around town), it's taken on an increasingly more overt presence, including gathering to watch Timbers matches at Seattle bars (including the awesomely named Angry

Beaver, a Canadian-themed hockey bar), and even attending Sounders matches not involving the Timbers in full Timbers regalia.

To Swearingen, the main divide between the Timbers Army and the ECS is cultural. He notes that Portland is more "DIY," compared to what he sees as a more corporate culture in Seattle. In his view, that's reflected by the Sounder in the capo-led ECS support, in the flame-spewing towers behind the goalpost that stadium operators in Seattle set off after each Sounders goal, and in virtually everything else that the Sounders and its fans do.

Swearingen notes that Portland gets its reputation as "the People's Republic of Portland" for being collectivist, but also notes that's part of what makes Timbers Army such a strong group. He's also critical of the ECS for having a separate supporters' group, Gorilla FC, spring up alongside them rather than being one unified group like Timbers Army. The FC in Gorilla FC, incidentally, stands for "football collective," and its website declares the group to be "an antifa (anti-fascist) supporters' group . . . opposed to acts of racism, sexism and homophobia."[5]

Paulson is very aware of and appreciative of Timbers Army culture; while he notes that Seattle's immediately massive soccer audience helped sell skeptical Portland City Council members to bet on soccer in the Rose City, he also picks up on the same cultural nuances separating Seattle from Portland that the Timbers Army espouse. "Having anything feel forced to supporters in Portland is death," he explains, and it is a philosophy that was put to the test when the team's original mascot (though that seems too simple a word to cover everything he did) "Timber Jim" Serrill retired in 2008 and was replaced by the team's current mascot, "Timber Joey" Webber. Serrill, who was originally invited to Timbers games by his father, immediately saw the appeal of what he characterized as "drinking beer and yelling at the goalie." Around the start of the 1978 season he approached the Timbers' front office with the greatest question ever asked of management by a fan: "Can I bring my chainsaw to the game?" Serrill and Timbers general manager Keith Williams discussed it and struck a deal: For two comp tickets a game, Timber Jim would come out from the dugout (for then, the stadium they played in was configured for baseball), pull out his chainsaw, and saw a slab off a giant log.

Later that season, his act evolved when—during a possession-heavy, low-scoring game—he decided to scale one of the stadium's 110-foot poles on which was the lighting was mounted, hooked a rope linking his pole to an adjacent pole, and then, as he explains, "I rappelled down, and inverted, and started swinging back and forth, and got a pretty good swing going. Then I fired up my chainsaw, and everyone was looking around to see where the noise was coming from. And that was a hit!" Throughout the years, he integrated new elements into his routine, including beating a giant drum, climbing a pole and staying on top of it until the Timbers scored their first goal, and doing handsprings in front of the assembled north end fans.

Timber Jim's story took a somber turn in 2004 when his teenage daughter Hannah died in a car accident while Jim was performing at a Timbers game. The singing of "You Are My Sunshine," a song Jim had sung to Hannah when she was a child, became integrated into the Timbers Army in-game routine, but he never quite felt the same way about being a mascot after the tragedy and retired in the early part of the 2008 season.

Webber, who had both a logging and a rugby background, became a soccer fan in 2001, when friends took him to a game. That's when he first saw Timber Jim, and initially remembers being "excited to see a chainsaw in the middle of downtown Portland." Upon seeing a 2007 news report that Timber Jim was retiring and the Timbers were looking for a replacement, Webber decided he wanted the tradition to continue, and since he knew his way around a chainsaw, he applied.

It was important to Paulson that Timber Jim bless the transition, and a halftime ceremony at a 2008 friendly between the Timbers and Juventus served as that. "It was a mixed bag," says Webber about officially becoming Timber Joey. "There were people telling me that I'd never be able to fill Timber Jim's shoes, and I never wanted to. There were also so many people, though, who were extremely kind, who welcomed me with open arms." Over time, though, Timber Joey's become an increasingly essential part of the Timbers' game-day atmosphere.

Timber Joey, unlike Timber Jim, doesn't scale poles or otherwise put his life in peril—he's typically circulating around the stadium and meeting fans when he's not as his post in front of the log along the stadium's north end. The slab-cutting ceremony at the heart of Timber Joey's act has evolved a bit, though—the log is now passed from Timber Joey to north end fans, circulating throughout the crowd before being awarded to the goal-scorer in a postmatch ceremony.

What was evident from the outset is that Cascadia fans were ready to come out and be part of the experience that supporters' groups were helping create, and that hasn't let up. In the Sounders' inaugural season, the team averaged over 30,000 for home matches at what was then called Qwest Field, and in 2015, set an attendance record with nearly 45,000 per game—even though upper portions of the stadium are only opened for select games each year, in part to manage traffic on days when the Mariners, next door at Safeco Field, share home game days with the Sounders.

The Whitecaps moved into B.C. Place toward the end of 2011, after spending most of the season at a temporary stadium in a city park. B.C. Place has an upper deck and lower deck situation akin to Seattle's; Lenarduzzi notes that a series of "sails" covering the stadium's upper sections was commissioned by his front office to create a more deliberate aesthetic than tarps. The Whitecaps averaged just fewer than 20,000 in its first full season at B.C. Place, using a 21,000-seat plan that can convert to a 27,500-seat configuration if demand warrants.

Due to its footprint, its downtown location, and the narrowness of some of its walkways, the Portland stadium is at a constantly sold-out 21,000, with a 10,000-person waiting list, though the Timbers do have a plan they could conceivably activate to get to 24,000.

The Sounders, first from Cascadia to the MLS party, made an auspicious debut in 2009. Led by two designated players in opposite directions of their careers—just-starting Colombian striker Fredy Montero (today with Sporting Lisbon) and now-retired Swedish midfielder Freddie Ljungberg (part of Arsenal's legendary Invincibles squad)—the team won a U.S. Open Cup, qualified for the playoffs, sold more than 22,000 season tickets (and sent out season packages that included a scarf proclaiming the bearer a 2009 season-ticket holder).[6] And were it not for the Dynamo's Brian Ching breaking a two-leg aggregate scoreless tie with an extra-time goal in the Houston-hosted second match, they might have faced the Galaxy (quickly emerging as its first MLS rival) in the Western Conference Finals.

The Timbers and Whitecaps' 2011 debuts weren't as successful on the field; Portland narrowly missed a playoff spot, while Vancouver was tied for last place in the league with New England.

Though 2011 had two true expansion teams in the Timbers and Whitecaps, the season also featured a reinvented team. Kansas City unveiled a new, stellar stadium to put its Arrowhead Stadium days to rest forever, and unveiled a new name that would create buzz to rival what Real Salt Lake had experienced—or, for that matter, what Kansas City itself had experienced when the franchise launched as the Wiz.

The Wizards had long been in need of a rebrand. Rob Thomson, who'd been involved with the club almost since its inception, notes, "There was no brand equity. We didn't have an identity, we didn't have a set demographic. We were last in the league in merchandising, below the generic MLS line. We had an order with Adidas, and they would send us fifty-five jerseys to sell for the season. That's all they'd give us. Now, we sell more jerseys in a halftime of a game than we'd sell in entire seasons with the Wizards."

The drive to rebrand was initiated in 2006 when a group of five local entrepreneurs bought the team from Hunt Sports Group. They informed the league a year later about the desire for the name change, which would eventually be timed with the opening of a desperately needed new soccer-specific stadium in 2011. On MLS's recommendation, Thomson met with a branding firm that the league had used. He recalls, "We had breakfast with them, and we told them everything about our club, about Kansas City, and what was important. They came down to Kansas City about a month later, they flew down, and presented to us. They said, we've got it, from now on, you'll be the Kansas City Bees, because the state insect of both Kansas and Missouri is the bee! And we're like, what in the world are they talking about?"

"We wanted something different that would unify the city, both sides of the state line into being part of a club," Thomson explains, and "Bees" was definitely not it. "We thought the best thing to do would be Sporting Kansas City, and we knew at the beginning people wouldn't understand it and it would be a lot to take in. The owners despised it, but we were confident."

One important facet of the club's marketing was buy-in from both the Kansas and the Missouri sides of the state line. The new club crest featured a graphic that subtly but surely emphasized how the state border specifically circumnavigated the city—and that diagonal line angling into a straight north-south bisection was important in defining the team's identity.

The opening ceremony, however, only vaguely articulated what the name change was about. CEO Robb Heineman told the thousand who braved wet and cold November weather for the unveiling, "Our goal is to revolutionize the way a professional sports team connects with fans through premier experiences and spaces. We believe a change in identify for the club was necessary to effectively live and breathe this vision. The name 'Sporting' represents our desire to become a dynamic organization focused on creating opportunities for social, cultural and athletic connections."

Ben Palosaari, with Kansas City alternative newspaper the *Pitch*, described the ceremony: "When a wall of soccer balls fell away to reveal the team's new crest, everybody for the most part cheered, before breaking out in a Wizards song. But those were the hardcore folks, the ones that would probably buy season tickets if the team's new logo was an orange cartoon platypus in cleats. Now that all the fans and media outlets have absorbed the news, the goodwill appears to have evaporated."[7]

Palosaari went on to describe incredulity from the *Kansas City Star*, which posed the possibility of calling the team the 'Tings, while high-profile sports website Deadspin offered the Fightin' Gerunds as a possibility.[8] Palosaari also described the team's post-announcement Facebook page as "a straight up cat fight, with haters pounding their keyboards with rage or simply looking for an explanation for the name and supporters coming back with 'Aw, shucks, it's not that bad' optimism."[9]

And the nickname also drew initial criticism from one of the city's sports integrity vanguards—Jack Harry of NBC affiliate KSHB-TV, who, in perhaps one of the highlights of his forty-year career covering sports in Kansas City, playfully referred to the team as "the Sporties."[10] Thomson notes that once the club was able to show that fans were gravitating toward the name and buying merchandise, Harry "went on air and did an impromptu thing where he said he was wrong. It was the first time he'd done that in about 70,000 years of sportscasting."

And Harry also acknowledged the team's success, lauding Sporting as "the only winning professional team in K.C." The team did, after all, advance to the 2011 Eastern Conference finals as its legitimate number 1 seed (before losing to the Dynamo, now also in the East).

The year 2011 brought a watershed moment for front office and supporters' group relationships. Dubbed FortGate, it involved the New England Revolution and two of its supporters' groups, the Midnight Riders and the Rebellion. The front office and supporters' groups were in ongoing discussions around what fans refer to in shorthand as "YSA"—the "You suck, asshole" chant that has unfortunately found its way to multiple MLS stadiums. The chant—directed toward a visiting team's goalie on any and all of his goal kicks—is seen as harmless tradition by some and a tired, infantile, or even vulgar (not to mention sponsor, broadcaster, and suite holder-offending) one by others.

Soccer magazine *Howler* attempted to find the origins of YSA for a 2012 podcast covering multiple facets of the chant, including an interview with veteran goalie Jon Busch and one with a sports psychologist to confirm its negligible effect on goalies. While they couldn't find a definitive source, theories they happened upon included it being gifted by then MetroStars fans around 2000 to the rest of the league, or Americanizations of even more offensive English or Mexican chants.[11]

Steve Stoehr, reporting for the SB Nation blog the Bent Musket, pieced together a narrative in which the Revolution front office cracked down on fans during a June 18 match against the Chicago Fire, despite efforts by the Riders and Rebellion leadership to try to eradicate YSA throughout the 2011 season. As Stoehr alleges in his story, "TeamOps [the stadium-hired security company], security and police descended on the Fort [two stadium sections occupied by supporters' groups] with what seemed to be extreme prejudice"—resulting in two arrests, more than twenty forcible ejections, and many more walkouts by fans throughout the course of the match.[12]

By the next week, in an article updating readers on the situation,

Stoehr opined, "If supporters' groups receive a clear message from their club's front office that a particular behavior will no longer be tolerated, it is their duty to work with that organization to either convince them that the request is unreasonable or implement a plan of attack that will allow them to accommodate the rulings of team officials."[13]

He did also, however, defend the Revs' supporters' groups for trying to work with the front office on eradicating YSA in the first place, and showcased shows of support, in tifo and banner form, from various supporters' groups around the nation, including Barra Brava and the Crew's Yellow Nation Army. Union fans even created a moment of silence in support of their what is typically one of their rival fan groups. The incident, and especially its aftermath, showed that a network that was once consigned to message boards and listservs was using a multitiered online approach, with websites and social media, to communicate and even mobilize.

Dittfurth, in an essay on the Timbers Army website in response to FortGate, offered this advice to fellow supporters' groups:

> We had a problem with the "You suck, asshole" chant years ago. It took almost two years to completely kill that thing and we didn't have as many years of doing it like the Revolution's supporters did. Our front office worked with us to kill off that chant long before MLS sniffed Portland. It didn't happen overnight and it didn't happen without some relapses and false starts. It took a lot of work from a lot of dedicated people. You won't hear that chant here because we've had enough time to educate people on why it's not used and the Timbers FO was a good faith partner who understood that working with us as equals and providing positive incentives was a smarter solution than threats and bans.[14]

Fran Harrington, current president of the Midnight Riders, noted that FortGate was important to help resolve long-standing and deep-seated differences between fans and the club. The Midnight Riders' website, for example, refers to "ongoing issues between the Riders and club management that contributed to growing frustration on both sides" in the 1996–99 section of its history, including a 1999 MLS Cup incident involving "unjustified harassment and the unfortunate, unnecessary arrest of some Riders."[15] FortGate necessitated a long-overdue meeting between front office reps and supporters' groups.

Harrington explains,

> This really is what changed the dynamic of the relationship we
> have with the front office. The first result of the blowback was a
> town-hall-type meeting where all supporters were invited and
> were able to directly ask questions to the Revs front office, security, and MLS officials. As a result of this meeting, we instituted
> meetings before every home match where members from the supporters' groups, FO, and security are all present. It's helped a lot,
> as now everyone really knows everyone. If there are issues on
> game day, they know to come to me and I feel much more comfortable going to them. This had helped on numerous occasions.
> I feel like before all this started, the FO was sort of a faceless bad
> guy in a lot of people's eyes. We still have issues from time to
> time, but now there's protocol in place to deal with them.

The Revs' red, white, and blue–clad fans came into league-wide focus in an unfortunate yet important episode in helping to define the supporters' group's role in defining MLS. But it would be another group of red, white, and blue–clad fans, not tied to any one MLS team, that would soon help a far greater number of Americans—casual fans of the game, as well as people falling for soccer for the first time—understand what supporters' groups did and why they were vital.

Chapter 11

THE BELIEVERS

In which the Americans battle snow and Central American teams to capture a burgeoning new fan base for soccer.

On October 21, 2012, 6,256 people shoveled dirt for two minutes on the site of a former factory across the street from the San Jose International Airport to break a Guinness world record for the largest participatory groundbreaking. The event was the precursor to something Earthquakes fans had long since hoped for: a new home stadium constructed specifically for their team. Fans joined San Jose city officials, team owner Lew Wolff, and a visiting Commissioner Garber in breaking ground for what ended up being a $100 million, fully privately financed, soccer-specific stadium with an array of features putting it into its own echelon of awesomeness.[1]

The Quakes, of course, spent the entirety of their first iteration in Spartan Stadium, and upon their reentry to the league, made a (smaller) home at Santa Clara University's Buck Shaw Stadium, with a capacity of just 10,500, venturing out to Stanford Stadium every year since 2012 for the California Clásico match against the Galaxy, and staging one-offs in other larger, football-oriented Bay Area stadiums.

According to Earthquakes president Dave Kaval, a new stadium was part of the plan when the Quakes 2.0 came back into the league in 2008. As matters developed, it would take four years to line up the approvals, permitting, and financing, but when it came time to do the groundbreaking, it was important to Kaval to have it be a communal event in which fans could actually participate. "We didn't just have a gold shovel ceremony for the high-falutin' one percent," Kaval explains. "We had a ceremony where everyone got to dig. We had seven thousand shovels. We're more of a community team."

The groundbreaking was a celebration of what was to come, but it was also a celebration of a 2012 season that was going incredibly well. The Quakes were decidedly outperforming expectations, winning seven of their first nine matches on the way to a Supporters' Shield–winning 19–6–9 record. They were doing more than just winning, though; they were coming back from deficits to win games and sometimes scoring incredibly late in matches to pull out victories. After one such victory that May—a 3–2 thriller against their archrival, the Galaxy—the Quakes' Steven Lenhart declared, "Goonies never say die!" in reference to the classic 1985 adventure movie featuring a band of misfits who prevail against long odds. The team then began dubbing themselves the Goonies—a nickname so beloved by Quakes fans that when the team created its new crest and uniforms to kick off the 2014 season, the back of the neckline—where many clubs choose to place a motto—was embossed with #NEVERSAYDIE.[2]

The Quakes' rivals would, however, once again arise as a nemesis.

The Galaxy, as the West's number 4 seed, needed to win its play-in wild card match against the number 5 Whitecaps to even get into the Western Conference bracket to face the Quakes. (In 2012, MLS simplified its playoff system, elevating the top five teams from each conference into the playoffs, and eliminating playoff seeding via the overall league table and the more-influential-than-perhaps-intended cross-conference migration of prior years.)

The Galaxy got past the Whitecaps, then dispatched the Quakes in a 3–2 aggregate win en route to a near déjà vu of the 2011 MLS Cup—this time, a 3–1 win against the Dynamo in the Home Depot Center, with Omar Gonzalez putting in an MVP performance and Landon Donovan converting the game-winning penalty kick.

In a major change that placed new emphasis on team seedings, the 2012 MLS Cup was the first to be played at the home stadium of the conference champion with the better regular-season record rather than at a predetermined neutral site—meaning that the 2011 Galaxy would be the last MLS champions to merely luck into playing the MLS Cup on their home field.

The 2012 MLS Cup would also be, as announced before the match,

David Beckham's final MLS appearance, in a season where he'd taken more of a complementary role than he had in 2011, but had still added to a lore of intermittent brilliance and tumult in his final two years. A Nick Firchau remembrance of Beckham on MLS's website recounted,

> He pinged San Jose's Sam Cronin with a ball from twenty-five yards in June and came perilously close to scrapping with the Quakes' mascot in a postgame shoving match. He missed an MLS game in Dallas in 2011 because he was a guest of honor at the biggest royal wedding in decades.
>
> He rolled into the closing ceremonies at the Beijing Olympics with rock god Jimmy Page, and four years later brought the Olympic flame down the River Thames in London. He sat courtside at Los Angeles Lakers games. He adorned a Times Square billboard in nothing but his H&M underwear. He scored from 70 yards at The Home Depot Center and pounded home amazing goals to ruin nights in expansion markets like Portland and Montreal.[3]

Chris Klein, who started his involvement with the Galaxy as a player arriving two weeks before Beckham (and moving into the front office in 2011, eventually becoming the club's president), reflects,

> It was something like I'd never seen before. We introduced one of the most famous people in the entire world into the league and into the club. I don't know that we were fully ready for it. Now we have designated players and big names—we're much more prepared for it. But we had to go through those times with having David here, with the media attention. But that project didn't really start to show the fruit until David was invested in the team and the Galaxy started to win. I think that's when you saw the real benefit. In terms of him choosing MLS, I don't even know if you can give it a value. Looking at guys like [Steven] Gerrard and [Frank] Lampard and [Andrea] Pirlo, who are now saying it's okay to come to MLS—[Beckham coming to MLS] was definitely one of those watershed moments.

While the word *dynasty* might have been premature to bestow upon the Galaxy after its second straight championship, there was a growing sense around the league that the team might be capable of that. Los Angeles–based soccer writer Josie Becker comments, "With the Supporters' Shield and the cups, there was a lot of talk that this was a dynasty from 2009–12. It certainly was a great group, but with MLS being such a young league, it just felt like LA needed to do more before putting them next to the D.C. United teams that won three out of the four first MLS Cups."

The 2012 season also brought two milestones for Canadians. Though it was only just for one game against the eventual champions, the Whitecaps bested their Canadian predecessors in Toronto by becoming the first team north of the border to make the playoffs. And in what was the sixth consecutive year of expansion—a string that started with Toronto FC in 2007—the Montreal Impact officially joined MLS.

Negotiations between the league and Impact owner Joey Saputo (of the Saputo family, involved with Montreal soccer since the North American Soccer League's Manic)—had been developing for more than a year before the official announcement was made in 2010.[4] Like the Timbers and Whitecaps, who entered the year prior, the Impact was a long-standing team with a local following. It started life in the American Professional Soccer League in 1993, and had a role in the A-League, the United Soccer League, the indoor National Professional Soccer League, and the newest iteration of the NASL before making its transition to MLS.

The move was "welcomed" by Toronto fans; while it would take a while to gather a history approaching what the Maple Leafs and Canadiens had between them, a similar sentiment was certainly already there. As Toronto supporter Mike Langevin simply puts it, "We dislike them on ice, we dislike them on grass, we dislike them in politics," adding that Toronto fans couldn't even muster solidarity for the Impact in a competition that would have reflected well on Canada—the Impact's deep run in the 2015 CONCACAF Champions League final, where the Impact reached the final before losing to Mexico's Club America on a 5–3 aggregate score.

American soccer fans came into the 2013 MLS season with divided attention; in early February, the U.S. national team lost its first match of the Hex, the ten-match home-and-away series involving the top six CON-CACAF teams to determine (in 2013's case) which three teams would automatically qualify for the World Cup and which team would have to enter a playoff with Oceania's top team. While many expected the Americans to advance, the result of the first match threw that into some doubt, and in the days prior to the match in Denver against Costa Rica, a *Sporting News* article by Brian Straus alleged disharmony among U.S. team members, some unhappy with head coach Jürgen Klinsmann's handling of certain players.[5] This led to team captain Michael Bradley having to address the article in a press conference prior to the game, with the requisite, expected allegiance to Klinsmann—perhaps, really, creating more of a sense of alarm and mystique around the Costa Rica game, a pop-up midterm exam for the Klinsmann era.

This did, of course, create a sense of urgency and interest around the game that rippled out to more casual American soccer fans. But there was another force generating interest in the hours before U.S. versus Costa Rica at Dick's Sporting Goods Park—a chance of snow at game time.

The 2010 World Cup in South Africa had captured American attention, in part because the United States had been drawn into a group with Algeria, England (to potentially revive War of 1812 smack talk), and Slovenia. Michael Lewis, writing for the *New York Daily News*, noted, "Some words were uttered Friday night that hadn't been heard at many, if any, World Cup draws" before quoting the Algeria and Slovenia coaches contending that the United States and England were the group favorites.[6]

But it would turn out that the United States would need a dramatic moment to advance out of the group in its final match against Algeria, coming in its final moments when a hard-charging Clint Dempsey had his point-blank shot blocked by the diving Algerian keeper, only to have a trailing Landon Donovan fire in the rebound for the 1–0 win. Fans reacted ebulliently in watch parties across America, and YouTube videos capturing those fan reactions circulated around the Internet. Doug McIntyre remembers celebrating for different reasons:

If in 2010 the U.S. hadn't gotten out of their group, it would have been a big blow to me professionally. We had just started a U.S. national team blog on ESPN's site, which goes on to this day. There was a question of are they going to continue this if the U.S. bombs out in the first round of this extremely easy group. So, I was watching the game in the offices of *ESPN The Magazine* in New York with my editor, behind closed doors, and when Landon Donovan scored, we were ecstatic, but it wasn't just because the U.S. advanced, it was because it saved our asses professionally!

Though the United States was ousted in its subsequent knockout match against Ghana, the 2010 World Cup captured many more viewers than in 2006—the 11.1 million average for the three group matches (including 17.1 million for the United States versus England) was a 66 percent jump from 2006's Nielsen numbers, and the 19.4 million who tuned in for the United States–Ghana knockout game were the most ever to watch a soccer match in the States. As in 2006 in Germany, South Africa's time zone placed Americans into daytime hours for match watching, but the United States' matches against England and Ghana were both Saturday games, which certainly didn't hurt viewership.

The 2010 American team had a number of past and present MLS standouts on the squad, though U.S. Soccer's official press release on the team boasted, "A record 19 players on the roster play professionally for clubs outside the United States," noting that all in all, clubs from ten different nations were represented by the U.S. Men's National Team. Some of the higher-profile players, including Clint Dempsey (with Fulham), Tim Howard (with Everton), and DaMarcus Beasley (with the Rangers), had all "graduated" from MLS teams to top-flight English and Scottish teams in what was characterized as a sign that American soccer players were beginning to make their mark on the world stage.[7]

The team looking to qualify for the 2014 World Cup was initially without Donovan—he'd taken an extended sabbatical from soccer following the 2012 MLS Cup, and though he'd worked out an arrangement with the Galaxy to return to the team in late March, his departure from the USMNT was indefinite.

I am one of the lucky people to have witnessed the United States–
Costa Rica game in person with the American Outlaws, the homegrown
U.S. supporters' group created for the match in Lincoln, Nebraska in
2007. The rumors of snow throughout the day began materializing as
buses provided by Centennial 38, the Rapids' supporters' group, shuttled
fans from downtown soccer bars to the tailgate party the group was hosting for American fans outside Dick's Sporting Goods Park.

The game was a Friday night ESPN-televised match, and the audience
numbers were fueled by excited social media chatter, encouraging people
to tune in for what were first snow showers and snow flurries and then
a veritable snow globe, and to watch athletes valiantly struggle and even
flail against those elements, which is about 95 percent of what is so fun
about games—any games—played in the snow.

Deadspin's Ryan O'Hanlon described the atmosphere this way:

> By kickoff, temperatures were near freezing. The field was coated
> in white and, gradually, cleated footsteps. John Deere mowers
> plowed the sidelines pre-game and then gave way to men with
> shovels who worked diligently to keep the sidelines and the 18-
> yard-box visible. The refs supplied a yellow ball, too, but that's
> about all that could be done to improve the conditions. For the
> fans, a flask—actually, many flasks—was the only thing that
> could be done to improve the conditions. The snow only got
> harder and heavier as the game went on, and it only got colder,
> too, because even during a sold-out soccer game, the world con-
> tinues to spin. There was no staying warm. There was only stay-
> ing slightly less cold.[8]

At the American Outlaws' end of the stadium, there was certainly a
growing sense that we were witnessing bizarre history, but there was also
a sense of frivolity that permeated the game. Before the game, as the
workers labored to clear the lines, we spontaneously started chanting,
"Sho-vel! Sho-vel!" When Dempsey scored the opening (and only) goal
of the game, at the opposite end of the stadium from us, we broke into
celebration, and then settled into a bubble of delirium reminiscent of Jack
London's story "To Build a Fire." When referees conferred with players

a few minutes into the second half to determine if the game should really continue, we spontaneously broke into a chant of "Let them play!" that was so impassioned that we almost believed it to be a mitigating factor in the decision to continue. Late in the second half, a fan next to me said, "Well, you know, our next sub's going to be Santa Claus, and they've got no answer for that," which sent me into delirious laughter. Balls kicked to the corner closest to us, by game's end, were skidding and then stopping behind the snowdrifts created in their wake, and this launched me into additional peals of laughter.

The postgame reaction was generally joyful and jingoistic, celebrating the win in the snow as a transcendent American triumph over the elements. The *Denver Post*'s Woody Paige wrote that the United States deserved a "home-snow advantage," and in response to Costa Rica's planned postgame protests over the conditions, asked, "If the match had been played in Costa Rica's National Stadium (a $100 million gift from China), could the Americans have protested because of heat, humidity, mosquitoes and sloth interference?"[9]

David Wegner of Centennial 38 noted that the match, while not necessarily growing the ranks of Rapids fans, did galvanize existing ones and gave its newly formed tailgate crew a formidable test that they passed admirably. He recalls,

> As for the residual effects of that game, it's kind of a funny thing and parallels a lot of the crossover issues from fans of European and English soccer. I think the game here was already growing exponentially regardless of the snow game, but what it did is it shored up existing fans' commitment to the game and to the USMNT going forward. I wouldn't say the growing support of the U.S. teams, or higher visibility of the English Premier League et al. has really spiked numbers. We actually own two sections in the stadium and our numbers didn't jump.
>
> There's a bit of elitism there though with local fans of that league that is frustrating since this team is their actual, attainable local club, yet the clamoring for squads 7000 miles away still trumps it. People have actual access to the actual players and staff of this team, but seem content with a long-distance TV relationship.

The following Tuesday, the United States was back in Hex competition, facing Mexico in Mexico City, and the combined audience numbers for both ESPN and Univision's American telecasts approached eight million viewers, "making it easily the most-viewed World Cup qualifier in American soccer history," according to a Soccer by Ives article—though the Spanish-language audience outpaced the English-language one by a nearly two-to-one margin.[10]

The remaining Hex qualifiers (and the Gold Cup tournament that summer, which is how Donovan reentered international play before being allowed to rejoin the team for its final few Hex matches) did two important things to place increased focus on American fandom and eventually help a wider circle of Americans gain greater awareness and understanding of supporters' groups.

First, the coverage that the American Outlaws were generating throughout 2013, and into the actual World Cup year, was placing the group—and the very idea of supporting with specific learned chants as a loud, passionate, standing collective of fans—into more living rooms than ever before.

Second, U.S. Soccer had wisely chosen to place all five home Hex qualifiers in MLS stadiums with solid fan bases and concrete supporters' groups. Many American Outlaws in MLS home cities are also members of their local MLS supporters' groups; the coordination of C38 with the American Outlaws in Denver was an example of how shared memberships, and the familiarity of local supporters' groups with their home stadiums, helped logistically.

Dan Wiersema, who handles communications for American Outlaws, notes that group has learned and taken cues from the various MLS supporters' groups it has coordinated with:

> If you look at MLS supporters—they're incredible. Game in and game out, the coordination and the tifos and the regularity of support and the creation of new chants and how the whole pipeline of support works, the local supporters' groups—it's incredible. It's admirable.
>
> They get that because they have regularity. Look at the Timbers Army. They have thirty-four games a year in Major League

Soccer. They get seventeen at home, in the north end, with the same people mostly, every time, with the same capos, who they probably recognize by first name. They have tifo committees, there are chants developed organically and inorganically, and they can practice them. A chant that may not get any traction in game one could be sung by two thousand people by mid-season or game seventeen. I'm jealous of that regularity.

When American Outlaws support, we have twenty games a year, we're in twenty different stadiums in twenty different cities with roughly twenty different crowds. There are always regulars, but if you're looking at a crowd of three thousand, maybe one hundred of them go to every single match, and that's being generous. So how do you take an incredible experience in one city to the next city and the next city? How do you get people to chant something beyond "I Believe?"

The season, played against the backdrop of the international tournaments, was incredibly close, with fifteen of the league's nineteen teams vying for playoff spots in the final two weeks of the season. Talk of a Galaxy dynasty would be suspended as Real Salt Lake defeated them in a conference semifinal matchup, with the Timbers ousting the Sounders in the other semifinals. The Dynamo and Sporting Kansas City lasted through overtime matches in their semifinal series to defeat the Red Bulls and Revolution, respectively.

Real Salt Lake and Sporting would advance to MLS Cup 2013, which turned out to be an endurance test thanks to its length and extreme conditions. The match went through ninety minutes of regulation, thirty minutes of overtime, and an incredible twenty penalty kicks before RSL's Lovel Palmer's penalty kick caromed off the bottom of the crossbar to seal the win for Kansas City and keep the goalies from having to face off against each other. It also gave MLS its version of the NFL's still-legendary Ice Bowl; as ESPN noted in its coverage, "It was the coldest MLS Cup in history with a game-time temperature of 22 degrees and a wind chill of 12, and that only dropped as the sun set and the game pressed through overtime."[11]

RSL coach Jason Kreis emerged from the locker room after the match to tell reporters, "I'd advise you if you have a choice not to go in there. It's bad, real bad."[12] One of the RSL players who did speak after the match, Javier Morales, called for a return to neutral-site MLS Cup stadiums, noting he was so cold he "couldn't talk at halftime." But he was apparently in distress even before then; he said, "My toes were freezing the first 20 minutes and I looked to the bench to give me something because I couldn't feel my toes."[13]

The late afternoon match—placing MLS's finale head-to-head against late-season NFL games—didn't draw particularly well for ESPN. World Soccer Talk's Christopher Harris reported, "The disappointing 505,000 viewing audience figure for the Sporting Kansas City against Real Salt Lake game follows the 29% decline in regular season MLS TV ratings on ESPN compared to last year, as well as a 8% decline on NBCSN." He then piled it on a bit, adding, "The 505,000 number is the same as the viewing audience for a repeat of *Everybody Loves Raymond*, which was shown on TBS at the same time as the second half of the 2013 MLS Cup."

But Harris's next sentence contains literally half the story—UniMas's Spanish-language telecast of the finals drew 514,000 viewers, the first time that the Spanish telecast surpassed the English telecast in MLS history.[14] Soccer America's account of the ratings noted that Kansas City and Salt Lake City TV markets drew 7.6 and 6.2 shares for the game—an indication that ratings might have only paled nationally compared to the prior Los Angeles–Houston matchups due to the size of the markets (and the Galaxy's Beckham factor.)[15]

Several days before the finals, TV ratings were a primary topic in Garber's State of the League address, along with the proclamation that the league was planning to expand to twenty-four teams by 2020, with Orlando City coming online in 2015, and other cities hinted at, starting with Atlanta and Miami (specifically, David Beckham's Miami).

"We've been growing our fan base," Garber told the media regarding the TV ratings. "We have to find a way to find a partner that gives us the right schedule, the right promotion and marketing, that is embracing us in a way that will allow us to have our programming be valuable and be a priority both for the broadcaster and for our fans." He called for greater consistency in week-to-week scheduling, and pointed to NBC's widely praised Premier League coverage as a model for how MLS could be promoted.[16]

The 2013 season also added to the evolving relationships—some positive, some less so—between front offices and supporters' groups. Despite the gains that Revs supporters' groups made in the wake of 2011's Fort-Gate, YSA (and the league and front office reactions to it) was still creating controversy. In a 2012 Sporting News interview, Garber had called for the chant to stop, concerned that it created issues with the Federal Communications Commission, and clearly expressing a personal dislike for it.[17] But for some supporters' groups, the debate about YSA went beyond the chant itself and into resistance toward front offices looking to curtail expression and sanitize the experience.

In July 2013 Deadspin's Barry Petchesky reported on letters that had gone out to at least two clubs' supporters' groups—Real Salt Lake and the New York Red Bulls—threatening sanctions (including rescinding parking passes, preventing fans from displaying banners, and eliminating use of megaphones and capo stands helping capos lead supporters in cheers) if supporters' groups did not work to eradicate YSA.

The article speculated, "The general feeling among fans is that this latest crackdown is directly tied to MLS's upcoming TV contract (deals with ESPN, NBC, and Univision all expire after 2014, so negotiations for the next deal are already ongoing). Garber has long pitched MLS as a family-friendly league, and the clearly audible profanities don't help that image in person, or on TV."[18]

The Red Bulls' front office took the engagement one step further. According to the *Village Voice*, the club promised each of its three South Ward–occupying groups (the Empire Supporters Club, Garden State Ultras, and Viking Army) five hundred dollars per game to not say the YSA chant for the entirety of the game. To ensure that it became habit rather than a one-time thing, the club said they'd have to string four games together to get a lump-sum two-thousand-dollar payment.[19]

"Two groups, the Empire Supporters Club and the Viking Army, publicly supported the initiative and have since qualified to receive $4,000 each," a *New York Times* follow-up article in September reported, while noting that the Ultras (who tend to present themselves as a more stern, hard-core supporters' group) was not on board. "At one game over the summer, it unfurled a sign—written on four twin-size bedsheets—that read, 'Not for sale.' The group, unlike the others, did not make a public statement on social media supporting the effort, and at the same time, a message appeared on the group's Facebook page that maligned the effort. In response, the club barred the group from taking its banners and flags to the games." As an Ultras leader going by the name Terror reasoned, "We don't do the chant, but we don't want money to be told not to do something."[20]

Empire Supporters Club board member Muller recalls,

> We eventually agreed that the chant needed to go, if not for the think-of-the-children crowd, for the fact that it was just played out at that point. At first, we tried to get people to say something else—for example, "You suck, Garber"—but to no avail. Again, sanctions were threatened, but they also came with this dangling carrot of money for YSA-free games. We figured the best way to get rid of it would be to just sing through the goal kicks. Whatever song we were doing, we'd just push through it. It took a bit of time. The main thing was getting the more vocal people in the section on board. Once the section leaders started singing through the goal kicks, most people followed suit. Once in a while, there will be a few YSAs that sneak through, but for the most part it's been eradicated.

Revs fans, displaying an admirable sense of humor in light of their FortGate experience, created an over-the-top alternative to YSA; according to Adam Sell of the Midnight Riders, the chant goes, "We all got together and decided that, among the two goalkeepers in this particular game, you are the one of lower skill and aptitude!" While it's difficult to execute—Sell suggested creating shirts with the text on the back, so a supporter can just read it from the supporter in the next row forward—it perhaps signals a sea change in the debate over YSA.

Another evolving front office and supporters' group saga, in Dallas, had its roots in the group's 2011 formation, but reached a major point of contention early in the 2014 season.

The group started early in the 2011 season when Andrew Gerbosi (who'd moved to Dallas in 2010 from Long Island, met members of the American Outlaws' Dallas chapter, and started going to FC Dallas games with them) came upon the idea to have a supporters' group for the beer garden (located on the stadium's north end, a concrete plank that doubles as a stage for music events). Gerbosi transformed a beat-up flag he'd found at the stadium into a banner that read FC DRUNK and, as he explained,

> We flew it at a U.S. Open Cup match against Orlando City. We had it hanging in the beer garden, and we added a few more people and a few more banners. We had as many as twenty people or maybe even more who kind of hung out and latched on. About three quarters of the way through the season, the front office said the banner wasn't exactly PC enough. We had to take it down. But we were still there every game, we still supported every game.
>
> At the end of the year, [then FC Dallas president] Doug Quinn had called me and thanked us for coming out, and said, "We want you to continue with this. Do you maybe want to do something a little more politically correct, like FC Brew Crew?" We thought that sounded like a softball team. He told us that Budweiser was looking to sponsor us, we could do something beer related but not inappropriate, and if we came up with something, they could get us some Adidas gear, shirts, scarves. I said, "Give us a week," and we sat around and talked about it, and we came up with Dallas Beer Guardians. We were in a beer garden, it just sort of fit us right, the way it rolled off the tongue sounded right.

By the start of the 2012 season, the group was officially christened, the club placed bleachers in the beer garden to allow for proper seating (or, at least, standing), and it flourished to become the club's largest supporters' group. Gerbosi recalls that Dirk Nowitzki once made an appearance in the DBG's section, as did Brek Shea (then still with FC Dallas) while serving a suspension. As the group grew, the tradition of beer showers began organically, with fans in a section of the beer garden tossing the contents of their cups in the air to celebrate goals.

Becky Chabot, a PhD candidate in religious and theological studies at the University of Denver and Iliff School of Theology, centered her dissertation on the social ethics of professional club soccer (and her fan typology) on the DBG, spending the 2014 and 2015 seasons with them to conduct ethnographic research on life in an MLS supporters' group. That May, as she recalls,

> The club banned fans from beer showers after a goal celebration, supposedly due to complaints. The leadership of Dallas Beer Guardians petitioned the club for over a year to get signage on the garden to warn fans they might get wet in the event of a goal. The celebration was only in the beer garden, which was a twenty-one-plus [age group] section, and is pretty tame as far as fan celebrations go around the world.
>
> Fans were informed through an e-mail to all members of registered SGs [supporter's groups], not through their leadership per the policy that the FO and SGs had in place. The e-mail informed fans that they would be given the equivalent of a red card for violating the policy: they would be ejected and suspended for the following home match. They also said the ban was retroactive, and they would be going through security footage to identify those who had beer showered in the past and suspend them; that threat never materialized. But at the first match after the ban was put in place, quite a few people were ejected, and security was not only increased but there were undercover security officers throughout the section.

Jay Neal, the DBG's director of community outreach, noted that signs were finally erected, as they'd requested, but rather than Sea World–style "splash zone" signs, they were signs explicitly prohibiting any beer throwing—which, as he says understatedly, was "not exactly what we wanted." The DBG mulled over a response, which included either an alternate form of shower, including glitter or silly string, or polite golf clapping and even dressing like soccer moms, to make the point that if the front office wanted tame, family-friendly fans, that's what they'd get.

The group instead decided to boycott beer purchases at the beer garden (a movement circulated in part, by a #BeerBoycott hashtag on Twitter), and put up a website publicizing the ban. For the first few games immediately following the ban, DBG members would still congregate outside the stadium for prematch tailgates, but the supporters' group was more dispersed throughout the stadium during the game, the north end's beer garden bleachers were noticeably more empty and, as Chabot recalls, goal celebrations were decidedly more muted: "It took about two months before the stadium sounded like a stadium again."

The group eventually found its way back to the beer garden as the team readied for a playoff run (after all, that's where its season tickets were), got a meeting with the front office several weeks after the initial meeting to discuss the situation, and has since successfully worked with the front office on other issues, even though the ban was never officially lifted and the club's policy is still in place.

And though the fans have brought back their spirited and sometimes coarse support, complete with a drum line and two trombone players whose go-to song is "Deep in the Heart of Texas," the beer showers are a thing of the past. "We have agreed to disagree," Gerbosi said. "But we know that if people throw beer now, they risk getting thrown out."

Overall, 2014 was a very good year for MLS—the season set an attendance record, with more than 19,000 fans per game. (The number would have approached the 20,000 mark had it not been for a troubled Chivas USA's absurdly low turnout of 7,063). Though Brazil was aligned with American time zones, many of the World Cup 2014 games were in the afternoon, limiting the overlap that some expected when Brazil won the rights to host the tournament.

The final twenty-three-man U.S. World Cup squad included ten MLS players, with two key players who'd made recent moves back to the league from overseas: Dempsey had signed with Seattle in August 2013—participating in an unveiling ceremony before a regular-season match in which he was interviewed by Sounders majority owner Joe Roth on the field before unzipping a hoodie to reveal a Sounders jersey underneath[21]— and Bradley had been sold to Toronto FC by Roma in January 2014.

But there was one MLS player notably left off the roster: Donovan.

Steven Goff, in a *Washington Post* article examining the shocking (or maybe not so shocking after all) admission, wrote,

> Despite his place in U.S. lore, not to mention 57 goals in 156 international matches, Donovan was not certain to make this year's team. Since taking a sabbatical from soccer two years ago, he has had to work his way back into Klinsmann's good graces. He featured in the CONCACAF Gold Cup last summer, joining several second-tier players, and returned to the primary group for the late stage of World Cup qualifying.
>
> This year, the first sign of Klinsmann's uncertainty about Donovan's World Cup status came last month when Donovan did not start in a friendly against Mexico, even though first-tier European-based players were not on the roster. Donovan had been hampered by a knee injury and did not show well in practice leading up to the match.
>
> In MLS, Donovan is scoreless in seven regular season matches. With his next goal, he will become the league's all-time leading scorer.
>
> Though neither side acknowledged it, there was persistent speculation in U.S. circles that Klinsmann questioned Donovan's commitment to the program and his coaching philosophy.[22]

Andrea Canales, writing about the decision, took a perspective that might have surprised some—how much Mexican fans would miss Donovan's presence in the World Cup:

> For Mexicans and Mexican-Americans on both sides of the border, Donovan has for so long been an icon of American soccer that they dubbed him "Captain America." It was immaterial to most that Donovan was not actually the U.S. team captain that often. But even as many who loved El Tri booed and chanted against Donovan, there was also an appreciation of his skills from the same people.
>
> Donovan's heritage was Irish-American, but he grew up in Southern California, speaking playground Spanish and learning

the game with a distinct Latin flair. His control on the dribble, his cutbacks, his quick passes, were skills that Mexicans could appreciate, because they valued such ability in their own players. Mexicans could get Donovan, in a way that often his fellow Americans did not. They understood his superstition of crossing himself before a penalty kick; they knew why he raced into open spaces instead of chasing the ball; they admired, for his small size, his eerily accurate heading ability. Even at the moment when he enraged the entire country, nailing a header to help eliminate Mexico in the 2002 World Cup, taking off his shirt to celebrate and screaming into the camera, "Where is Mexico?" they could understand him, because he said it in Spanish.[23]

Canales reflects, on the article, "It's a kind of interesting dichotomy that that respect for Donovan was so much more obvious to Latino fans. In LA he'd constantly get recognized by Mexican fans, and Americans would ask, 'Who is this guy?' It's almost a 'prophet is ignored in its own homeland' type of thing."

One thing that Donovan's omission from the USMNT did do was suddenly bolster a Galaxy team that needed bolstering. "Honestly, that gave the team an advantage to rally back from the middling start to the season," Canales says. "They hadn't expected Donovan to be available, and all of a sudden, here he was, still playing. And in some ways, he said that was therapeutic too. He was glad to be there, and glad the season was still going on. Had he been on a European team, that wouldn't have happened."

And even though Donovan announced in August that 2014 would be his last season, and there was certainly an added impetus for the Galaxy to rally, there was something even more profoundly emotional affecting the team. As Canales remembers, "There was also the very emotional impact of A. J. DeLaGarza's baby, who had been born with hypoplastic left heart syndrome. His brief life and death, and the team pulling together for the charity they established, Luca Knows Heart, was important. It was kind of a continuation of all these emotional elements for the team that created this tight bond. It all made them feel life is very precious—carpe diem, seize the moment—and they carried that through to the final and the championship."

The World Cup included a record 26.5 million Americans watching the finals between Argentina and Germany (with nearly 10 million of those watching in Spanish on Univision),[24] and the United States had record numbers watching the men tie Portugal in a weekend group-stage game and then losing a heartbreaker in extra time in the Round of 16 to Belgium to crash out of the tournament. The Belgium match drew nearly 16.5 million ESPN viewers and more than 5 million Univision viewers, for a combined audience of 21.6 million, though at one least one analyst surmised that figuring in watch parties at bars and homes would bring the total closer to 30 million.[25]

The tournament was also what FIFA president Sepp Blatter proclaimed "the first truly mobile and social World Cup," with 280 million posts on Facebook, and one match alone—Germany's surprise 7–1 trouncing of Brazil—generating more than 35 million tweets, breaking Twitter's all-time record for single-game traffic.[26]

The 2014 playoffs came down to two heated rivalries in an aggregate system that was now using away goals as the first tiebreaker for series tied at the end of the second game's regulation period. On one side were the Red Bulls, in what would be Thierry Henry's last MLS season, against a Revolution bolstered by the midseason signing of Jermaine Jones (returning to the United States after finishing out a contract in Turkey) and enjoying a breakout season from Vietnamese American midfielder Lee Nguyen, who'd played professionally in Denmark, the Netherlands, and Vietnam before returning to the United States. On the other, it was the Sounders versus the Galaxy.

In the East finals, the Revs got past the Red Bulls on a 4–3 aggregate, while the Sounders were done in on an away goal in the second half of the West finals' second leg; an especially boisterous group of Seattle fans had to reconcile beating the Galaxy 2–1 at home, having a 2–2 tie on aggregate, and yet not advancing to their first-ever finals.

The Revolution were in store for their own heartbreak. In their fifth MLS Cup, as visitors traversing the country to attempt to spoil Donovan's final match, they did take the Galaxy to extra time via a 1–1 score-line. But a mere nine minutes from going to penalty kicks for a second straight MLS Cup, Robbie Keane scored the decisive goal, robbing the Revolution of a chance to finally taste success in the finals, but giving Donovan the storybook ending that even rivals felt he deserved.

The dynasty question reemerged after the finals, but with a more de-finitive yes answer. As Becker reasons, "A dynasty needs a constant. If we're talking from '09 on, then it's Bruce Arena's dynasty, and three titles certainly makes that case. If we're talking from Landon Donovan's ar-rival and those four MLS Cups, then that's a decade where LA appeared in half the MLS Cup and won all but one. I think both are acceptable, and both are worthy of praise."

"Now," she adds, "we get to see if the Arena dynasty survives Dono-van's retirement or if Donovan's is the only one that stands the test of time. For me, MLS's two decades are divided into the DC years and the LA years, pretty much down the middle. And it's the 2014 championship which sealed that."

Despite the gains that MLS made in this chapter of its history, 2014 did lose a team at season's end, the first since the dark days of the January 2002 contraction that left Florida without a team. Earlier in the year, Chivas USA had been sold back to the league to operate, and just one day after the team's final regular-season match—a 1–0 victory over the Quakes that locked up seventh place in the West for the doomed fran-chise—MLS told the world Chivas USA was no more. Specifically, Garber announced "a new strategy for the Los Angeles market," which Brooks Peck, on the Dirty Tackle website, pithily observed "sounds more like the introduction of a revamped McDonald's menu than the shutting down of a sports team" as part of an article titled "MLS Shuts Down Chivas USA and a Cold World Shrugs."[27]

But Los Angeles wouldn't technically be losing a second team—rather than the team dissolving entirely, a new ownership group would rebrand, reshape, and relaunch it in 2017, even though the players would be dis-persed to the rest of the league and the name would disappear (and be burned with fire if at all possible).

The new ownership group included Vincent Tan, the Malaysian businessman who was at the time of the announcement embroiled in a major conflict of his own making with Cardiff City FC fans. In 2012, shortly after buying the Welsh club, Tan pushed for a rebranding, changing the century-plus-old club's kits from blue to red and placing a red Welsh dragon in a dominant position on the crest, demoting the team's namesake bluebird to the crest's bottom.[28] The standoff lasted until January 2015; Tan told the media he'd decided to give the fans what they wanted, to revert to blue home kits, based on the counsel of his mother.[29]

The year 2015 would reveal the full extent of the new plan—a team called LAFC, with its own stadium to be built in downtown Los Angeles, a smart black-and-gold art-deco influenced logo, with actor Will Ferrell as part of an extended ownership group, giving the team a distinctive shift from what Chivas USA was at its outset and what it had become.

The twentieth-anniversary year would reveal so much more, including the question Becker posed about Arena's dynasty versus Donovan's dynasty, how two new franchises would fare, and a frightening, looming possibility that the season might not start on time—or indeed at all.

Chapter 12

THE ANNIVERSARY

In which MLS turns twenty, a generational birthday,
and achieves new levels of symbolic solvency.

The Tuesday before the 2015 Major League Soccer season started, the *New York Times* ran an article that led with the good news of "the start of eight-year television deals with Fox, ESPN and Univision worth $90 million a year," which also established more of the predictable weekly pattern Don Garber had sought in his late 2013 State of the League address, and heralded the news that "the league's new expansion teams, Orlando City and New York City F.C., are to face off Sunday on ESPN2 in front of more than 60,000 fans at the sold-out Citrus Bowl."

But it then veered into a dark place, noting that "all that good news might get buried, for at least a little while, if M.L.S. players go on strike over free agency and higher salaries. The players' union and the league have been negotiating a new collective bargaining agreement for weeks, and have been in talks with the aid of a federal mediator since Sunday in Washington. But a strike could be called as early as Wednesday to keep the teams that are scheduled to play Friday from traveling to game sites that would be shuttered."[1]

In a nutshell, the dispute revolved around salary increases (from the league minimum $36,500), each team's salary cap being raised (from the current $3.1 million) and, most important, free agency provisions that—under MLS's single-entity system—didn't exist the way they did in other pro sports.

The two sides were able to come to an agreement just days before the start of the season. As the *Los Angeles Times* reported,

Neither the league nor the union released details of the collective bargaining agreement, which still must be formally ratified by the players. But several media reports said the five-year deal, approved only 50 hours before the season was scheduled to begin, includes a raised salary cap, a higher minimum wage and restricted free agency, all items the union demanded to avoid a walkout.

Yet, while the union won on every major point, some players apparently believed it didn't push hard enough for more concessions, especially on free agency, something the league had steadfastly said it would not consider.[2]

In many respects, the resolution was a relief; in the immediate term, any delay in the season starting would have deprived MLS fans of witnessing how far the league had come with the initial matchup between 2015's two expansion teams. On the purple Orlando side, Brazil and Real Madrid veteran midfielder Kaká was the captain and the clear star on a team with its origins in the USL, for a franchise that five years earlier was playing in a high school stadium in Austin, Texas, against the likes of the El Paso Patriots and the Laredo Heat. On the sky-blue New York City Football Club (NYCFC) side, Spain and Barcelona veteran forward David Villa was the other captain, the first of three highly prized international players featured on the squad, for a franchise born of the alliance between Manchester City Football Club and the New York Yankees. Probably none of that was discussed as a possibility for MLS when Alan Rothenberg and Mark Abbott were building the league out of a promise to FIFA in the early 1990s.

For Orlando City SC, hosting the home opener was a chance to show the world that Florida was once again ready for MLS. For club president Phil Rawlins, the home opener was the culmination of a strategy to take the team he'd purchased in 2008 (the Austin Stampede, which was then rebranded as the Austin Aztex) and drive it toward the MLS on-ramp.

"We started to open a dialogue with MLS, and it was fairly obvious from what they were saying that they wanted at least one team in the Southeast," Rawlins remembers. "That helped immensely with figuring out where we should locate. We did a due diligence exercise, looked at several marketplaces, and Orlando just started to rise to the top of the list, and by the end of the exercise, it was the obvious choice."

Rawlins announced in late 2010 that the USL team would move to Orlando, but at that additional announcement, made clear the goal was to graduate to MLS—and had contacted the league about its intentions. "We simply asked them what we had to do to bring a franchise to Orlando," Rawlins explains. "They gave us an outline, and we went toward checking off all the boxes during the next three years."

These included being able to "prove the marketplace" in both numbers of fans and commitment of corporate sponsors, putting a funding plan in place for a downtown soccer stadium, and assembling an ownership group that could sustain the club in the long term. The team's success in USL helped draw fans; for its 2013 championship game, the club launched a campaign (dubbed #Mission15k) to have at least 15,000 fans in the stadium; more than 20,000 witnessed the team's triumph in the Citrus Bowl, making it the best-attended minor-league sporting event to date.

The organization checked enough boxes for MLS to announce the arrival of Orlando City SC in late 2013, with a plan to play in the Citrus Bowl until the team's 100 percent privately funded stadium (accommodating 25,500) came online in the summer of 2016. Majority owner Flavio Augusto da Silva, described on OCSC's official website as "a wealthy Brazilian entrepreneur with a deep passion for the game,"[3] was not only able to fulfill MLS's ownership requirements but was able to bring Kaká over to the team, after nearly eighteen months of negotiations and logistical coordination, as its first truly bankable star. The team also repeated its #Mission15k campaign on a much grander scale for the inaugural home opener, with a campaign to do what soccer hadn't done in Orlando since World Cup '94.

"It was obviously incredibly emotional," Rawlins says of the first match. "We'd launched #FillTheBowl six to eight weeks beforehand, with the goal of getting over 62,000 people to the game, which was an audacious goal. Our front office felt confident we could do it. We sold out the stadium with more than ten days to go. Had we had limitless capacity, we projected that we could have sold 80,000 tickets. But it was also emotional because up until the week of the game, with the CBA [collective bargaining agreement] negotiations, we weren't sure the game was going to continue. So there was a lot going on!"

The league's other 2015 expansion team, NYCFC, was announced in May 2013—with the Manchester City–Yankees partnership surprising some observers who'd thought that New York's other baseball franchise, the Mets, would be involved. NYCFC, billed as the first team that would actually play in New York City (a not-so-subtle dig at the Jersey-based MetroStars/Red Bulls), was definitely intertwined with Manchester City. The November 2014 jersey reveal showed NYCFC would play in jerseys essentially identical to its parent club, sky blue with Etihad Airways as the kit sponsor, and this set off a fair amount of Twitter snark. (The best of these came from Seth Vertelney, who posted a side-by-side picture of both kits, with a Photoshopped arrow pointing to the NYCFC badge, and underneath it, "#branding."[4])

Though the initial announcement came on the heels of a Manchester City–Chelsea exhibition played in Yankee Stadium four days later, the club didn't officially announce that it would be the home for their inaugural season (and beyond, despite the distinct possibility of a soccer-specific stadium somewhere in New York's five boroughs) until April 2014—at which time it laid out specifics on how the baseball-to-soccer transition would take place, including the dismantling of the pitcher's mound (which turned out to not be necessary; the mound ended up as part of the sideline, painted to function as an advertisement for season tickets).[5]

The Third Rail, NYCFC's supporters' group, described its birth coinciding with the club announcement and happening when "prospective fans took to Twitter, Facebook and blogs to share their excitement." Its website said, "Known at the time as 'New York City FC Supporters Group,' it began as a loosely-knit group interacting first on social media, then increasingly in public meet-ups, pub crawls and other events."[6]

But the Third Rail didn't just seek traditional (read: twenty- and thirty-something male) supporters; the group also created a space for families under its umbrella, called Light Rail. According to the current "conductor" of Light Rail, Jenny Lando, the group doesn't have a designated family-friendly section but does encourage kids and parents to congregate for pregame face-painting, arranges with the club for members to have the opportunity to be player escorts and ball kids, and generally invites parents to fully participate in whichever level of soccer culture they deem appropriate, be it rated G, PG, or otherwise.

NYCFC defined itself in its first season through three extremely high-profile players presumably preparing to make the Big Apple their final professional soccer destination. The first, arriving in June 2014, was David Villa, best known as a Barcelona player, though he'd most recently played with Atlético Madrid. The signing came early enough to not only generate stateside buzz about the team but also allow him to spend time at another of Manchester City's recently acquired entities, Melbourne City of Australia's A-League, to prepare for life in MLS.

The second, Frank Lampard, proved to be a slightly more contentious acquisition with American fans thanks to how he was initially utilized. Lampard, who'd played with Chelsea from 2001 to 2014 as one of the club's most celebrated players, was let go by the club, and NYCFC signed Lampard in July 2014. Ten days after the signing, Manchester City announced that NYCFC would loan Lampard to the parent club for the remainder of the calendar year, to participate in a title race against his former club. Then, before that deadline arrived, Manchester City announced that the loan was being extended to the end of the Premier League season in May—when the MLS season Lampard was supposed to have signed on for was well underway.

But NYCFC wasn't done yet. With its third and final designated player slot, the club signed Juventus and Italian national team legend Andrea Pirlo in July to a contract keeping him in New York until the end of the 2016 season.

Other teams also strove for relevancy via the Designated Player market. Toronto FC brought in still-in-his-prime Italian striker Sebastian Giovinco from Juventus during the offseason. Initially he was supposed to wait until the Serie A season finished to come over, but Juventus allowed him to leave early in time for the start of the MLS season; Giovinco pounced on the opportunity with twenty-two goals, winning an MVP in a season where Columbus Crew mainstay (and season-long Golden Boot rival) Kei Kamara was also making a case for himself. In July, Montreal brought in Didier Drogba, the former Chelsea and Ivory Coast star (whose "Drogba Legend" banner followed him from Stamford Bridge to Stade Saputo) and made a spirited playoff run in which he featured significantly. Portland brought in Argentine international Lucas Melano, also a July addition, who would figure into a particularly important playoff moment.

The Galaxy had brought in its own designated player of note, Liverpool mainstay Steven Gerrard, who, upon learning he would be gradually phased out of the only club he'd ever known, arranged to make the same move that David Beckham had made eight years earlier.

Chris Jones, writing for ESPN FC on Gerrard's July 4 welcome at StubHub Center, gave the impression that the veteran Premier Leaguer would enjoy MLS:

> Steven Gerrard takes his seat in the front row of a private box at StubHub Center and settles in to watch his first game as a stateside member of the Los Angeles Galaxy. It's July Fourth, and the stadium is sold out, 27,000 strong and festive. The Riot Squad, one of the more notable L.A. supporters' groups, has been wellrefreshed by the truckload of California beer that Gerrard bought them for their tailgate—veteran move, that—accompanied by a hand-signed letter: "I look forward to meeting you at tonight's match," Gerrard wrote. He is more than getting his wish. This isn't Anfield, and Gerrard is essentially sitting in the crowd, separated only by a low cement wall. A steady stream of fans stop by for autographs and pictures; a few of them are already wearing Gerrard's No. 8 in Galaxy white. "That's a bit of a gamble," he says. "They haven't seen me play yet."[7]

Gerrard debuted well, looking sharp in his first official Galaxy match—a U.S. Open Cup 1–0 loss to Real Salt Lake—and then scored and assisted on another goal in a July 18 California Clásico win against the San Jose Earthquakes.

But it was another Galaxy signing, requiring the league to create another mechanism to allow it, that proved to be impactful and controversial, while allowing the Galaxy to meaningfully reach a whole new fan base.

It's helpful to understand, in discussing this, that the evolution of MLS signing rules draws some level of skepticism from longtime observers of the league. Some prominent soccer journalists, for instance, have looked askance at signings of the past several seasons—regardless of how well they've served the league and its competitive balance—to insinuate that the league is participating in some level of orchestration.

For example, in an August 5, 2013, article detailing how Dempsey recently signed to Seattle (instead of Los Angeles or Toronto, other potential destinations), Wahl quoted Roth as saying, "I think it was important that [Clint Dempsey] ended up . . . how do I say this politely? . . . not in Los Angeles. Because from a perception standpoint it would make MLS look essentially like a one-team league when it came to important international players."[8]

In the summer of 2014, when Jermaine Jones became available, both the Chicago Fire (who would go on to finish ninth in the East) and New England Revolution (who would go on to the MLS Cup finals) coveted him, and the league needed to determine where he'd go.

Goff cynically observed, "From the league that introduced weighted lotteries, homegrown signings, discovery selections, re-entry drafts, the SuperDraft, designated players, allocation orders and designated players exempt from allocation orders, MLS unveiled a new acquisition mechanism Sunday: the blind draw."

Goff noted that Jones, like Dempsey and Michael Bradley before him, wouldn't need to go through the allocation process because, as MLS rules stated, "Designated Players of a certain threshold—as determined by the League—are not subject to allocation ranking."

As he explained,

Protocol, however, requires the league to run a player's name through the entire membership to identify other clubs financially capable and interested. Historically reluctant to spend big bucks, New England stepped forward at some point and became an unexpected suitor. Chicago suddenly had competition.

Jones preferred to play for the Fire—closer to his family in Los Angeles, a home stadium with natural grass, an established dialogue with Chicago brass—but because MLS could not ensure his destination if multiple teams were interested, Jones backed away last week.

MLS wanted him badly and increased the offer. His salary would be the same whether he landed in Foxborough or Bridgeview. The rub: Jones would have to drop his demand to play for Chicago and allow the process to play out.[9]

The random draw sent Jones to the Revs on a contract through the end of 2015; his 2015 season ended on an unhappy note when he was sent off after shoving referee Mark Geiger in the dying moments of the Revs' playoff-ending loss to D.C. United, and Jones posted wistfully to Instagram several days later, a black-and-white picture of him walking past a stadium brick wall, captioned, "I am so thankful what has happened in one and a half years with the club, the teammates & fans, the city of Boston! I appreciate the love from everybody! I'm going home now and finally enjoying my family! Very excited to see what will be the next step in our life!"[10] (This led more than one fan to post a message along the lines of "Don't go!" in response; but Jones would indeed go, ending up in Colorado to start the 2016 season.)

When the Galaxy signed Gerrard, it reached its maximum of three designated players per MLS rules, as Gerrard joined Roy Keane and U.S. national team defender Omar Gonzalez. On July 7, though—via an article on MLS's own website—Mexican national star Giovani dos Santos, playing with Villarreal in La Liga, confirmed that the Galaxy was interested in his services but was coy about reports that he had already signed.

The next day, MLS announced new salary cap rules allowing a team to spend an additional $500,000 above the $3.49 million salary cap, and the ability to buy down the contracts of existing DPs, through what the league termed "targeted allocation money." The MLSSoccer.com article detailed a key provision of the rule: "Teams may also use Targeted Allocation Money to convert a Designated Player to a non-Designated Player by buying down his salary budget charge to below the maximum salary budget charge. When using Targeted Allocation Money to free up a Designated Player slot, a club must simultaneously sign a new Designated Player at an investment equal to or greater than the player he is replacing."[11]

As ESPN.com floated, "The new rule opens the door for a club such as LA Galaxy to pay Omar Gonzalez's cap hit with these funds to get below the DP threshold, then add another big earner, such as Mexican national team star Giovani dos Santos, who is reportedly in advanced discussions with the club."[12]

By the next week, the Galaxy had done exactly that. While Galaxy fans were thrilled with what dos Santos could bring to a team fighting for playoff position in a competitive Western Conference, detractors saw the move as a rich-getting-richer situation (which would have most certainly been the complaint had, say, Dempsey found his way to Los Angeles rather than Seattle in 2013).

Fusion's Kevin Brown, in an article snarkily titled, "The L.A. Galaxy Signed Giovani dos Santos Because Rules are for Chumps," remarked,

> The midfielder joins a Galaxy team that already features the league limit of three designated players . . . so the league had to create a new mechanism (drink!) to make all of this legal. Targeted allocation money to help pay for expensive players is a thing now. The only relevant detail from a fan perspective is it means better (or at least more famous) players have another pathway to join MLS.
>
> The sort of person who gets angry at MLS finding ways to improve the on-field product either a) made a poor choice and supports a cheap franchise (shout out to Colorado), b) finds valor in pointing out the obvious that "MLS is weird," but has no real intention of watching less of it, or c) is unfortunately a member of the players union and is starting to realize that the last round of collective bargaining agreement negotiations wasn't the breakthrough they thought it was. For you, the fan who invests time and energy in search of entertainment, this is a win.[13]

Speaking of the targeted allocation money provision (TAM), Grant Wahl comments, "It does make you laugh, with some of the communist-era names that they come up with at MLS headquarters. And based on the timing, it does seem that this was allowing the Galaxy to have four designated players." Yet he notes that TAM hasn't just favored the

Galaxy but rather has positive for the league so far in that it's allowed a number of teams to bring in good players, and is increasing the overall collective star power within MLS.

For the Galaxy, Giovani dos Santos was more than just an attacking midfielder with a high motor who could fortify the team's 2015 playoff position and play a role in what the club would coin the #RaceForSeis. Seeing that dos Santos has been a captain and one of the highest-profile players on El Tri, and seeing that the Galaxy probably wouldn't mind galvanizing Mexican American support before a still-coalescing LAFC has a chance to sign players, the move is fan minded as well as field minded.

"The impact of him coming to our club has changed us," Chris Klein explains. "It's changed the way that the marketplace is looking at us. It's enhanced our relevancy in the market. The real test is going to be the success of Gio and how he produces, because as we've seen, you can't just have a player who comes for marketing. But certainly, we're getting fans who have traditionally supported their clubs in Mexico that are now supporters of the Galaxy."

And yet, despite the focus on the dos Santos signing coming right before the All-Star Game, it was still a celebration of the designated players who had come into the league to kick off the 2015 season.

The twentieth edition of the MLS All-Star Game, had injuries not interfered with plans, would have served as the coming out party for Gerrard and Lampard. Even though they had only finished their Premier League seasons that May, and neither had played a minute in MLS, Garber named the two English stars to the All-Star squad as commissioner's selections. Injuries would claim them, as well as Bradley, Keane, Sebastian Giovinco, and Chris Tierney. Jozy Altidore, a late substitution for Giovinco, ended up also adopting Giovinco's number 10 jersey as his own customary number 17 (plus many other reasonable jersey numbers) had long since been claimed.

And yet, the setting of Dick's Sporting Goods Stadium on a perfect Colorado summer evening, with an opening ceremony reminiscent of the pregame ceremony at the first-ever MLS game in San Jose, heralded the twentieth season with appropriate pomp, even if all the special guests couldn't be on the field as planned. The game itself pitted the MLS All-Stars against traveling English Premier League team Tottenham Hotspur, with Kaká (the game's MVP) and David Villa scoring for the All-Stars and breakout Spurs star Harry Kane getting on the score sheet in the losing effort. The event also featured Landon Donovan in his coaching debut the night before the All-Star Game, overseeing the MLS Homegrown team (of top young academy players) against the Club America U-20s.

The Gerrard and Lampard saga took an additional twist on August 23, when the two of them were supposed to face off with NYCFC's trip to StubHub Center to face the Galaxy. Despite shirts and posters that celebrated the renewal of the rivalry—the StubHub Center's store sold shirts that read RENEWED RIVALRY underneath their names and faces—Lampard failed to make the NYCFC eighteen-man squad.

It's maybe just as well; after being lucky to only be down 1–0 at half-time, NYCFC let in four second-half goals and turned a dubious penalty call into a David Villa penalty kick to make the final 5–1 scoreline slightly less lopsided than it should have been. Keane's exclamation-point goal was the Galaxy's thousandth goal, making the Galaxy the first MLS team to reach that milestone.

But one of the more intriguing elements of the game played out in ESPN's broadcasting center. The broadcast, scheduled to start at 3:00 p.m. ET, was held off by the Junior League World Series finals, in which a team representing Chinese Taipei was bettering a team representing Virginia, 10–0, in the seventh inning. American Soccer Twitter came alive with commentary, with expectations that they'd get soccer when and only when Chinese Taipei recorded the final inevitable out. Even the broadcasters commented on soccer in passing—namely, how it'd been years since they'd personally played it—on the way to saying they'd stay with the game until its corporeal end.

Then at 3:15 ET, minutes before kickoff, ESPN broke abruptly from preadolescent baseball, proclaimed it time for soccer, went to a quick pregame commercial, and then the game was on. ESPN soccer producer Chris Alexopoulus tweeted, "I've never seen ESPN dump out of an event in the 20 years I've worked there,"[14] and Jonathan Tannenwald, who wrote extensively on soccer coverage on TV during his time at Philly.com, tweeted in response that it was "among the most stunning moments in MLS history" with no sign of sarcasm whatsoever.[15]

"I hesitate to say something grandiose along the lines of 'It was the moment when Major League Soccer finally arrived,'" Tannenwald comments. "But it was a moment in which people could say here is an event within MLS that ESPN will draw a large-enough audience to be bigger than a little league baseball game. ESPN has a fairly hard and fast rule that it will not jump out of live programming to go to other live programming, except for something really drastic. They always let whatever game they are televising finish." Though Gerrard versus Lampard didn't materialize, and though the game ultimately showed viewers that three world-class DPs do not a great team make, MLS fans got to feel, at least for a moment, some acknowledgment that their sport merited a moment of sports TV history.

MLS also got its newest cathedral in 2015. Avaya Stadium opened with features reflecting a mindfulness of all elements of the league's fan base. Dave Kaval said the stadium design was inspired by European stadiums—they'd scouted a number of them in their preparations for the $100 million project—with the steepest seat grading of any MLS stadium and with overhanging roofs to help capture noise. One end of the stadium is designed with the team's four different supporters' groups in mind; the other end features North America's largest outdoor bar, replete in reclaimed redwood, underneath the stadium's giant double-sided videoboard. The stadium's eighteen suites are, in a novel move that might be trendsetting for future stadiums, at field level and incorporate porches that butt up to the sidelines, meaning that those paying top dollar for seats are closest to the action as opposed to literally and metaphorically above it all.

And, since Avaya is a "cloud-based solutions provider" in the heart of Silicon Valley, the stadium also bills itself as the "first cloud-enabled stadium in MLS."[16]

As stellar as the stadium is—in the league's tradition of showcasing the new, it was selected to host the 2016 All-Star Game—the Quakes had a bittersweet end to the 2015 season, just missing out on the sixth playoff spot in the West in their final regular-season game. The 2015 edition of the playoffs brought in twelve of the league's twenty teams, with the top two teams in each conference receiving byes. Though a system in which 60 percent of the league advances seems generous—or, as some complained, dismissive of regular-season results—the 2015 playoffs brought some of the most entertaining, epic finishes in the league's history.

Some criticized the fact that opening-round games, including the showcase Sounders–Galaxy match, were telecast exclusively on UniMas; for English-speaking audiences who weren't aware of the SAP feature providing alternative commentary, or who couldn't get the feature to work, the game provided impromptu Spanish lessons with the action. Beyond the opening rounds, though, the league's other two broadcast partners, ESPN and Fox Sports, were involved in telecasting matches. The numbers for 2015 only upticked slightly from 2014's; those who watched, though, saw MLS at its best.

The Timbers—playing in their smart retro third kits for their entire Western Conference playoff run—set themselves up as a potential team of destiny with a first-round match against Sporting Kansas City that went to penalty kicks. Kansas City had already won the U.S. Open over the Union via PKs early in the year, and of course, had recently won an MLS Cup that way. But this shootout was happening in the north end of Providence Park, directly underneath a full-throated Timbers Army. The ensuing PKs went eleven players deep, with Timbers keeper Adam Kwarasey converting his kick and then returning to goal to save Sporting keeper Jon Kempin's shot. Sporting defender Saad Abdul-Salaam, with a chance to win the match earlier in the PK session, fired a shot that hit one post, caromed across goal to the other post, and bounced out, to the terror and/or delight of everyone watching.

In the following playoff game the next week, the Timbers Army (who adopted a Kenny Powers–themed tifo motif for the playoffs, under the slogan "Cup bound and down") commemorated the moment by creating a giant tifo, directed at the visiting Whitecaps, that read THE POWER OF KWARASEY STOPS YOU HOSERS. But when fans discovered that Kwarasey would be out until the following week's return leg, enterprising Timbers Army fans created an additional sign that read NEXT WEEK to hoist next to the original one.

That match, which finished 0–0, included an eighty-ninth-minute shot by the Timbers' Max Urruti that bounced off the far post. Abdul-Salaam hilariously Tweeted (from his couch, presumably), "Wow those posts in Portland are something else #ishouldknow,"[17] which earned him appreciative responses from a good number of Timbers fans.

Though it looked as if the Timbers and Sounders might be on course for an epic Western Conference finals, top-seeded FC Dallas had other ideas. Seattle won the opening leg at home 2–1, meaning that a scoreless tie would send Seattle through, a 2–1 Dallas win would send the game into extra time, and the other likely scorelines would bring the confusing-to-outsiders away goal rule into effect.

For eighty-four minutes, the match in Frisco, Texas, remained scoreless. Then, Tesho Akindele scored a header for Dallas, and the stadium roared as a 1–0 win sent Dallas through by virtue of the away goal rule. Six minutes later, on the cusp of stoppage time, Chad Marshall scored a header on a corner kick, Seattle took the aggregate lead, and the stadium deflated. But less than two minutes later, with the Sounders just needing to hang on through stoppage time, central defender Walker Zimmerman scored, the crowd found life once more, and after a scoreless thirty minutes of extra time, Dallas keeper Jesse Gonzalez saved two of Seattle's five penalty kicks to propel his team to a finals with Portland.

The Western Conference finals provided a continuation of the earlier rounds' drama. Portland won the opening leg, 3–1, at home, including a beautiful goal (Dairon Asprilla's twenty-seven-yard parabola, recommended for any MLS evangelist collecting YouTube clips to bring fans over to the league) and two ugly ones by centerbacks either falling into or away from the goal. The return leg in Dallas started slowly and with thin crowds, partially due to unseasonably cold, rainy weather (on Twitter, some newer fans wondered if the match would be canceled), but mostly due to a security bottleneck—a cautionary measure due to the terrorist attacks in Paris earlier that month. The Timbers increased their aggregate lead with a Fernando Adi goal early in the second half, but FC Dallas scored twice after that, leading to a frantic final fifteen minutes in which Dallas chased the equalizer before late-game sub Lucas Melano killed Dallas's hopes with a stoppage-time goal in which he swerved around Gonzalez to the end line and chipped in from an extremely acute angle.

In the East, the Red Bulls were dominant over D.C. United in getting to the Eastern Conference finals, while Columbus needed to go to extra time in the second leg with Montreal for a Kei Kamara winning goal, after Kamara had missed a second-half penalty that would have put the Crew through without extra time. Columbus won the first leg at home, 2–0, with Justin Meram scoring the opening goal just nine seconds in, and for 92-½ minutes the teams were scoreless in the return leg at Red Bull Arena. Then, Anatole Abang broke through for the Red Bulls to score with ninety seconds officially left in stoppage time, though the officials let the match play out an extra minute. In the dying throes, with the ball bouncing around the Columbus box, Bradley Wright-Phillips attempted a header, which slipped past keeper Steve Clark but bounced off the post, where Kamara then met the ball and cleared it.

The 2015 MLS Cup, which sold out the day after the conference championships, included two thousand Timbers Army fans creating an enclave on the stadium's south end and bringing portable tifo to the game. Timber Joey did travel to Columbus with log in tow, just in case any Portland goals needed acknowledgment, but, according to a Massive Report article, "Crew SC Director of Stadium Operations and Merchandise Dan Lolli pointed out on Twitter that 'chainsaws' and 'Logs of any wooden variety' are against MAPFRE Stadium policy."[18] (In fact, those two items topped the list in what seemed like a hasty amendment to have some fun with the opponent.) The Timbers ended up bringing the log to Columbus and featuring it at the tailgate party but not inside the stadium.

The match itself featured three stunning goals in the first seventeen minutes. Portland's Diego Valeri scored the fastest goal in MLS Cup history, just twenty-seven seconds into the match, when he saw Columbus goalie Steve Clark dawdling with the ball in front of goal, charged, and took a chance slide at the ball, and swept it in. Six minutes later, on a sequence in which the Timbers had clearly gone out of bounds with the ball but were allowed to continue play, Melano found Rodney Wallace with a far-post pass that he headed in. The Crew benefited from a seventeenth-minute lapse by Kwarasey, who fell after awkwardly punching a ball into rather than away from danger. Kamara pounced on the mistake, winning the ball, creating a bit of space, and then firing into the net to bring the Crew back to 2–1.

But the score would remain there for the entirely of the game, despite several tantalizing chances—most notably a shot that, on review, clearly struck a parked-on-the-goal-line Columbus defender Michael Parkhurst on his outstretched arm before ricocheting down to his foot, where he cleared it, avoiding a red card and a Portland penalty kick in the process.

The Timbers' victory, a feel-good story for everyone but Crew and Sounders fans, capped off a year with one fitting success for its twentieth year: the league finally broke through the 20,000 average attendance ceiling that had evaded it in years past and that even haunted it through its early years of trying to get traction with American audiences. The Sounders led the way with 44,247, placing the team second in the Western Hemisphere, higher than Liverpool, and besting its own record from two years earlier. Ten teams averaged above 20,000, and even the lowest-attended teams still averaged around the 16,000 mark.

The attendance numbers were strong enough to bring MLS to seventh in the world, past top-flight leagues in Argentina, Brazil, France, and the Netherlands. While there's still a clear striation between the top professional soccer leagues in the world and MLS, there's a growing sense—made more defensible with numbers like this—that the league born of a promise to FIFA in order to host the World Cup is cementing a place among the world's leagues, staying stridently American yet being solidly part of a global community.

One more piece of news, coming just a week after the MLS Cup (but hinted at three weeks before), was another pivotal moment in MLS history—the announcement that Dynamo minority owner Gabriel Brener bought out majority owner Anschutz Entertainment Group to take a controlling interest in the club.[19] This left AEG owning just the Galaxy, and for the first time in the league's history, each of the twenty teams in MLS was owned by a separate, distinct ownership group.

For Abbott, turning twenty is more than a number. Reflecting philosophically, he says,

When you're in your twenties you can't imagine twenty years later. It's not comprehensible. You can't sit there and say, in twenty years, I dream to be this. Ultimately, for the kind of league we want to have, you have to show that you're viable and sustainable. People are not going to give their hearts and their passions to something that will fail. Once you've got to twenty years, you've done a full generational turn. We joke about it all the time in the office. We have people here who grew up as kids going to MLS games as fans, and who went to All-Star Games on vacations —we laughed at that. But that's what the truth is. Many of our interns were not born or barely born when the league started. They don't see it the way you or I might see it, which is that it's still a relatively new thing. It's always been there for them. Soccer's always been there. They don't get people who think it isn't a popular sport, because it has been for them. It's the sustainability of having reached that. And now, people are making that association.

THE FUTURE

In which MLS, its proponents, and its detractors
seek to write the next chapter in American
soccer history, one keystroke at a time.

To UNDERSTAND THE FUTURE OF MAJOR LEAGUE SOCCER, IT REQUIRES A
bit of a look back—to 2008, a time when desktop web browsing held a
two-to-one advantage over mobile browsing and social media was still
in its relative infancy. Facebook was emerging from its early identity as a
photo-gathering locus and relationship-status notifier to its current status
of being completely, culturally ubiquitous. Twitter was still pretty adherent
to its creators' original vision of it as a "microblogging" site, versus the
rough beast it has evolved into today, and Instagram was still just a twin-
kle in a developer's eye, a full two years away from launching.

In 2008, Sunil Gulati was teaching at Columbia University, and Chris
Schlosser was a Columbia MBA student who decided to stop by Gulati's
office hours with an idea for taking MLS headlong into the Internet age.
Schlosser, who wrote up a business plan following his meeting with Gulati, successfully convinced the league to embark on a different path from
letting Major League Baseball handle its digital platform, which is what
was happening prior to the summer of 2008.

Schlosser was brought on to head what is now arguably the league's
most important arm for fan outreach. He started where the league was
initially focused, on its website content, by bringing on Greg Lalas of
Goal.com (also, notably, Alexi's brother) to build a team that has expanded from 5.5 million users in 2010 to 20 million users five years later.

MLS's digital presence—now encompassing a robust website with both written and video content, numerous social media platforms (including standbys like Facebook and Twitter, but current enough to include Snapchat), and an online channel airing live MLS games—is more than just a way to reach fans. The digital space is where fans connect, and is arguably as vital to the American soccer experience in 2016 as stadiums and supporters' groups are.

And soccer, particularly MLS, is witnessing the importance of the digital sphere, embracing it in a way that other American sports have emulated but haven't as adeptly mastered. "Soccer wouldn't exist the way it does in this country without the Internet," Schlosser explains. "If radio built baseball, and TV built the NFL, we're going to look back, and I think we can already say, that the Internet built MLS. It connected—it really was the secret thing that connected everyone."

Part of that connectivity, according to Greg Lalas, comes from a DIY aesthetic that makes soccer fans from the 1990s to the present day analogous to indie music fans of the 1980s and early 1990s. Back when Top 40 acts ruled the radio airwaves and record label system of production and distribution, well before the Internet, there was a diasporic network of indie music fans who communicated through the creation of fanzines, which helped communication move from localized scenes built around college radio stations, alternative weekly publications, and indie-friendly venues.

He notes that in the years when MLS evolved from idea to actualized league, American soccer fans were much like indie music fans in the 1980s and 1990s; major media was heaping so much attention on mainstream sports that it couldn't be bothered to give soccer attention, coverage was accessible only through out-of-the-way channels, and fans were left to create their own avenues for expanding knowledge about the sport. The emerging Internet provided an ideal way to bridge the physical distance between like-minded fans. He reflects,

> That notion back in the '80s was that you were alone, and everyone was alone. All these soccer fans across the country were alone, they might have had their high school buddy who was a soccer fan, but that was really it. But the whole main-

stream world was talking about football, baseball, basketball, even poker for a little while. The only place you could go to have that communication with like-minded people was in the digital space.

So, originally, it was on the boards, like on Big Soccer, where a number of people in the community first came together. Then, it shifted to the comment area on websites like Goal.com, and then eventually, it shifted to social media, to Twitter, Facebook, wherever the latest one is.

So the soccer community was almost stitched together by the digital world. Those fed off each other—chicken or the egg, it's hard to say which was which. To be a soccer fan in America in general fifteen years ago meant you were a little bit off the beaten path, you might have been ahead of everything on the curve on digital stuff. You were the first one to have an Apple, or an iPhone, so we've even seen on the analytics how much more advanced the soccer fan and the MLS fan are in terms of using smartphones and being digitally savvy. We know that for a fact. And so, that's what they communicated differently. It was a digitally savvy group, because they were forced to by circumstance.

Amanda Vandervort, MLS's senior director of social media, says, "I would add that soccer fans are interested in all kinds of innovation, in ways that allow us to explore our creativity, and different ways to engage them and bring them into our content and our community." She also notes that soccer is full of "open and welcoming communities"—communities that, after all, create supporters' groups from the diverse patchwork of people who forged the Screaming Eagles and Barra Brava community in Washington, DC, the Section 8 Chicago community, and the many fan communities that followed.

One example of this innovation came from the redesigned MLS logo at the centerpiece of the MLS Next event, held in September 2014 to showcase the branding and marketing upgrades the league was making in order to reach fans in the digital space as well as the stadiums.[1]

As Vandervort notes,

You can see in the logo, in the crest, the way it's designed, there's an empty space in the bottom corner. When we released it, we didn't really address that space or tell fans what would be done in that space. What's so cool is that fans really embraced it—they took the mark and really made it their own. So fans would put in their avatar, or their favorite club, or their hometown, or lightning bolts—they used those as avatars, and brought it into their own social world. That's an example of how the brand is welcomed into their own social sphere, into the conversation.

One of the most poignant examples of how MLS Digital enhances actual MLS fandom is in its gamecasts. The MLS Digital team characterizes it as an ideal "second-screen" experience—if the televised (or web-projected) game is the first screen, then the gamecast provides a second screen for the fan to watch, to help augment the live game action he or she is seeing telecast or videocast. The gamecast is essentially a curated Twitter experience—MLS employees use proprietary software to sort through the tweets that fans are pushing out during a game, select the best ones, and add them to a running timeline of the game, providing a digital commentary to the action.

Though the tweets range from off-the-cuff comments from unaffiliated MLS fans, to in-stadium observations from home and away supporters, to insights from analysts and soccer journalists, MLS employees select tweets that help capture the ebbs and flows of the games. Lalas describes the criteria for gamecast elevation thus: show emotion, be funny, and/or tell us something we don't know.

While the gamecasts can work for someone trying to follow a game without watching it on TV, it's curated with the second-screen experience in mind. Research has shown the MLS team that those seeking out gamecasts are more likely to be with a second screen, most likely a smartphone, in hand as they're watching a game.

While written content is still important, there's been an increased emphasis on video—in part to respond to the need for what Vandervort terms "platform-specific content" as well as video's increasing impor-

tance across social media, and in part to showcase the emphasis on quality that MLS Digital strives for.

The content doesn't necessarily start and end with soccer, either;
Rachel Bonnetta, a twenty-something Canadian with a quirky sense of
humor and a comfortable rapport with pretty much everyone across the
MLS spectrum, created some of the MLS site's most noteworthy content
over the course of the 2015 season. Some of the videos relate directly to
soccer and fan culture; she previewed the 2015 playoffs, for instance, by
interviewing herself dressed as fans from all twenty MLS teams, including
a hilarious spoof of former Crew player and current Columbus Crew SC
brand ambassador Frankie Hejduk. But another series, *Off Topic with
Rachel Bonnetta* (sponsored by AT&T) features her with soccer personalities doing decidedly nonsoccer things like ice-skating in New York with
then-Toronto forward Herculez Gomez, shoe shopping with Union midfielder Maurice Edu, and inhaling helium with Fox Sports commentator
Rob Stone (in order to record helium-voiced conference final previews).

Bonnetta emphasizes that she's a sports fan, but also wants to get to
know athletes as people, and sometimes, traditional sports journalism
doesn't allow for that:

> I'm curious to know what they like to do off the pitch, what
> makes them tick. You see these guys getting asked the exact same
> questions over and over, and they're so programmed to say the
> same thing every single time. You're not learning anything about
> them, and some of them have really amazing stories. My whole
> philosophy was to pull that out. I'm a soccer fan, and if I think
> that's interesting, you're going to think that's interesting. That
> was my philosophy going into it.
>
> The beautiful thing about working in the digital space is that
> you can have an idea that's outside the box, and throw it against
> the wall. If it sticks, great; if not, try something else.

Bonnetta notes that the access she's been able to get to MLS players—and their willingness to go along with some of her wackier ideas—
is due to the desire of everyone within MLS to grow the sport. "We're
able to give the fans more," she says. "I hope that it never gets to the

point where it becomes an NFL or NBA, where we don't have that access. It's a beautiful thing. The supporters' groups are right next to the pitch, and players can go up to them and hug them after scoring a goal. Every part of MLS is accessible, because they want to get bigger. I just hope that if they get bigger, we can still have that intimate Major League Soccer that we know and love."

Bonnetta has since moved on from MLS, but is still creating original content featuring MLS players and fans. She was reportedly sought by both ESPN and Fox Sports after the 2015 season, and she opted for Fox, where, in addition to content creation, she hosts live video halftime and postgame chats tied to the network's Champions League broadcasts, hosted on the Fox Soccer Facebook page.

American soccer fans' engagement with the sport does, of course, extend beyond MLS. Soccer, for all its increasing popularity in the United States, is still a diaspora of passionate fans (dwarfed in numbers by pro and college football fans) who now have the means to connect across geographical boundaries digitally and instantly. Fans deeply passionate about soccer won't just gravitate to a single MLS team; they're also adopting Premier League teams, La Liga teams, and Bundesliga teams, and with more soccer on TV than ever before, fans are able to have first-screen as well as second-screen relationships with soccer.

There's a reciprocal effect starting to happen as well. In part because Britain's Sky Sports started carrying MLS matches in the 2015 season, there's now an audience tuning in late at night to watch American soccer in the same way that American fans get up early to watch English soccer. In October 2015 the *New York Times* profiled a group of three English MLS fans who launched a website, MLSGB.com, directed at British fans of the league.[2]

And of course, online platforms are where conversations about how to make soccer better are happening. One prime example of this is the ongoing promotion and relegation (pro/rel) debate.

Ted Westervelt, a Denver-based veteran of Washington, DC, political campaigns (as a Democratic political consultant) is passionate about soccer, and specifically, about the adoption of a promotion and relegation system that top European leagues employ in the interest of teams being competitive with each other; he is leading a campaign for U.S. Soccer to adopt a pro/rel system across all its leagues, including MLS, with his @soccerreform Twitter account.

Westervelt's campaign—often voiced with the stridency of a partisan fund-raising e-mail in the last hours before a quarterly deadline—paints MLS as a league frightened of competition and desperate to guard its D1 status; frequently retweets screenshots from @emptyseatspics if there's visibly poor attendance at any MLS game; and engages with soccer personalities, journalists, fans, and virtually anyone who Tweets about pro/rel. Westervelt initially turned to the Big Soccer boards to start conversations in 2007, got kicked off Big Soccer, and then found Twitter to be an ideal platform for his campaign.

Westervelt explains,

> When I started, I thought it would be an education process—you know, Americans just don't get promotion/relegation." We need to educate them on it, and the further I got into it, I realized I need to give a lot more credit to Americans. Most anybody who's been a soccer fan for any amount of time gets promotion/relegation. What we got, initially back in the day, was the excuse that MLS wasn't ready. One of the best things that's happened since then, with people hemming and hawing about it, is that those excuses have gone by the wayside. All that's really left is this idea that we owe MLS owners, that's why they invested in the sport, and we have to do it that way because that's the way they want it.

Specifically, the campaign is an appeal to U.S. Soccer to adopt promotion/relegation for all its existing leagues, making participation in the system a requirement for MLS to keep its Division I status. He believes that the current system is "suffocating" the development of U.S. soccer, and if every club in the United States had the same opportunity, "it will explode the game."

Commissioner Garber, though certainly aware of the noise that the pro/rel camp is making, dismisses it as a small, vocal minority that doesn't understand that the economics of the twenty-year-old MLS differ vastly from the economics of a Football Association hierarchy (to use the most familiar example of pro/rel for its American fans) in its second century. He comments,

> I get asked a lot and read a lot about soccer promotion and relegation. It is coming from a handful of media people and a very small set of fans who are very active on social media. It is not something that is resonating in our fan base. It is not something that I get asked about by the traditional soccer press or sports media, ever. So it has, in many ways, taken on a life within a very vocal group of people.
>
> Passionate fans are what drive professional sports, so I don't dismiss it as being meaningless. However, none of them are engaged every day as we are in growing this league and managing this league, so that we can ensure that we are here for generations to come. Because if we stay to our plan and do it right, MLS will be one of the big soccer leagues in the world, and one of the top major sports leagues here in America.
>
> All the pro leagues here in the U.S. don't have promotion/ relegation. Their playoffs rate anywhere from two times to five times their regular season. Their championship events are some of the biggest events on television that year, sports or otherwise. And every team is fighting hard to win every game and to win a championship. So I don't believe that just because it's existed in the rest of the world for one hundred years, that it means that it needs to be part of the American soccer solution. There's no reason American soccer can't be defined by what makes our leagues great. They're looked at by the rest of the world as the way sports leagues should be structured. So I dismiss entirely this view that just because it works in the rest of the world in football means that it needs to work here in the United States.
>
> I believe a lot of people are very engaged in global football, and they think that anything that's going on in global football means it's an all-for-one and one-for-all solution. I think we've learned in many ways that just because it's part of the culture of international soccer doesn't make it a one-size-fits-all solution.

We have a system of a player draft. We have union agreements. We have investors that have committed billions. They are partners in Soccer United Marketing. They have agreed to certain rules that have bound them, a wide variety of rules and regulations that are a phone book thick, commitments that they make to each other as partners. To think that somebody can come in or out of that partnership just because of the [team's] performance, just because it exists in international football, is a structural and legal impossibility.

While there is some striation now developing in American soccer leagues, it's the result of an expanding partnership between MLS and the USL, considered the third-tier league in the USSF hierarchy. The twenty-nine-team league includes a number of teams with clear ties to their parent clubs (like the LA Galaxy II, nicknamed Los Dos; the Portland Timbers 2; and Orlando City B), and others with more slightly veiled brands (including Kansas City's playfully named Swope Park Rangers, Salt Lake City's slightly redundant Real Monarchs SLC, and Montreal's simply named FC Montreal).

Though the latest iteration of the North American Soccer League, launched in 2011, is considered the second-tier league by the USSF, it operates independently from the bridged MLS and USL, and its eleven teams in 2016 will reduce by one when Minnesota United FC moves to MLS in 2017 or 2018 (likely rebranding to, more simply, Minnesota FC). This edition of the NASL, like the prior one, has a New York Cosmos, a Fort Lauderdale Strikers, and a Tampa Bay Rowdies; it also has additional Florida franchises in Miami and Jacksonville, Canadian franchises in Ottawa and Edmonton, and the oddly named Rayo OKC—majority owned by the owner of La Liga team Rayo Vallecano—coexisting in the same small market (though with stadiums more than an hour apart) with the USL's OKC Energy.

The NASL bolstered its profile by signing a TV deal with beIN Sports for the 2016 season, announced at the end of March 2016, but USL announced its own TV deal with ESPN (albeit involving its ESPN3 streaming service) three weeks later. There might be a future where all three leagues coexist, and some pro/rel advocates have even gone as far as to imagine what the composition of the 2016 leagues might look like based on 2015 results. But there also might be a future in which the NASL eventually folds or is at least partially absorbed into the USL.

Pro/rel isn't the only debate around the future of MLS playing out among fans and thought leaders. Some feel that adopting the August to May calendar that the other major pro leagues around the world use will allow MLS to access a greater—and better overall—pool of players, whereas others blanch at the thought of attending MLS matches in January and February and feel that soccer in the summer months is a distinct element of MLS's appeal.

And there are, of course, more and more cities that want to be involved in the league, even as some caution that the expansion beyond twenty-four teams might dilute the product. Atlanta United FC, LAFC, and Minnesota are progressing toward their opening days, while in Miami the David Beckham–led group, as of the start of the 2016 season, is working toward connecting all the dots on a plan that would allow them to be team 24 and coexist (or not) with the NASL's Miami FC, which began play in 2016.

The league announced, from meetings the day before the 2015 MLS Cup, that the Beckham group has a stadium plan that has met MLS approval; it would now just be up to the group to work matters out with South Florida's governmental entities to move forward toward, optimistically, the 2018 season.

The league also made it known that day that it was open to a future with twenty-eight teams—a message that has continued on into 2016.

That certainly has buoyed cities with MLS aspirations. Sacramento has been campaigning for a team for years; its USL team, the Sacramento Republic, lays out its aspirations on a page on its website, complete with a #BuiltForMLS hashtag. In April 2016, Garber visited Sacramento and according to an MLSSoccer.com article, gave quite strong hints that Sacramento will be team 25. As Evan Ream noted,

Sacramento Republic FC supporters gathered . . . for a block party thrown by the soccer club in downtown Sacramento, where hundreds of fans packed closed-down L Street between 15th and 16th in hopes of influencing MLS's expansion decision.

As MLS Commissioner Don Garber took to the stage at the south end of the block, the massive crowd held up signs of the team's "#BuiltForMLS" motto as well as giant cardboard cutouts of the commissioner's face.

"We are making the announcement today that we will go to 28 teams," Garber said to massive applause. "We hope and really we expect that Sacramento will be one of the next four [teams].

"The last piece of that is the process of that and the timing of that . . . is still to be determined," he added. "But the good news is, I'm very, very impressed and excited by everything you guys have done."[3]

San Antonio has also thrown its hat in the ring—provided everyone forgets all that 2005 unpleasantness—by buying Toyota Field (an 8,000-seat stadium built to easily be expanded to 18,000 should the city be awarded an MLS franchise), and partnering with Spurs Sports & Entertainment, which runs the dynastic NBA franchise. The new partnership, upon conclusion of the NASL Scorpions' 2015 season, folded the Scorpions, and created a new Spurs-run USL team, San Antonio FC, positioning it for a potentially easier transition into MLS.

Detroit Pistons owner Tom Gores and Cleveland Cavaliers owner Dan Gilbert announced their intentions to bring an MLS franchise to Detroit in April 2016, yet it wasn't met with the enthusiasm you might expect from the city's more hard-core supporters. "Detroit's soccer hipsters are upset," wrote Ty Duffy for the Big Lead. "The 'Northern Guard,' the Supporters' Group for fourth-division Detroit City FC, is adamantly opposed to MLS coopting its precious brand,"[4] referencing a Facebook post that declared, "Just because it's the 'top' league doesn't mean it's actually worthwhile, and settling for MLS because you think it's the best you can get just means you'll never get anything better. The biggest and best-smelling turd on the buffet is still a turd you shouldn't consume." The Facebook post also noted "all of the options for moving up out of the National Premier Soccer League have major flaws. That's not our club's fault, but it's a sign of the miserable state of American soccer that there's no obvious place for a club built on passion rather than profit to continue its growth."[5]

And a *Detroit Free Press* editorial, not quite sharing the Northern Guard's invective for MLS, nevertheless groused, "It matters little that nearly 110,000 people filled Michigan Stadium two years ago, when Real Madrid played Manchester United—only two of the five most valuable sports franchises in the world. But just because there's a soccer audience in this area doesn't make it a sustainable market for an MLS franchise. It'll be cute for a while because it's new. But then even the heartiest soccer fans will realize that the quality of the MLS is mediocre, at best. And mediocrity only sells in Detroit sports if it comes from a team you've embraced your entire life."[6] (Should Detroit not welcome an MLS franchise, St. Louis, San Diego, Cincinnati and Indianapolis have all expressed interest in Garber's pledge to grow the league to twenty-eight teams.)

Yet despite MLS's growth and the increasing demand for its franchises, the league still maintains an accessibility to its players and its front office that is unparalleled among American sports leagues (which I would argue that MLS can now be counted among).

Sons of Ben president Ami Rivera, reflecting on the relationship the supporters' group has with the team it helped launch, notes, "The fans here, in regards to the relationship we have with the front office and the players, is unlike anything I've witnessed before. We hang out with the players. We know these guys. We know their families. They come out to every [charity] event that we try to do—they're willing to donate and actually be a physical part of it, which is huge. You don't see that among any other sports groups. The Philadelphia Eagles aren't coming out to some small supporters' group's benefit."

Even with the demands of an MLS owner with a brand-new stadium, the Quakes' Dave Kaval still maintains Tuesday afternoon "office hours," born out of his belief in "being transparent and open," having an open door, "almost over-communicating via social media," and being upfront with fans to help build up trust. In office hours, "any fan can just come and meet me face to face, and talk about any issue they want to, to allow people to understand what we're doing and why we're doing it, and what was the path—how we were going to get to the point to open a world-class stadium and put a team on the field that people could be proud of."

Office hours have gotten Kaval the eclectic mix you might expect;

some fans come to him with starting lineups employing twelve or fourteen players, but he's also met a local bank representative who became a sponsor, an analyst whom the club hired for a time, and in the process, he says, "It's allowed me to have a really good feel for the pulse of the team and the fan base, and it also allowed me to talk to people who were irate, to discuss things . . . and to build an army of ambassadors and evangelists who have really gone out there to spread the message about what we do for soccer in the community."

Not every front office around the league is willing to talk formations with fans, of course, but there's a shared sense of the fan experience being vital to the future of MLS and to each club in particular, and different paths to get there. In Toronto, a major stadium renovation completed in May 2016 placed a roof over the seating areas to shield the fans from inclement weather. In Chicago, the Pub to Pitch bus is taking fans to Fire games, making the trip from soccer-friendly bars in downtown Chicago to Bridgeview and back in an effort to bolster numbers in the stadium. In Frisco, Texas, the entire south end of FC Dallas's stadium is being transformed via a $39 million project with an end-of-2017 target completion date; at its conclusion, the stadium's seating will be integrated into the design of the National Soccer Hall of Fame Museum, showcasing a century-plus worth of American soccer history.

As MLS continues its evolution, the supporters' groups will certainly continue to be central to what happens in the league's twenty and counting stadiums—sometimes brash, sometimes irreverent, sometimes even at loggerheads with the front office, but ultimately dedicated to the American version of the world's sport, whether it's the league they've known all their lives or the league they feared might not outlast them. Major League Soccer, unlike any of the leagues before it, seems positioned to remain intact and supported.

SOURCES

Chapter 1

1. Michael Janofsky, "U.S. Awarded '94 World Cup Tourney in Soccer," New York Times, July 5, 1988.

2. Associated Press, "NASL Down to Two Teams, Won't Play for This Season," Eugene Register-Guard, March 29, 1985.

3. Janofsky, "U.S. Awarded '94 World Cup Tourney."

4. "Alan I. Rothenberg," Sports Business Institute Biographies, University of Southern California Marshall School of Business, http://www.marshall.usc.edu/faculty /centers/board/alan-i-rothenberg.

5. Filip Bondy, "To Practice for 1994, a U.S. Cup Next June," New York Times, November 27, 1992.

6. "FIFA Confederations Cup Archive," FIFA, http://www.fifa.com/confederationscup /archive/saudiarabia1992/.

7. Beau Dure, Long-Range Goals: The Success Story of Major League Soccer (Washington, DC: Potomac, 2010).

8. Julie Cart, "Soccer's Brain Trust Begins Tackling Issues: Proposed U.S. Professional League and World Cup Point System Are at Top of the Agenda," Los Angeles Times, December 16, 1993.

9. Michael Lewis, "Looking Back at the 1994 FIFA World Cup Draw," December 3, 2013, U.S. Soccer, http://www.ussoccer.com/stories/2014/03/17 /13/44/131203-mnt -1994-wc-draw.

10. Tom Farrey, "Seattle Misses First MLS Cut—But Bid Isn't Dead," Seattle Times, June 15, 1994.

11. Darris Blackford and Connie A. Higgins, "City Nets Pro Soccer Franchise," Columbus Dispatch, June 16, 1994.

12. Farrey, "Seattle Misses First MLS Cut."

13. "1994 FIFA World Cup USA," FIFA, http://www.fifa.com/worldcup /archive/usa1994/index.html.

14. Seth Vertelney, "That Wonderful Summer," March 4, 2014, SBNation, http://www.sbnation.com/longform/2014/3/4/5466056/world-cup-usmnt-1994-usa -soccer-history.

15. Kevin Baxter, "World Cup in 1994 Gave U.S. Soccer the Kick in the Pants It Needed," Los Angeles Times, May 31, 2014.

16. "MLS Inaugural Draft—1996," MLS, http://www.mlssoccer.com/history /draft/1996-inaugural.

17. Graeme L. Jones, "MLS Teams Gain Identities in 'Unveiling' Soccer: League Will Open Play April 6. Marco Etcheverry is the Biggest Signing Announced," Los Angeles Times, October 18, 1995.

18. David Payne, "Inaugural Match in S.J.; Clash Kick Off Season April 6

against Undetermined Opponent at Spartan Stadium," *San Jose Mercury-News*, October 18, 1995.

19. Ann Killion, "MLS May Be Offering Too Little, Too Late," *San Jose Mercury-News*, October 18, 1995.

20. Bill Ward, "Mutiny under Scrutiny as MLS Team Announced," *Tampa Tribune*, October 18, 1995.

21. Bob Luder, "Wiz GM Adjusts to Name," *Kansas City Star*, October 19, 1995.

22. Darris Blackford, "Name Game Begins for Soccer Team—White Castle Backs Columbus Slyders Proposal with Offer," *Columbus Dispatch*, June 17, 1994.

23. Jack Williams, "The Motley Crew: The Stories behind America's Wackiest Football Club Names," March 4, 2015, *Eight by Eight*, http:/ /8by8mag.com /motley-crew/.

24. "The Clubs, the Facts and the Origin of Their Names," February 12, 1996, FIFA, http://www.fifa.com/live-scores/news/y=1996/m=2/news=the-clubs-the-facts-and-the-origin-their-names-71411.html.

Chapter 2

1. Associated Press, "Wynalda Strikes Late in Opener," *New York Times*, April 7, 1996.

2. Gary Peterson, "Kick of an Opener, But Will League Fly?," *Contra Costa Times*, April 7, 1996.

3. Mark Ziegler, "Wynalda Rescues MLS Debut with Goal," *San Diego Union-Tribune*, April 7, 1996.

4. Graeme L. Jones, "Just in Kick of Time for MLS," *Los Angeles Times*, April 7, 1996.

5. Ross Atkin, "American Pro Soccer Gets Another Shot at Success," *Christian Science Monitor*, April 5, 1996.

6. Jones, "Just in Kick of Time for MLS."

7. Ibid.

8. Atkin, "American Pro Soccer Gets Another Shot at Success."

9. Nick Green, "Were You at the Galaxy's First Game at the Rose Bowl?" July 28, 2009, Insidesocal.com, http://www.insidesocal.com/soccer/2009/07/28 /were-you-at-the-galaxys-first/.

10. David Litterer, "The Year in American Soccer, 1996," American Soccer History Archives, http://homepages.sover.net/~spectrum/year/1996.html.

11. "1996 Season Recap," MLS, http://www.mlssoccer.com/history/season/1996.

12. David Neilsen, "Will District Stand United behind Latest Pro Franchise?" *Washington Times*, October 18, 1995.

13. Jeff Bradley, "New York–DC United Rivalry Dates Back to Gritty Glory Days of MLS," March 15, 2013, MLS, http://www.mlssoccer.com/post /2013/03/15/word-new-york-dc-united-rivalry-dates-back-gritty-glory-days-mls.

14. Mark Sappenfield, "Soccer's Foul Weathered Friends," *Christian Science Monitor*, October 22, 1996.

15. "D.C. United's First Fan and Founder of the Screaming Eagles," August 23, 2011, MLS, http://www.mlssoccer.com/post/2011/08/23/dc-uniteds-first-fan-and-founder-screaming-eagles.

16. Matthew Doyle, "Top 50 MLS Moments: #1, I Am Legend," November 20, 2011, MLS, http://www.mlssoccer.com/post/2011/11/20/top-50-mls-cup-moments -1-i-am-legend.

17. Kevin Acee, "Galaxy Go Thud In Mud," *Los Angeles Daily News*, October 22, 1996.

18. Associated Press, "Fans Overwhelm DC Soccer Champs," *Press of Atlantic City*, October 22, 1996.

19. Associated Press, "No Offense: MLS Has One Goal," *St. Paul Pioneer Press*, April 7, 1996.

20. Jere Longman, "Questions Are More Plentiful for MLS," *New York Times*, July 9, 1997.

21. Ibid.

22. Joseph White, "MLS Optimistic Despite Drop in Crowds, Ratings— Changes Considered for Next Tear," *Gazette* (Colorado Springs, CO), October 28, 1997.

23. Mark Asher, "It's Still Early in the Game," *Washington Post*, October 22, 1997.

Chapter 3

1. Grahame L. Jones, "MLS to Add Teams in Miami and Chicago," *Los Angeles Times*, April 10, 1997.

2. DeSimone, Bonnie. "Name Game Ends: It's Fire; New MLS Franchise Balks at Nike Suggestion," *Chicago Tribune*, October 9, 1997.

3. Barry Jackson and Karen French, "Will Fusion Play at OB? Lease Disagreement Turns Ugly after Owner Horowitz Balks," *Miami Herald*, July 25, 1997.

4. "Fusion to Broward? Courtship Heating Up," *Miami Herald*, August 30, 1997.

5. "1998 Miami Fusion," MLS, http://www.mlssoccer.com/history/club /miami /1998.

6. Jeff Rusnak, "Fusion's Lockhart Stadium Stint Paved Way for New MLS Venues," *Sun-Sentinel*, October 12, 2008.

7. Mark Sappenfield, "World Cup '98: MLS Faces a Tough Decision," *Christian Science Monitor*, February 26, 1997.

8. Richard Farley, "Major League Soccer Players' Absence from the 2010 World Cup," July 28, 2010, SBNation, http://www.sbnation.com/2010/7/28 /1591752 /major-league-soccer-players-absence-2010-world-cup.

9. Sam Pierron, "The History," Supporters' Shield, http://supportersshield .org/the-history/.

10. Bernie Lincicome, "MLS Cup Runneth Over with Nonsense," *Chicago Tribune*, October 25, 1998.

Chapter 4

1. "Columbus Crew Set for May 15 Opener," May 11, 1999, Soccer America, http://www.socceramerica.com/article/8891/mls-columbus-crew-stadium-set-for-may-15-opener.html.

2. Michelle Kauffman, "MLS: It's Time to Kick It into High Gear," *Miami Herald*, March 21, 1999.

3. Mark Ziegler, "It Could Be Do or Die for MLS," *San Diego Union-Tribune*, March 17, 1999.

4. Bob Greene, "MLS Ditches Logan, Replaces Him with NFL Executive," August 5, 1999, Associated Press Archive.

5. Craig Merz, "League to Tap New Commissioner's Marketing Skills," *Columbus Dispatch*, August 5, 1999.

6. "About," Section 8 Chicago, http://www.s8c.org/about/.

7. Gus Martins, "United Take It, Gladly—Mistakes Doom Galaxy," *Boston Herald*, November 22, 1999.

8. Jimmy Golen, "D.C. United an MLS Dynasty in the Making," November 22, 1999, Associated Press Archive.

9. David Zeitlin, "The Legend of the Rochester Raging Rhinos, the Last Underdog to Win the US Open Cup," June 16, 2015, MLS, http://www.mlssoccer.com/post /2015 /06/16/legend-rochester-raging-rhinos-last-underdog-win-us-open-cup-word.

10. Ibid.

11. Alex Yannis, "MLS Is Making Changes," *New York Times*, November 18, 1999.

12. Associated Press, "In MLS, Nobody Beats the Wiz," *Charleston Daily Mail*, October 16, 2000.

13. Steven Goff, "Quakes on Shaky Ground?," *Contra Costa Times*, December 30, 2000; "MLS Considering Cutting Teams, Mutiny May Be Out," *Tampa Tribune*, December 30, 2000.

14. Michelle Kauffman, "Future Not Looking So Bright for Fusion," *Miami Herald*, December 31, 2000.

Chapter 5

1. "Remaining MLS Regular Season Games Canceled; MLS Cup Playoffs Will Start September 20," September 13, 2001, U.S. Soccer, http://www.ussoccer.com /stories/2014/03/17/13/24/remaining-mls-regular-season-games-canceled-mls-cup -playoffs-will-start-september-20.

2. Greg Cote, "At a Time When Magic Was Required, Fusion Pulled a Disappearing Act," *Miami Herald*, October 18, 2001.

3. Bill Ward, "Mutiny's Kinnear to Take Coaching Job," *Tampa Tribune*, February 3, 2001.

4. "San Jose Nabs Donovan in Complex Loan Deal with Bayer Leverkusen," March 30, 2001, Soccertimes.com, http://www.soccertimes.com /mls/2001 /mar30.htm.

5. Dwight Chapin, "Earthquakes' Victory Is Extra Special—DeRosario's Goal in Overtime Clinches MLS Title," *San Francisco Chronicle*, October 22, 2001.

6. Marc Stein, "MLS Nearly Folded in 2001—FC Dallas President Dan Hunt," April 12, 2016, ESPN FC, http://www.espnfc.us/major-league-soccer /story/2848878 /mls-nearly-folded-in-2001-fc-dallas-president-dan-hunt.

7. "ABC, ESPN, Inc., and MLS Ink Multi-Year Deal," January 3, 2002, ABC Sports, http://espn.go.com/abcsports/pressreleases/s/2002/0103 /1305097.html.

8. Steven Wine, "MLS Folds Fusion, Mutiny," *USA Today*, January 9, 2002.

9. Rodney Page, "Mutiny Folded by MLS," *St. Petersburg Times*, January 9, 2002.

10. "Super Bowl Hero Takes a Slice of Man Utd," March 2, 2003, BBC News, http://news.bbc.co.uk/2/hi/business/2813439.stm.

11. "Glazer Wins Control of Man United," May 12, 2005, BBC News, http://news .bbc.co.uk/2/hi/business/4540939.stm.

Chapter 6

1. "ABC/ESPN Announce World Cup 2002 Broadcast Schedule," May 1, 2002, U.S. Soccer, http://www.ussoccer.com/stories/2014/03/17/12 /12/abcespn-announce-world-cup-2002-broadcast-schedule.

2. Ed Farnsworth, "Looking Back at the U.S. Soccer Team's Historic 2002 World Cup," May 9, 2014, Philly.com, http://www.philly.com /philly/sports/soccer/worldcup /Looking_back_at_the_US_soccer_teams_historic_2002_World_Cup.html.

3. Tom Goldman, "Soccer Fans around the World to Watch the World Cup Tournament, Which Begins Tomorrow," May 30, 2002, National Public Radio, http://www .npr.org/templates/story/story.php?storyId=1144183.

4. "The Boys of Soccer," *New York Times Magazine*, May 23, 2002, http://www .nytimes.com/slideshow/2002/05/23/magazine/26fash.slideshow_1.html?_r=0.

5. Brian Phillips, "Red, White & Blue Steel," August 9, 2013, Grantland, http:/ /grantland.com/features/usmnt-new-york-s-magazine-greatest-photo-shoot-history/.

6. Landon Donovan, "I've been waiting for this day," August 11, 2015, Twitter, @landondonovan.

7. "Korea Rally to Deny U.S," June 10, 2002, BBC News, http://news.bbc.co .uk/sport3/worldcup2002/hi/matches_wallchart/south_korea_v_usa/default.stm.

8. "World Cup Soccer, U.S. TV Viewership, 1994–2006," Nielsen.

9. Gary Davidson, "It's a Revolution in New England Where Five All-Stars Are Obtained from Dispersal Drafts," January 11, 2002, Soccertimes.com, http://www .soccertimes.com/mls/2002/jan11.htm.

10. John Haydon, "Colorful Hudson Takes Over as United Coach," *Washington Times*, January 10, 2002.

11. Nate Thompson, "Dream Season Comes to an End," *Taunton Daily Gazette*, October 21, 2002.

12. "Burn to Play at Dragon Stadium in Southlake in 2003; Team Announces Ticket Prices for 2003 Season," January 14, 2003, Our Sports Central, http://www.our sportscentral.com/services/releases/burn-to-play-at -dragon-stadium-in-southlake-in -2003-team-announces-ticket-prices-for-2003-season/n-1982817.

13. "Dallas Burn to Return to Cotton Bowl for 2004 MLS Season," November 14, 2003, Our Sports Central, http://www.oursportscentral.com/services /releases/dallas -burn-to-return-to-cotton-bowl-for-2004-mls-season /n-2707294.

14. Nick Green, "Up and Running—Carson's $150 Million Sports Complex Is Expected to Pick Up Recognition as It Opens Today with a Nationally Televised Track Event," *Daily Breeze* (Torrance, CA), June 1, 2003.

15. Nick Green, "Win Kick-Starts Home Depot—Galaxy's First Home Game Yields Win," *Daily Breeze* (Torrance, CA), June 8, 2003.

16. Soccer America, *Soccer's Cathedral: Guide to the Home Depot Center*, adver-

tising circular, LA84 Foundation, http://library.la84.org/SportsLibrary/SoccerAmerica/2003/sa1553s.pdf.

17. Dylan Hernandez, "Down by 2, 4, Then . . . 5 Goals Push Quakes Onward; San Jose into West Final after Furious Comeback," *San Jose Mercury-News*, November 10, 2003.

Chapter 7

1. Brice Wallace, "Checketts Vows No double-Zs," *Deseret News*, August 6, 2004.

2. Peter Richins, "Major League Soccer: Highlanders Hold the High Ground," *Salt Lake Tribune*, August 11, 2004.

3. Doug Alden, "Utah Team Named Real Salt Lake," *USA Today*, October 9, 2004.

4. Leigh Dethman and Amelia Nielson-Stowell, "A Groundbreaking Day: 'This Is the Place,' Checketts Says of Decision to Build Sandy Stadium," *Deseret News*, August 13, 2006.

5. Associated Press, "Galaxy Trade Ruiz to Dallas, Donovan Returning to L.A.?" *USA Today*, March 30, 2005.

6. Associated Press, "Major League Soccer Ends Talks with San Antonio," *USA Today*, June 9, 2005.

7. Simon Romero, "What's in a Brand Name? Houston Just Found Out," *New York Times*, January 27, 2006.

8. Bernardo Fallas, "Houston Soccer Team Will 86 its 1836 Name," *Houston Chronicle*, February 15, 2006.

9. "Robertson Stadium," Houston Cougars, http://www.uhcougars.com /facilities/hou-robertson.html.

10. Jordan Robertson, "A's Owners Test Stadium Waters by Bringing Back MLS Soccer," May 24, 2006, SFGate.com, http://www.sfgate.com /sports/article/A-s-owners-test-stadium-waters-by-bringing-back-2534290.php.

11. Jack Bell, "Red Bull Is New Owner, and Name, of MetroStars," *New York Times*, March 10, 2006.

12. Julie Bosman, "First Stadiums, Now Teams Take a Corporate Identity," *New York Times*, March 22, 2006.

13. Michael Davies, "Welcome to World Cup Football," June 12, 2006, ESPN, http://espn.go.com/espn/page2/story?page=davies/060612.

14. Ronald Blum, "Czechs Steamroll U.S. 3–0 at World Cup," *Washington Post*, June 13, 2006.

15. Amy Lawrence, "De Rossi Draws Blood as Three Sent Off," *Guardian*, June 17, 2006.

16. Michael Davies, "America, the Beautiful," June 17, 2006, ESPN, http://espn.go.com/espn/page2/story?page=davies/060617.

17. "U.S. Eliminated from World Cup as Ghana Wins," June 22, 2006, U.S. Soccer, http://www.ussoccer.com/stories/2014/03/17/11/16/u-s-men-eliminated-from-world-cup-following-2-1-loss-vs-ghana.

18. "1975–1978 Toronto Metros-Croatia," Fun While It Lasted, http://www.funwhileitlasted.net/tag/toronto-metros-croatia/.

Chapter 8

1. Jack Bell, "David Beckham Is Coming to America," *New York Times*, January 12, 2007.

2. Jen Chang, "Debunking the Myths behind Beckham's Contract," January 12, 2007, ESPN Soccernet, http://www.espnfc.us/story/399597 /debunking-the-myths-behind-beckhams-contract.

3. Paul Kennedy, "Beckham Is MLS Expansion Story du Jour," May 20, 2013, SoccerAmerica, http://www.socceramerica.com/article/51723/beckham -is-mls-expansion-story-du-jour.html.

4. "Rocky Mountain High: Celtic vs. MLS in All-Star Game in Colorado," January 25, 2007, Big Apple Soccer, http://www.bigapplesoccer.com/leagues /mls2.php ?article_id=8525.

5. "Beckham Boosts Traffic to Official U.S. Major League Soccer Website to Over One Million," August 30, 2007, ComScore, www.comscore.com/Insights /PressReleases/2009/08/Beckham-Major-League-Soccer-Website-Traffic.

6. "Beckham to Join AC Milan on Loan in January," October 30, 2008, ESPN Soccernet, http://www.espnfc.us/story/587422/beckham-to-join-ac-milan-on-loan-in -january.

7. "Beckham Confronts Fans after Boos," July 20, 2009, BBC Sport, http://news .bbc.co.uk/sport2/hi/football/8158547.stm.

8. José Miguel Romero, "Real Salt Lake Wins MLS Cup on Penalty Kicks," *Seattle Times*, November 22, 2009.

9. David Winter, "David Beckham's Injury Is a Desperately Sad Way to End His World Cup Dream," *Telegraph*, March 15, 2010.

10. Steven Goff, "Colorado Rapids Beat FC Dallas in Overtime for First Major League Soccer Title," *Washington Post*, November 22, 2010.

11. "2010 MLS Cup: FC Dallas vs. Colorado Rapids," November 21, 2010, MLS, http://www.mlssoccer.com/history/mls-cup/2010?autoplay=true.

Chapter 9

1. Steven Wells, "US Soccer Punks 1, McFans 0," *Guardian*, June 6, 2007.

2. Bryan James, "A Fan's Perspective—Bryan James, President of Sons of Ben," November 9, 2009, Original Winger, http://theoriginalwinger .com/2009/11/a-fans-[erspective-bruan-james-president-of-sons-of-ben/.

3. Ibid.

4. Dave Zeitlin, "Philadelphia Union Owner Jay Sugarman Says Nick Sakiewicz Firing 'Right Decision' for Club's Future," October 2, 2015, MLSSoccer.com, http://www.mlssoccer.com/post/2015/10/02/philadelphia-union-owner-jay-sugarman-says-nick-sakiewicz-firing-right-decision.

5. Jonathan Tannenwald, "Sons of Ben President Discusses Protest March," May 17, 2015, Philly.com, http://www.philly.com/philly/blogs /sports/union/Sons-of-Ben-president-discusses-protest-march.html.

6. "Statement from CEO and Cofounding Partner Nick Sakiewicz regarding Sons of Ben 'We Deserve Better' Message," May 17, 2015, PhiladelphiaUnion .com,http://www.philadelphiaunion.com/post/2015/05/17 /statement-ceo-and-cofounding-partner-nick-sakiewicz-regarding-sons-ben-we-deserve.

7. Dave Zeitlin, "New Sons of Ben President Ami Rivera Wants to Welcome All Fans to the Fun at PPL Park," November 24, 2015, MLSSoccer.com, http://www.mlssoccer.com/post/2015/11/20/new-sons-ben-president-ami-rivera-wants-welcome-all-fans-to-fun-ppl-park.

8. "Songs and Chants," Sons of Ben, http://www.sonsofben.com/songs-and-tifo/.

Chapter 10

1. Les Carpenter, "How Soccer Saved the Seattle Seahawks," *Guardian*, January 14, 2015.

2. José Miguel Romero, "MLS Seattle Fans Can Write In Vote for Team Name," *Seattle Times*, March 25, 2008.

3. "Seattle Sounders FC Selected as Team Name," April 6, 2008, Seattle Sounders FC, http://www.soundersfc.com/post/2008/04/07/seattle-sounders-fc-selected-team-name.

4. "History," Timbers Army, http://timbersarmy.org/aboutus/history.

5. "Who is Gorilla FC?," Gorilla FC, http://www.gorillafc.com/#!whoisgfc/c19zy.

6. Zach Slaton, "E Pluribus Sounders (Part 3): Connecting to Old and New Fans," *Forbes*, August 6, 2012.

7. Ben Palosaari, "Sporting Kansas City's Name Not a Hit with Fans and Media," 18 November 2010, Pitch, http://www.pitch.com/news/article /20578346/sporting-kansas-citys-name-not-a-hit-with-fans-and-media.

8. Barry Petchesky, "Kansas City MLS Team's New Name Is Impossibly Awful," November 18, 2010, Deadspin, http://deadspin.com/5693456 /kansas-city-mls-teams-new-name-is-impossibly-awful.

9. Palosaari, "Sporting Kansas City's Name Not a Hit."

10. Jack Harry, "I Feel Compelled to Address My Lack of Covering Sporting Kansas City," September 29, 2011, KSHB-TV, http://www.kshb.com/sports/jacks-smack   /jacks-smack-i-feel-compelled-to-address-my-lack-of-covering-sporting-kansas-city.

11. "Episode 2: You Suck Asshole," December 18, 2012, Howler Radio, http://www.howlermagazine.com/howler-radio-2-you-suck-asshole/.

12. Steve Stoehr, "Fracas in the Fort: Revolution Supporters Banned and Arrested for Profane Chants," June 20, 2011, Bent Musket/SBNation, http://www.thebentmusket.com/2011/6/20/2234298/fracas-in-the-fort-revolution-supporters-banned-and-arrested-for.

13. Steve Stoehr, "FortGate: One Week Later," June 26, 2011, Bent Musket /SBNation, http://www.thebentmusket.com/2011/6/26/2245114/fortgate-one-week-later-revolution-support-the-fort.

14. Garrett Dittfurth, "You Suck . . ." June 21, 2011, Timbers Army, https://timbersarmy.org/you-suck.

15. "History," Midnight Riders, http://www.midnightriders.com/about-us/history/.

Chapter 11

1. "Quakes Set Guinness World Record on Groundbreaking Day," October 21, 2012, San Jose Earthquakes, http://www.sjearthquakes.com/post/2012/10/21/quakes-set-guinness-world-record-groundbreaking-day.

2. Geoff Lepper, "In New Look, San Jose Earthquakes Make Effort to Acknowledge Past, Present and Future," January 31, 2014, MLS, http://www.mlssoccer.com/post/2014/01/31/new-look-san-jose-earthquakes-make-effort-acknowledge-past-present-and-future.

3. Nick Firchau, "MLS Cup to Be David Beckham's Final Match with Galaxy," November 19, 2012, MLS, http://www.mlssoccer.com/post/2012 /11/20 /mls-cup-be-david-beckhams-final-match-galaxy.

4. Jonah Freedman, "'Passionate' Montreal Named as 19th MLS City," May 7, 2010, MLS, http://www.mlssoccer.com/post/2010/05/07/passionate-montreal-named-19th-mls-city.

5. Brian Straus, "Friendly Fire: U.S. Coach Jurgen Klinsmann's Methods, Leadership, Acumen in Question," March 19, 2013, Sporting News, http://www.sportingnews.com/soccer-news/4486437-jurgen-klinsmann-us-mens-soccer-coach-national-team-usa-american-world-cup-2013.

6. Michael Lewis, "World Cup 2010 Draw: U.S. Soccer Joins England, Slovenia, Algeria in Group C," *New York Daily News*, December 4, 2009.

7. "U.S. Head Coach Bob Bradley Names 23 Players to Represent the United States at the 2010 FIFA World Cup in South Africa," May 26, 2010, U.S. Soccer, http://www.ussoccer.com/stories/2014/03/17/12/25/us-head-coach-bob-bradley-names-23-players-to-represent-the-us-at-the-2010-fifa-world-cup.

8. Ryan O'Hanlon, "Snow Clash: Watching Soccer Get Weird at 5,000 Feet," March 26, 2013, Deadspin, http://deadspin.com/snow-clash-watching-soccer-get-weird-at-5-000-feet-458755115.

9. Woody Paige, "Snow Job in World Cup Qualifier Sweet for U.S. Soccer," *Denver Post*, March 24, 2013.

10. Ives Galarcep, "Ratings for USA–Mexico Shatter Records," March 27, 2013, Soccer by Ives, http://sbisoccer.com/2013/03/ratings-qualifier-records.

11. Associated Press, "Sporting KC Outlasts RSL for Title," December 6, 2013, ESPN FC, http://www.espnfc.com/major-league-soccer/story /1642681/mls-cup-sporting-kc-defeats-real-salt-lake-in-shootout-for-title.

12. Ibid.

13. Simon Borg, "Citing the Frigid Weather, Real Salt Lake's Javier Morales Wants a Return to Neutral Venue," December 7, 2013, MLS, http://www.mlssoccer.com/post/2013/12/08/mls-cup-citing-frigid-weather-real-salt-lakes-javier-morales-wants-return-neutral.

14. Christopher Harris, "MLS Cup 2013 Down 44% in Viewership; Sets Record as Least-Viewed MLS Cup Ever," December 10, 2013, World Soccer Talk, http://worldsoccertalk.com/2013/12/10/mls-cup-2013-down-44-in-viewership-sets-record-as-least-viewed-mls-cup-ever/.

15. Paul Kennedy, "MLS Cup Viewers on UniMas Surpass Those on ESPN," December 10, 2013, Soccer America, http://www.socceramerica .com/article/55322/mls-cup-viewers-on-unimas-surpass-those-on-espn.html.

16. Brian Straus, "Garber Touches on MLS Expansion, Academies, Transparency and More in Address," December 3, 2013, *Sports Illustrated*, http://www.si.com /soccer/planet-futbol/2013/12/03/don-garber-mls-state-of-the-league.

17. Brian Straus, "Sporting News Conversation Part Two: Don Garber," July 21, 2012, Sporting News, http://www.sportingnews.com/soccer-news/3890242 -sporting-news-conversation-don-garber-part-ii.

18. Barry Petchesky, "MLS Threatens Fans: No More 'You Suck, Asshole' Chants," July 9, 2013, Deadspin, http://deadspin.com/mls-threatens-fans-no-more -you-suck-asshole-chants-708117042.

19. Albert Samaha, "Red Bulls Will Pay Fan Clubs Not to Chant 'You Suck, Asshole.'" *Village Voice*, July 9, 2013.

20. Andrew Keh, "M.L.S. Tries to Mute Fans' Vulgar Chants," *New York Times*, September 19, 2013.

21. Seattle Sounders FC, "Sounders FC Introduce Clint Dempsey," August 3, 2013, YouTube, https://www.youtube.com/watch?v=zFr5MM7EdGw.

22. Steven Goff, "2014 World Cup: Juergen Klinsmann Finalizes Roster, Cuts Landon Donovan from U.S. National Team," *Washington Post*, May 22, 2014.

23. Andrea Canales, "Mexico Fans Will Miss Donovan," May 26, 2014, ESPN FC, http://www.espnfc.us/fifa-world-cup/4/blog/post/1833313/andrea-canales-dissects -landon-donovans-omission-from-usa-world-cup-squad-from-a-mexican-perspective.

24. "World Cup Final Sets U.S. TV Record," July 15, 2014, ESPN, http://www .espnfc.us/fifa-world-cup/story/1950567/world-cup-final-most-watched-soccer-game -in-us-history-more-than-26-million-viewers.

25. Richard Dietsch, "USA vs. Belgium Draws Another Huge American TV World Cup Audience," *Sports Illustrated*, July 2, 2014.

26. Stuart Dredge, "Germany's World Cup Hammering of Brazil Broke Twitter Records," *Guardian*, July 9, 2014.

27. Brooks Peck, "MLS Shuts Down Chivas USA and a Cold World Shrugs," October 27, 2014, Yahoo! Sports, http://sports.yahoo.com/blogs/soccer-dirty-tackle /mls-shuts-down-chivas-usa-and-a-cold-world-shrugs-203926859.html.

28. "Cardiff City to Change Kit from Blue to Red amid Financial Invest-ment," June 6, 2012, BBC Sport, http://www.bbc.com/sport/football /18324804.com.

29. James Corrigan, "Cardiff to Wear Blue Again after Vincent Tan Takes Advice from His Mum," *Telegraph*, January 9, 2015.

Chapter 12

1. Richard Sandomir, "M.L.S., Facing Possible Strike, Finds Labor Strife at Its Door," *New York Times*, March 3, 2015.

2. Kevin Baxter, "Labor Deal Averts MLS Player Strike," *Los Angeles Times*, March 4, 2015.

3. "History," Orlando City SC, http://www.orlandocitysc.com/club/history.

4. Nate Scott, "NYCFC Reveals New Jersey and It Looks Exactly Like Man-chester City," *USA Today*, November 13, 2014.

5. "New York City FC Announces Yankee Stadium to Be Home Field for 2015 Season," April 21, 2014, MLS, http://www.mlssoccer.com/post /2014/04/21/new -york-city-fc-announce-yankee-stadium-be-home-field-2015-season.

6. "Who We Are," Third Rail, http://www.thirdrail.nyc/who-we-are/.

7. Chris Jones, "Steven Gerrard, from Liverpool to L.A., Is Still Just a Boy Who Loves Football," July 28, 2015, ESPN FC, http://www.espnfc.us/club/la-galaxy/187 /blog/post/2533763/steven-gerrard-final-act-with-la-galaxy.

8. Grant Wahl, "How Seattle's Stunning Clint Dempsey Deal Got Done," *Sports Illustrated*, August 5, 2013.

9. Steven Goff, "Jermaine Jones Joins New England Revolution. Here's How," *Washington Post*, August 25, 2014.

10. Jermaine Jones, "I am so thankful what has happened in one and a half years with the club, the teammates & fans, the city of Boston! I appreciate the love from everybody! I'm going home now and finally enjoying my family! Very excited to see what will be the next step in our life!" Instagram, October 30, 2015.

11. "MLS Announces Additional Investment in Club Rosters with Introduction of Targeted Allocation Money," July 8, 2015, MLS, http://www.mlssoccer.com /post /2015/07/08/mls-announces-additional-investment-club-rosters-introduction -targeted-allocation.

12. Doug McIntyre, "MLS Rule Opens Door for More 'High-Earning' Players," July 8, 2015, ESPN FC, http://www.espnfc.us/major-league-soccer /story/2516355 /mls-rule-opens-door-for-more-high-earning-players-at-clubs.

13. Kevin Brown, "The L.A. Galaxy Signed Giovani dos Santos Because Rules Are for Chumps," July 15, 2015, Fusion, http://fusion.net/story/167406 /giovani-dos-santos -signs-with-la-galaxy-mls/.

14. Chris Alexopoulos, "I've never seen ESPN dump out of an event in the 20 years I've worked there," August 23, 2015, Twitter, @chriszop.

15. Jonathan Tannenwald, "Among the most stunning moments in MLS history RT @svertelney: Whoa . . . did ESPN just break their own policy and cut away from a live event?" August 23, 2015, Twitter, @thegoalkeeper.

16. "San Jose Earthquakes Announce New Club Facility Naming Rights: Avaya Stadium," Avaya, http://www.avaya.com/usa/sponsorship/sports /earthquakes2.html.

17. Saad Abdul-Salaam, "Wow those poss in Portland are something else# iwouldknow," November 1, Twitter, @Saad-Abdul..

18. Patrick Guldan, "Timber Joey's Log Won't Be Inside MAPFRE Stadium for MLS Cup," Massive Report, December 1, 2015. http://www.massiverepo.com /2015/12/2/9833816/timber-joeys-log-wont-be-inside-mapfre-stadium-for-mls-cup.

19. "Gabriel Brener Acquires AEG's Interests in Houston Dynamo, BBVA Compass Stadium and Houston Dash," December 15, 2015, Houston Dynamo, http://www.houstondynamo.com/post/2015/12/15/gabriel-brener-acquires-aeg %E2%80%99s-interests-houston-dynamo-bbva-compass-stadium-and

Epilogue

1. Associated Press, "MLS Unveils New Shield Logo That Includes a 'Tail.'" *New York Daily News*, September 18, 2014.

2. Ken Belson, "In England, Embracing M.L.S. for What It Is, Not What It Isn't," *New York Times*, October 27, 2015.

3. Evan Ream, "Commissioner Don Garber Visits Sacramento to Survey MLS Expansion Quest." April 15, 2016, MLSSoccer.com, http://www.mlssoccer.com/post /2016/04/15/commissioner-don-garber-visits-sacramento-survey-mls-expansion-quest.

4. Ty Duffy, "MLS to Detroit Already Facing Battle with Soccer Hipsters, County Officials," May 2, 2016, Big Lead, http://thebiglead.com/2016/05 /02/mls-to-detroit -already-facing-battle-with-soccer-hipsters-county-officials/.

5. Northern Guard Supporters Facebook Page, April 30, 2016.

6. Drew Sharp, "Major League Soccer Not a Good Fit for Detroit," *Detroit Free Press*, May 3, 2016.

INTERVIEWS

Mark Abbott, New York City, September 17, 2015

Josie Becker, via e-mail, November 29, 2015

Randy Bernstein, via phone (Los Angeles), April 4, 2016

Brett Bird, via phone (Vancouver, BC), November 16, 2015

Rachel Bonnetta, Austin, May 7, 2016

Ben Burton, via phone (Chicago), November 4, 2015

Jeremy "Truman" Cadmus, via e-mail, November 28, 2015

Andrea Canales, via phone (Los Angeles), September 14, 2015

Becky Chabot, Denver, July 28, 2015, and via e-mail, November 29, 2015

Dave Checketts, via phone (New York City), April 25, 2016

Brian Ching, via phone (Houston), November 30, 2015

Elizabeth Cotignola, via e-mail, November 30, 2015

Don Crafts, via phone (Chicago), November 12, 2015

Garrett Dittfurth, via e-mail, October 12, 2015

Landon Donovan, Austin, August 1, 2015, and via-email, November 23, 2015

Mark Fishkin, via e-mail, November 28, 2015

Trey Fitz-Gerald, via phone (Sandy, Utah), September 23, 2015 and April 22, 2016

Gabe Gabor, via phone (Miami), October 16, 2015

Don Garber, New York City, September 15, 2015

Andrew Gerbosi, Frisco, Texas, November 8, 2015

Nick Green, via phone (Los Angeles), August 24, 2015

Kenny Hanson, via phone (Philadelphia), October 12, 2015

Fran Harrington, via e-mail, October 26, 2015

Ken Horowitz, via phone (Palm Beach, Fla.), October 7, 2015

Ray Hudson, via phone (Ft. Lauderdale), September 11, 2015

Dan Hunt, via phone (Frisco, Texas), September 11, 2015 and December 2, 2015

Jay Igiel, via phone (Washington, DC), October 23, 2015

Bryan James, via phone (Philadelphia), November 25, 2015 and May 12, 2016

Dave Kaval, via phone (San Jose, Calif.), October 21, 2015

Chris Klein, via phone (Carson, Calif.), November 6, 2015

Mirek Krupa, via e-mail, November 17, 2015

Alexi Lalas, via phone (Los Angeles), November 24 and 25, 2015

Greg Lalas, New York City, September 15, 2015

Jenny Lando, via phone (New York City), November 27, 2015

Mike Langevin, via e-mail, September 8, 2015

Rick Lawes, via phone (Pittsburgh), September 2, 2015

Bob Lenarduzzi, via phone (Vancouver, BC), October 30, 2015

Scott MacKay, via e-mail, November 27, 2015
Bill Manning, via phone (Toronto), November 25, 2015
Matt Mathai, via e-mail, October 31, 2015
Sean McConnell, via phone (Seattle), September 22, 2015
Frank McDonald, via e-mail, July 14, 2015 and November 19, 2015
Doug McIntyre, via phone (New York City), August 17, 2015
Jennifer Muller, via e-mail, November 30, 2015
Liam Murtaugh, via phone (Chicago), October 21, 2015
Jay Neal, Frisco, Texas, November 8, 2015
Merritt Paulson, via phone (Portland, Oregon), October 6, 2015
Kevin Payne, via phone (Charleston, SC), October 13, 2015
Sam Pierron, via phone (Kansas City), November 9, 2015
Tab Ramos, Austin, May 8, 2016
Phil Rawlins, via phone (Orlando), October 31, 2015
Ami Rivera, via phone (Philadelphia), October 9, 2015
Alan Rothenberg, via phone (Los Angeles), October 15, 2015
Nick Sakiewicz, via phone (Philadelphia), April 20, 2016
Chris Schlosser, New York City, September 15, 2015
Adam Sell, via phone (Boston), April 27, 2016
Adam Serrano, via e-mail, November 30, 2015
"Timber Jim" Serrill, via phone (Portland, Oregon), October 14, 2015
Steve Sirk, via e-mail, October 19, 2015
Paul Sotoudeh, via phone (Washington, DC), September 28, 2015
Scott Swearingen, via phone (Portland, Oregon), November 11, 2015
Jonathan Tannenwald, via phone (Philadelphia), October 28, 2015
Rob Thomson, via phone (Kansas City), September 2, 2015
Amanda Vandervort, New York City, September 15, 2015
Grant Wahl, via phone (New York City), May 11, 2016
"Timber Joey" Webber, via phone (Portland, Oregon), October 13, 2015
David Wegner, via e-mail, June 29, 2015
Ted Westervelt, via phone (Denver), August 28, 2015
Dan Wiersema, Austin, September 4, 2015
Peter Wilt, via phone (Indianapolis), October 22, 2015
Eric Wynalda, via phone (Los Angeles), November 3, 2015

INDEX